C-2845 CAREER EXAMINATION SERIES

This is your
PASSBOOK for...

Teaching Assistant (ATAS)

Test Preparation Study Guide
Questions & Answers

COPYRIGHT NOTICE

This book is SOLELY intended for, is sold ONLY to, and its use is RESTRICTED to individual, bona fide applicants or candidates who qualify by virtue of having seriously filed applications for appropriate license, certificate, professional and/or promotional advancement, higher school matriculation, scholarship, or other legitimate requirements of education and/or governmental authorities.

This book is NOT intended for use, class instruction, tutoring, training, duplication, copying, reprinting, excerption, or adaptation, etc., by:

1) Other publishers
2) Proprietors and/or Instructors of "Coaching" and/or Preparatory Courses
3) Personnel and/or Training Divisions of commercial, industrial, and governmental organizations
4) Schools, colleges, or universities and/or their departments and staffs, including teachers and other personnel
5) Testing Agencies or Bureaus
6) Study groups which seek by the purchase of a single volume to copy and/or duplicate and/or adapt this material for use by the group as a whole without having purchased individual volumes for each of the members of the group
7) Et al.

Such persons would be in violation of appropriate Federal and State statutes.

PROVISION OF LICENSING AGREEMENTS – Recognized educational, commercial, industrial, and governmental institutions and organizations, and others legitimately engaged in educational pursuits, including training, testing, and measurement activities, may address request for a licensing agreement to the copyright owners, who will determine whether, and under what conditions, including fees and charges, the materials in this book may be used them. In other words, a licensing facility exists for the legitimate use of the material in this book on other than an individual basis. However, it is asseverated and affirmed here that the material in this book CANNOT be used without the receipt of the express permission of such a licensing agreement from the Publishers. Inquiries re licensing should be addressed to the company, attention rights and permissions department.

All rights reserved, including the right of reproduction in whole or in part, in any form or by any means, electronic or mechanical, including photocopying, recording, or by any information storage and retrieval system, without permission in writing from the Publisher.

Copyright © 2024 by
National Learning Corporation

212 Michael Drive, Syosset, NY 11791
(516) 921-8888 • www.passbooks.com
E-mail: info@passbooks.com

PUBLISHED IN THE UNITED STATES OF AMERICA

PASSBOOK® SERIES

THE *PASSBOOK® SERIES* has been created to prepare applicants and candidates for the ultimate academic battlefield – the examination room.

At some time in our lives, each and every one of us may be required to take an examination – for validation, matriculation, admission, qualification, registration, certification, or licensure.

Based on the assumption that every applicant or candidate has met the basic formal educational standards, has taken the required number of courses, and read the necessary texts, the *PASSBOOK® SERIES* furnishes the one special preparation which may assure passing with confidence, instead of failing with insecurity. Examination questions – together with answers – are furnished as the basic vehicle for study so that the mysteries of the examination and its compounding difficulties may be eliminated or diminished by a sure method.

This book is meant to help you pass your examination provided that you qualify and are serious in your objective.

The entire field is reviewed through the huge store of content information which is succinctly presented through a provocative and challenging approach – the question-and-answer method.

A climate of success is established by furnishing the correct answers at the end of each test.

You soon learn to recognize types of questions, forms of questions, and patterns of questioning. You may even begin to anticipate expected outcomes.

You perceive that many questions are repeated or adapted so that you can gain acute insights, which may enable you to score many sure points.

You learn how to confront new questions, or types of questions, and to attack them confidently and work out the correct answers.

You note objectives and emphases, and recognize pitfalls and dangers, so that you may make positive educational adjustments.

Moreover, you are kept fully informed in relation to new concepts, methods, practices, and directions in the field.

You discover that you are actually taking the examination all the time: you are preparing for the examination by "taking" an examination, not by reading extraneous and/or supererogatory textbooks.

In short, this PASSBOOK®, used directedly, should be an important factor in helping you to pass your test.

TEACHING ASSISTANT

INTRODUCTION

Purpose of This Preparation Guide

This preparation guide is designed to help familiarize candidates with the content and format of the Assessment of Teaching Assistant Skills (ATAS). Educators may also find the information in this guide useful as they discuss the test with candidates.

This preparation guide illustrates some of the types of ATAS questions; however, the set of sample questions does not necessarily define the content or difficulty of an entire actual test. All test components (e.g., directions, content, and question formats) may differ from those presented here. The program is subject to change.

Organization of This Preparation Guide

The ATAS objectives appear on the pages following this introduction. The objectives list the content that is eligible to be assessed by the ATAS. Each objective is followed by focus statements that provide examples of the range, type, and level of content that may appear on the ATAS. Following the objectives is information about the sample questions for the ATAS and a set of sample directions for the ATAS.

The sample multiple-choice questions are presented next. The correct answer and an explanation of the correct answer follow at the end.

The Assessment of Teaching Assistant Skills (ATAS)

The purpose of the Assessment of Teaching Assistant Skills (ATAS) is to assess knowledge and skills in the following four areas:
- Reading
- Writing
- Mathematics
- Instructional Support

The Assessment of Teaching Assistant Skills consists of 100 multiple-choice questions.

Strategies for Taking the ATAS

Be On Time
Arrive at the test center on time so that you are rested and ready to begin the test when instructed to do so.

Follow Directions
At the beginning of the test session and throughout the test, follow all directions carefully. This includes the oral directions that will be read by the test administrator and any written directions in the test booklet. If you do not understand something about the directions, do not hesitate to raise your hand and ask your test administrator.

Pace Yourself
The test schedule is designed to allow sufficient time for completion of the test. Each test session is three hours in length. Furthermore, the test is designed to allow you to

allocate your time within the session as you need. You will be required to return your materials at the end of the three-hour session.

Since the allocation of your time during the test session is largely yours to determine, planning your own pace for taking the test is very important. There will be 100 multiple-choice questions for the ATAS. Do not spend a lot of time with a multiple-choice test question that you cannot answer promptly; skip that question and move on. If you skip a question, be sure to skip the corresponding row of answer choices on your answer sheet. Mark the question in your test booklet so that you can return to it later, but be careful to appropriately record on the answer sheet the answers to the remaining questions.

You may find that you need less time than the three hours allotted in a test session, but you should be prepared to stay for the entire time period. Do not make any other commitments for this time period that may cause you to rush through the test.

Read Carefully
Read the directions and the questions carefully. Read all response options. Remember that the test questions call for the "best answer"; do not choose the first answer that seems reasonable. Read and evaluate all choices to find the best answer. Read the questions closely so that you understand what they ask. For example, it would be a waste of time to perform a long computation when the question calls for an approximation.

Read the test questions, but don't read into them. The questions are designed to be straightforward, not tricky. Often your first and most direct opinion, based on your knowledge, is the best answer.

Mark Answers Carefully
Your answers for the multiple-choice questions will be scored electronically; therefore, the answer you select must be clearly marked and the only answer marked. If you change your mind about an answer, erase the old answer completely. Do not make any stray marks on the answer sheet; these may be misinterpreted by the scoring machine. You may use any available space in the test booklet for notes, but **your answers must be clearly marked on your answer sheet. ONLY ANSWERS THAT APPEAR ON YOUR ANSWER SHEET WILL BE SCORED.** Answers in your test booklet will not be scored.

IF YOU SKIP A QUESTION, BE SURE TO SKIP THE CORRESPONDING ROW OF ANSWER CHOICES ON YOUR ANSWER SHEET.

Guessing
As you read through the response options, do your best to find the best answer. If you cannot quickly find the best answer, try to eliminate as many of the others as possible. Then guess among the remaining answer choices. Your score on each test is based on the number of test questions you have answered correctly. There is no penalty for incorrect answers; therefore, it is better to guess than not to respond at all.

Reading Passages
Some test questions are based on reading passages. You may want to employ some of the following strategies while you are completing these test questions.

One strategy is to read the passage thoroughly and carefully and then answer each question, referring to the passage only as needed. Another strategy is to read the questions first, gaining an idea of what is sought in them, and then read the passage with the questions in mind. Yet another strategy is to review the passage to gain an overview of its content, and then answer each question by referring back to the passage for the specific answer. Any of these strategies may be appropriate for you. You should not answer the questions on the basis of your own opinions but rather on the basis of the ideas and opinions expressed in the passage.

Check Accuracy
Use any remaining time at the end of the test session to check the accuracy of your work. Go back to the test questions that gave you difficulty and verify your work on them. Check the answer sheet, too. Be sure that you have marked your answers accurately and have completely erased changed answers.

ATAS OBJECTIVES

Sub-area I—Reading

0001 Understand the meaning of general vocabulary words
For example:
- Determining the meaning of commonly encountered words presented in context
- Identifying appropriate synonyms or antonyms for words
- Recognizing the correct use of commonly misused pairs of words (e.g. their/there, to/too)

0002 Understand the stated main idea of a reading passage
For example:
- Identifying the stated main idea of a passage
- Identifying the topic sentence of a passage
- Recognizing introductory and summary statements of a passage
- Selecting an accurate restatement of the main idea of a passage

0003 Understand the sequence of ideas in a reading passage
For example:
- Identifying the order of events or steps described in a passage
- Organizing a set of instructions into their proper sequence
- Identifying the cause-and-effect relationships described in a passage

0004 Interpret textual and graphic information
For example:
- Interpreting information from tables, line and bar graphs, and pie charts
- Recognizing appropriate representations of written information in graphic or tabular form
- Recognizing differences between fact and opinion

Sub-area II—Writing

0005 Understand the standard use of verbs
For example:
- Identifying standard subject-verb agreement (e.g. number, person)
- Identifying verb tense (e.g. present, past)
- Recognizing consistency of verb tense (e.g. verb endings)

0006 Understand the standard use of pronouns and modifiers
For example:
- Identifying agreement (number, gender, person) between a pronoun and its antecedent
- Using possessive pronouns (e.g. its vs. it's), relative pronouns (e.g. that, which) and demonstrative pronouns (e.g. this, that)
- Using comparative and superlative modifiers (e.g. good/better/best)

0007 Understand standard sentence structure and punctuation
For example:
- Distinguishing between sentence fragments and complete sentences
- Distinguishing between run-on sentences and correctly divided sentences
- Identifying correct and incorrect punctuation

0008 Understand the standard use of capitalization and spelling
For example:
- Identifying standard capitalization at the beginning of sentences
- Identifying standard capitalization of proper words and titles
- Recognizing standard spelling of commonly encountered words presented in context

Sub-area III—Mathematics

0009 Understand number concepts
For example:
- Identifying the place value of digits (e.g. hundreds, tens, ones, tenths)
- Identifying correctly rounded numbers
- Identifying equivalent weights and measures in different units (e.g. feet and inches, quarts and pints, kilograms and grams)
- Estimating the solution to a measurement problem (e.g. height, perimeter)

0010 Understand the addition and subtraction of whole numbers
For example:
- Solving problems involving the addition of whole numbers
- Solving problems involving the subtraction of whole numbers
- Applying principles of addition and subtraction of whole numbers to solve problems encountered in every day life

0011 Understand multiplication and division of whole numbers
For example:
- Solving problems involving the multiplication of whole numbers
- Solving problems involving the division of whole numbers
- Applying principles of multiplication and division of whole numbers to solve problems encountered in every day life

0012 Understand operations involving fractions, decimals and percents
For example:
- Solving problems involving fractions, decimals and percents
- Solving problems involving conversions between fractions, decimals and percents

0013 Understand classroom instruction related to reading
For example:
- Providing support under the guidance of classroom teachers to match student needs, styles of learning and background experiences (e.g. drilling, using pictorial or video materials, relating reading materials to real-life contexts)
- Helping students use instructional resources (dictionaries, encyclopedias, multimedia) to support reading
- Helping students use a variety of approaches to understand what they read (e.g. skimming, questioning to tap prior knowledge, monitoring understanding, reviewing, summarizing)
- Gathering information about students' progress as readers to support the teacher's planning, assessment and instruction

0014 Understand classroom instruction related to writing
For example:
- Understanding drafting, editing and proofreading written work
- Helping students focus their writing
- Helping students use instructional resources (dictionaries, grammar books, library and technological resources) to support writing
- Gathering information about students' progress as writers to support the teacher's planning, assessment and instruction

0015 Understand classroom instruction related to mathematics
For example:
- Relating mathematics to everyday situations
- Identifying and correcting basic errors in addition, subtraction, multiplication and division
- Helping students use instructional resources (hands-on materials, rulers, money, charts, graphs) to support mathematical learning
- Gathering information about students' progress in mathematics to support the teacher's planning, assessment and instruction

SAMPLE QUESTIONS

Along with each sample question, this guide presents the correct response and an explanation of why the correct response is the best available response. Keep in mind when reviewing the questions and response options that there is one *best* answer to each question. Remember, too, that each explanation offers one of perhaps many perspectives on why a given response is correct or incorrect in the context of the question; there may be other explanations as well.

EXAMINATION SECTION

DIRECTIONS: Each question or incomplete statement is followed by several suggested answers or completions. Select the one that BEST answers the question or completes the statement. *PRINT THE LETTER OF THE CORRECT ANSWER IN THE SPACE AT THE RIGHT.*

Questions 1 through 3 refer to the following passage:

    Children can benefit greatly from learning how to play chess. Through studying and playing chess, they strengthen their thinking, learn how to deal with competitive situations and develop important social skills.
    Playing chess requires hard thinking. Players must analyze moves and decide on the best one to play. Then they must live with their decision no matter how good or bad the move.
    Players must set goals and fight their way toward achieving them. Usually, the first player to make a bad move loses the game, but not always. Staying focused on winning the game and overcoming setbacks are valuable experiences for young people.
    Chess also helps children improve their social skills. Learning to win graciously is just as important as learning to be a good loser. Both of these skills help children interact successfully with other people.
    Chess can be a great deal of fun to play. It can also teach children valuable skills that they can use for the rest of their lives.

1. Read the sentence below, taken from the fourth paragraph of the passage; then complete the exercise that follows:

    "Learning to win graciously is just as important as learning to be a good loser."

    Select the best definition of the word <u>graciously</u> as it is used in the sentence above.
    - A. quietly
    - B. courteously
    - C. happily
    - D. humorously

1._____

2. What is the *topic sentence* of the passage?
   A. Children can benefit greatly from learning how to play chess
   B. Through studying and playing chess, they strengthen their thinking, learn how to deal with competitive situations and develop important social skills
   C. Chess can be a great deal of fun to play
   D. It can also teach children valuable skills that they can use for the rest of their lives

3. According to the passage, how do children develop social skills while playing chess?
   A. By staying focused on winning the game and overcoming setbacks they encounter
   B. By having fun playing with other children
   C. By living with the decisions they make during each game
   D. By learning how to behave appropriately whether they win or lose a game

4. Use the graph below to answer the question:

Annual Student Suspension Report

(Line graph showing Number of Suspensions by Month: Sept=4, Oct=4, Nov=7, Dec=5, Jan=3, Feb=5, Mar=6, Apr=3, May=4, Jun=6)

What was the total number of student suspensions during the three-month period of September, October and November?
   A. 8
   B. 11
   C. 12
   D. 15

5. Which sentence is in the present tense?
   A. The grocery bag still stood where he left it.
   B. Melissa asks for a little more sugar in her tea.
   C. Conrad reflected on the meaning of the story.
   D. He came home soon after we arrived.

6. Choose the best word to complete the sentence below:

   The new principal, _____ speaks four languages, has some exciting ideas to suggest.
   A. that
   B. whom
   C. which
   D. who

7. Which of the following is NOT a complete sentence? 7._____
   A. Making a lesson plan is necessary.
   B. First, define the objectives.
   C. The usual standards for evaluation.
   D. Nothing is more important.

8. Which word is spelled *incorrectly*? 8._____
   A. critisism
   B. judicial
   C. scholastic
   D. recognition

9. How many centimeters are in 7 meters? 9._____
   A. 10
   B. 70
   C. 100
   D. 700

10. A cashier has $42 in his cash drawer at the beginning of his shift. During 10._____
    his shift, he collects $815. How much money is in his drawer at the end
    of his shift?
    A. $773
    B. $815
    C. $839
    D. $857

11. What is the remainder when 53 is divided by 9? 11._____
    A. 6
    B. 7
    C. 8
    D. 9

12. What is 60% written as a fraction? 12._____
    A. 2/5
    B. 3/5
    C. 2/3
    D. 5/6

13. A teaching assistant in a second-grade class is taking a small group of 13._____
    students to the school library to find information needed to complete an
    assignment on whales. Which of the following would be the best way for
    the teaching assistant to help the students with their project?
    A. Make sure the students remain quiet and behave appropriately
       while they are in the library
    B. Have the students choose information resources on their own, and
       help them use the resources to complete their assignments
    C. Show the students how to find the entry on whales in a dictionary,
       and transfer that information to their notebooks
    D. Find a story about whales, read it aloud to the students, then have
       them discuss what they learned from the story

14. Ms. Perrotta, a teaching assistant in a seventh-grade English class, has been asked to supervise a small group of students while they each edit the first drafts of short stories they are writing based on personal experiences. Which of the following pieces of information would be most helpful for Ms. Perrotta to provide to the teacher about the students' work during this session?

14._____

    A. What kinds of help the students needed
    B. Which story Ms. Perrotta thinks is the most creative
    C. Which student Ms. Perrotta thinks is the best writer
    D. How well the students worked together

15. Mr. Barry has just introduced his third-grade class to the concept of division. After several days, most of the students seem to have grasped the concept, but Louisa is still confused. Mr. Barry asks Ms. Salem, his teaching assistant, to help Louisa. Which of the following approaches would best help Louisa understand the basic idea of division?

15._____

    A. Show Louisa how to do division problems using a calculator
    B. Have Louisa read the section in the textbook on division and ask Ms. Salem if she has any questions
    C. Have Louisa separate a large pile of pennies into smaller piles of equal numbers
    D. Give Louisa a worksheet with several simple division problems

ANSWERS AND EXPLANATIONS

1. B

   To be gracious is to behave in a kind and polite manner to others. Thus, of the choices available, "courteously" most closely fits the meaning of the word graciously as it appears in the passage.

2. A

   The topic sentence of a passage introduces the central idea that the rest of the passage develops. This passage talks about a variety of ways in which playing chess benefits children. Therefore, A best states the central idea.

3. D

   In the fourth paragraph, the author points out that, whether children win or lose at chess, they gain experience in interacting with other people.

4. D

   The graph indicates that there were four students suspended in September, four more in October, and seven more in November. Thus, the total was 15.

5. B

   When a verb is in the present tense, it expresses action that is taking place right now, rather than in the past or in the future. To express the present tense with a singular noun, an *s* or an *es* is usually added to the verb. Among the alternatives, only B contains a verb in the present tense.

6. D

   The pronouns "that" and "which" are generally used to refer to a thing or an idea. The pronouns "who" and "whom" are used to refer to a person. Specifically, the pronoun "who" is used when the person being referred to is the subject of a phrase or sentence, and the pronoun "whom" is used when the person being referred to is the object of a phrase or sentence. In this sentence, "who" refers to "principal," which is the subject of the opening phrase.

7. C

   A complete sentence is a group of words that expresses a complete thought. Only C does not express a complete thought.

8. A

   Choice A, "critisism," is not spelled correctly. The correct spelling is "criticism."

9. D

   There are 100 centimeters in a meter, therefore there are 700 centimeters in 7 meters.

10. D

    In order to determine how much money the cashier has in his cash drawer at the end of the day, add the amount at the beginning of the day ($42) to the amount added during the day ($815). The result is $857.

11. C

The remainder is what is left over when one number is divided by another number. When 53 is divided by 9, the result is 5, with 8 left over.

12. B

Sixty percent means 60 out of 100, or 60/100, which is the same as 6/10, which is the same as 3/5.

13. B

The goal of this activity is to have the students use the school library to gather information to complete an assignment on whales. By allowing the students to select information resources on their own, then showing them how to use these resources effectively, the teaching assistant helps students learn basic research skills while providing the assistance needed to complete their assignments.

14. A

The fundamental purpose of the work that the teacher has assigned is to help students learn how to edit their own work, a complex skill that the students will continue to learn and practice over many years. Response A, providing information on the kinds of problems that the students are experiencing as they try to edit their own work, represents the best way of helping the teacher plan the continuing instruction that the students will need.

15. C

The teacher has asked his teaching assistant to provide extra help to a student who is having difficulty understanding a new mathematical concept. The activity described in Response C is best suited to this goal because it introduces the concept of division in a simple, concrete manner. By using familiar objects in a hands-on activity, Louisa can more easily grasp the fundamental idea of division before applying the concept to specific problems.

HOW TO TAKE A TEST

I. YOU MUST PASS AN EXAMINATION

A. *WHAT EVERY CANDIDATE SHOULD KNOW*

Examination applicants often ask us for help in preparing for the written test. What can I study in advance? What kinds of questions will be asked? How will the test be given? How will the papers be graded?

As an applicant for a civil service examination, you may be wondering about some of these things. Our purpose here is to suggest effective methods of advance study and to describe civil service examinations.

Your chances for success on this examination can be increased if you know how to prepare. Those "pre-examination jitters" can be reduced if you know what to expect. You can even experience an adventure in good citizenship if you know why civil service exams are given.

B. *WHY ARE CIVIL SERVICE EXAMINATIONS GIVEN?*

Civil service examinations are important to you in two ways. As a citizen, you want public jobs filled by employees who know how to do their work. As a job seeker, you want a fair chance to compete for that job on an equal footing with other candidates. The best-known means of accomplishing this two-fold goal is the competitive examination.

Exams are widely publicized throughout the nation. They may be administered for jobs in federal, state, city, municipal, town or village governments or agencies.

Any citizen may apply, with some limitations, such as the age or residence of applicants. Your experience and education may be reviewed to see whether you meet the requirements for the particular examination. When these requirements exist, they are reasonable and applied consistently to all applicants. Thus, a competitive examination may cause you some uneasiness now, but it is your privilege and safeguard.

C. *HOW ARE CIVIL SERVICE EXAMS DEVELOPED?*

Examinations are carefully written by trained technicians who are specialists in the field known as "psychological measurement," in consultation with recognized authorities in the field of work that the test will cover. These experts recommend the subject matter areas or skills to be tested; only those knowledges or skills important to your success on the job are included. The most reliable books and source materials available are used as references. Together, the experts and technicians judge the difficulty level of the questions.

Test technicians know how to phrase questions so that the problem is clearly stated. Their ethics do not permit "trick" or "catch" questions. Questions may have been tried out on sample groups, or subjected to statistical analysis, to determine their usefulness.

Written tests are often used in combination with performance tests, ratings of training and experience, and oral interviews. All of these measures combine to form the best-known means of finding the right person for the right job.

II. HOW TO PASS THE WRITTEN TEST

A. NATURE OF THE EXAMINATION

To prepare intelligently for civil service examinations, you should know how they differ from school examinations you have taken. In school you were assigned certain definite pages to read or subjects to cover. The examination questions were quite detailed and usually emphasized memory. Civil service exams, on the other hand, try to discover your present ability to perform the duties of a position, plus your potentiality to learn these duties. In other words, a civil service exam attempts to predict how successful you will be. Questions cover such a broad area that they cannot be as minute and detailed as school exam questions.

In the public service similar kinds of work, or positions, are grouped together in one "class." This process is known as *position-classification*. All the positions in a class are paid according to the salary range for that class. One class title covers all of these positions, and they are all tested by the same examination.

B. FOUR BASIC STEPS

1) Study the announcement

How, then, can you know what subjects to study? Our best answer is: "Learn as much as possible about the class of positions for which you've applied." The exam will test the knowledge, skills and abilities needed to do the work.

Your most valuable source of information about the position you want is the official exam announcement. This announcement lists the training and experience qualifications. Check these standards and apply only if you come reasonably close to meeting them.

The brief description of the position in the examination announcement offers some clues to the subjects which will be tested. Think about the job itself. Review the duties in your mind. Can you perform them, or are there some in which you are rusty? Fill in the blank spots in your preparation.

Many jurisdictions preview the written test in the exam announcement by including a section called "Knowledge and Abilities Required," "Scope of the Examination," or some similar heading. Here you will find out specifically what fields will be tested.

2) Review your own background

Once you learn in general what the position is all about, and what you need to know to do the work, ask yourself which subjects you already know fairly well and which need improvement. You may wonder whether to concentrate on improving your strong areas or on building some background in your fields of weakness. When the announcement has specified "some knowledge" or "considerable knowledge," or has used adjectives like "beginning principles of…" or "advanced … methods," you can get a clue as to the number and difficulty of questions to be asked in any given field. More questions, and hence broader coverage, would be included for those subjects which are more important in the work. Now weigh your strengths and weaknesses against the job requirements and prepare accordingly.

3) Determine the level of the position

Another way to tell how intensively you should prepare is to understand the level of the job for which you are applying. Is it the entering level? In other words, is this the position in which beginners in a field of work are hired? Or is it an intermediate or advanced level? Sometimes this is indicated by such words as "Junior" or "Senior" in the class title. Other jurisdictions use Roman numerals to designate the level – Clerk I, Clerk II, for example. The word "Supervisor" sometimes appears in the title. If the level is not indicated by the title, check the description of duties. Will you be working under very close supervision, or will you have responsibility for independent decisions in this work?

4) Choose appropriate study materials

Now that you know the subjects to be examined and the relative amount of each subject to be covered, you can choose suitable study materials. For beginning level jobs, or even advanced ones, if you have a pronounced weakness in some aspect of your training, read a modern, standard textbook in that field. Be sure it is up to date and has general coverage. Such books are normally available at your library, and the librarian will be glad to help you locate one. For entry-level positions, questions of appropriate difficulty are chosen -- neither highly advanced questions, nor those too simple. Such questions require careful thought but not advanced training.

If the position for which you are applying is technical or advanced, you will read more advanced, specialized material. If you are already familiar with the basic principles of your field, elementary textbooks would waste your time. Concentrate on advanced textbooks and technical periodicals. Think through the concepts and review difficult problems in your field.

These are all general sources. You can get more ideas on your own initiative, following these leads. For example, training manuals and publications of the government agency which employs workers in your field can be useful, particularly for technical and professional positions. A letter or visit to the government department involved may result in more specific study suggestions, and certainly will provide you with a more definite idea of the exact nature of the position you are seeking.

III. KINDS OF TESTS

Tests are used for purposes other than measuring knowledge and ability to perform specified duties. For some positions, it is equally important to test ability to make adjustments to new situations or to profit from training. In others, basic mental abilities not dependent on information are essential. Questions which test these things may not appear as pertinent to the duties of the position as those which test for knowledge and information. Yet they are often highly important parts of a fair examination. For very general questions, it is almost impossible to help you direct your study efforts. What we can do is to point out some of the more common of these general abilities needed in public service positions and describe some typical questions.

1) General information

Broad, general information has been found useful for predicting job success in some kinds of work. This is tested in a variety of ways, from vocabulary lists to questions about current events. Basic background in some field of work, such as sociology or economics, may be sampled in a group of questions. Often these are principles which have become familiar to most persons through exposure rather than through formal training. It is difficult to advise you how to study for these questions; being alert to the world around you is our best suggestion.

2) Verbal ability

An example of an ability needed in many positions is verbal or language ability. Verbal ability is, in brief, the ability to use and understand words. Vocabulary and grammar tests are typical measures of this ability. Reading comprehension or paragraph interpretation questions are common in many kinds of civil service tests. You are given a paragraph of written material and asked to find its central meaning.

3) Numerical ability

Number skills can be tested by the familiar arithmetic problem, by checking paired lists of numbers to see which are alike and which are different, or by interpreting charts and graphs. In the latter test, a graph may be printed in the test booklet which you are asked to use as the basis for answering questions.

4) Observation

A popular test for law-enforcement positions is the observation test. A picture is shown to you for several minutes, then taken away. Questions about the picture test your ability to observe both details and larger elements.

5) Following directions

In many positions in the public service, the employee must be able to carry out written instructions dependably and accurately. You may be given a chart with several columns, each column listing a variety of information. The questions require you to carry out directions involving the information given in the chart.

6) Skills and aptitudes

Performance tests effectively measure some manual skills and aptitudes. When the skill is one in which you are trained, such as typing or shorthand, you can practice. These tests are often very much like those given in business school or high school courses. For many of the other skills and aptitudes, however, no short-time preparation can be made. Skills and abilities natural to you or that you have developed throughout your lifetime are being tested.

Many of the general questions just described provide all the data needed to answer the questions and ask you to use your reasoning ability to find the answers. Your best preparation for these tests, as well as for tests of facts and ideas, is to be at your physical and mental best. You, no doubt, have your own methods of getting into an exam-taking mood and keeping "in shape." The next section lists some ideas on this subject.

IV. KINDS OF QUESTIONS

Only rarely is the "essay" question, which you answer in narrative form, used in civil service tests. Civil service tests are usually of the short-answer type. Full instructions for answering these questions will be given to you at the examination. But in case this is your first experience with short-answer questions and separate answer sheets, here is what you need to know:

1) **Multiple-choice Questions**

Most popular of the short-answer questions is the "multiple choice" or "best answer" question. It can be used, for example, to test for factual knowledge, ability to solve problems or judgment in meeting situations found at work.

A multiple-choice question is normally one of three types—
- It can begin with an incomplete statement followed by several possible endings. You are to find the one ending which *best* completes the statement, although some of the others may not be entirely wrong.
- It can also be a complete statement in the form of a question which is answered by choosing one of the statements listed.

- It can be in the form of a problem – again you select the best answer.

Here is an example of a multiple-choice question with a discussion which should give you some clues as to the method for choosing the right answer:

When an employee has a complaint about his assignment, the action which will *best* help him overcome his difficulty is to
   A. discuss his difficulty with his coworkers
   B. take the problem to the head of the organization
   C. take the problem to the person who gave him the assignment
   D. say nothing to anyone about his complaint

In answering this question, you should study each of the choices to find which is best. Consider choice "A" – Certainly an employee may discuss his complaint with fellow employees, but no change or improvement can result, and the complaint remains unresolved. Choice "B" is a poor choice since the head of the organization probably does not know what assignment you have been given, and taking your problem to him is known as "going over the head" of the supervisor. The supervisor, or person who made the assignment, is the person who can clarify it or correct any injustice. Choice "C" is, therefore, correct. To say nothing, as in choice "D," is unwise. Supervisors have and interest in knowing the problems employees are facing, and the employee is seeking a solution to his problem.

2) True/False Questions

The "true/false" or "right/wrong" form of question is sometimes used. Here a complete statement is given. Your job is to decide whether the statement is right or wrong.

SAMPLE: A roaming cell-phone call to a nearby city costs less than a non-roaming call to a distant city.

This statement is wrong, or false, since roaming calls are more expensive.

This is not a complete list of all possible question forms, although most of the others are variations of these common types. You will always get complete directions for answering questions. Be sure you understand *how* to mark your answers – ask questions until you do.

V. RECORDING YOUR ANSWERS

Computer terminals are used more and more today for many different kinds of exams.
For an examination with very few applicants, you may be told to record your answers in the test booklet itself. Separate answer sheets are much more common. If this separate answer sheet is to be scored by machine – and this is often the case – it is highly important that you mark your answers correctly in order to get credit.
An electronic scoring machine is often used in civil service offices because of the speed with which papers can be scored. Machine-scored answer sheets must be marked with a pencil, which will be given to you. This pencil has a high graphite content which responds to the electronic scoring machine. As a matter of fact, stray dots may register as answers, so do not let your pencil rest on the answer sheet while you are pondering the correct answer. Also, if your pencil lead breaks or is otherwise defective, ask for another.

Since the answer sheet will be dropped in a slot in the scoring machine, be careful not to bend the corners or get the paper crumpled.

The answer sheet normally has five vertical columns of numbers, with 30 numbers to a column. These numbers correspond to the question numbers in your test booklet. After each number, going across the page are four or five pairs of dotted lines. These short dotted lines have small letters or numbers above them. The first two pairs may also have a "T" or "F" above the letters. This indicates that the first two pairs only are to be used if the questions are of the true-false type. If the questions are multiple choice, disregard the "T" and "F" and pay attention only to the small letters or numbers.

Answer your questions in the manner of the sample that follows:

32. The largest city in the United States is
    A. Washington, D.C.
    B. New York City
    C. Chicago
    D. Detroit
    E. San Francisco

1) Choose the answer you think is best. (New York City is the largest, so "B" is correct.)
2) Find the row of dotted lines numbered the same as the question you are answering. (Find row number 32)
3) Find the pair of dotted lines corresponding to the answer. (Find the pair of lines under the mark "B.")
4) Make a solid black mark between the dotted lines.

VI. BEFORE THE TEST

Common sense will help you find procedures to follow to get ready for an examination. Too many of us, however, overlook these sensible measures. Indeed, nervousness and fatigue have been found to be the most serious reasons why applicants fail to do their best on civil service tests. Here is a list of reminders:

- Begin your preparation early – Don't wait until the last minute to go scurrying around for books and materials or to find out what the position is all about.
- Prepare continuously – An hour a night for a week is better than an all-night cram session. This has been definitely established. What is more, a night a week for a month will return better dividends than crowding your study into a shorter period of time.
- Locate the place of the exam – You have been sent a notice telling you when and where to report for the examination. If the location is in a different town or otherwise unfamiliar to you, it would be well to inquire the best route and learn something about the building.
- Relax the night before the test – Allow your mind to rest. Do not study at all that night. Plan some mild recreation or diversion; then go to bed early and get a good night's sleep.
- Get up early enough to make a leisurely trip to the place for the test – This way unforeseen events, traffic snarls, unfamiliar buildings, etc. will not upset you.
- Dress comfortably – A written test is not a fashion show. You will be known by number and not by name, so wear something comfortable.

- Leave excess paraphernalia at home – Shopping bags and odd bundles will get in your way. You need bring only the items mentioned in the official notice you received; usually everything you need is provided. Do not bring reference books to the exam. They will only confuse those last minutes and be taken away from you when in the test room.
- Arrive somewhat ahead of time – If because of transportation schedules you must get there very early, bring a newspaper or magazine to take your mind off yourself while waiting.
- Locate the examination room – When you have found the proper room, you will be directed to the seat or part of the room where you will sit. Sometimes you are given a sheet of instructions to read while you are waiting. Do not fill out any forms until you are told to do so; just read them and be prepared.
- Relax and prepare to listen to the instructions
- If you have any physical problem that may keep you from doing your best, be sure to tell the test administrator. If you are sick or in poor health, you really cannot do your best on the exam. You can come back and take the test some other time.

VII. AT THE TEST

The day of the test is here and you have the test booklet in your hand. The temptation to get going is very strong. Caution! There is more to success than knowing the right answers. You must know how to identify your papers and understand variations in the type of short-answer question used in this particular examination. Follow these suggestions for maximum results from your efforts:

1) Cooperate with the monitor

The test administrator has a duty to create a situation in which you can be as much at ease as possible. He will give instructions, tell you when to begin, check to see that you are marking your answer sheet correctly, and so on. He is not there to guard you, although he will see that your competitors do not take unfair advantage. He wants to help you do your best.

2) Listen to all instructions

Don't jump the gun! Wait until you understand all directions. In most civil service tests you get more time than you need to answer the questions. So don't be in a hurry. Read each word of instructions until you clearly understand the meaning. Study the examples, listen to all announcements and follow directions. Ask questions if you do not understand what to do.

3) Identify your papers

Civil service exams are usually identified by number only. You will be assigned a number; you must not put your name on your test papers. Be sure to copy your number correctly. Since more than one exam may be given, copy your exact examination title.

4) Plan your time

Unless you are told that a test is a "speed" or "rate of work" test, speed itself is usually not important. Time enough to answer all the questions will be provided, but this does not mean that you have all day. An overall time limit has been set. Divide the total time (in minutes) by the number of questions to determine the approximate time you have for each question.

5) Do not linger over difficult questions

If you come across a difficult question, mark it with a paper clip (useful to have along) and come back to it when you have been through the booklet. One caution if you do this – be sure to skip a number on your answer sheet as well. Check often to be sure that you have not lost your place and that you are marking in the row numbered the same as the question you are answering.

6) Read the questions

Be sure you know what the question asks! Many capable people are unsuccessful because they failed to *read* the questions correctly.

7) Answer all questions

Unless you have been instructed that a penalty will be deducted for incorrect answers, it is better to guess than to omit a question.

8) Speed tests

It is often better NOT to guess on speed tests. It has been found that on timed tests people are tempted to spend the last few seconds before time is called in marking answers at random – without even reading them – in the hope of picking up a few extra points. To discourage this practice, the instructions may warn you that your score will be "corrected" for guessing. That is, a penalty will be applied. The incorrect answers will be deducted from the correct ones, or some other penalty formula will be used.

9) Review your answers

If you finish before time is called, go back to the questions you guessed or omitted to give them further thought. Review other answers if you have time.

10) Return your test materials

If you are ready to leave before others have finished or time is called, take ALL your materials to the monitor and leave quietly. Never take any test material with you. The monitor can discover whose papers are not complete, and taking a test booklet may be grounds for disqualification.

VIII. EXAMINATION TECHNIQUES

1) Read the general instructions carefully. These are usually printed on the first page of the exam booklet. As a rule, these instructions refer to the timing of the examination; the fact that you should not start work until the signal and must stop work at a signal, etc. If there are any *special* instructions, such as a choice of questions to be answered, make sure that you note this instruction carefully.

2) When you are ready to start work on the examination, that is as soon as the signal has been given, read the instructions to each question booklet, underline any key words or phrases, such as *least, best, outline, describe* and the like. In this way you will tend to answer as requested rather than discover on reviewing your paper that you *listed without describing*, that you selected the *worst* choice rather than the *best* choice, etc.

3) If the examination is of the objective or multiple-choice type – that is, each question will also give a series of possible answers: A, B, C or D, and you are called upon to select the best answer and write the letter next to that answer on your answer paper – it is advisable to start answering each question in turn. There may be anywhere from 50 to 100 such questions in the three or four hours allotted and you can see how much time would be taken if you read through all the questions before beginning to answer any. Furthermore, if you come across a question or group of questions which you know would be difficult to answer, it would undoubtedly affect your handling of all the other questions.

4) If the examination is of the essay type and contains but a few questions, it is a moot point as to whether you should read all the questions before starting to answer any one. Of course, if you are given a choice – say five out of seven and the like – then it is essential to read all the questions so you can eliminate the two that are most difficult. If, however, you are asked to answer all the questions, there may be danger in trying to answer the easiest one first because you may find that you will spend too much time on it. The best technique is to answer the first question, then proceed to the second, etc.

5) Time your answers. Before the exam begins, write down the time it started, then add the time allowed for the examination and write down the time it must be completed, then divide the time available somewhat as follows:
   - If 3-1/2 hours are allowed, that would be 210 minutes. If you have 80 objective-type questions, that would be an average of 2-1/2 minutes per question. Allow yourself no more than 2 minutes per question, or a total of 160 minutes, which will permit about 50 minutes to review.
   - If for the time allotment of 210 minutes there are 7 essay questions to answer, that would average about 30 minutes a question. Give yourself only 25 minutes per question so that you have about 35 minutes to review.

6) The most important instruction is to *read each question* and make sure you know what is wanted. The second most important instruction is to *time yourself properly* so that you answer every question. The third most important instruction is to *answer every question*. Guess if you have to but include something for each question. Remember that you will receive no credit for a blank and will probably receive some credit if you write something in answer to an essay question. If you guess a letter – say "B" for a multiple-choice question – you may have guessed right. If you leave a blank as an answer to a multiple-choice question, the examiners may respect your feelings but it will not add a point to your score. Some exams may penalize you for wrong answers, so in such cases *only*, you may not want to guess unless you have some basis for your answer.

7) Suggestions
   a. Objective-type questions
      1. Examine the question booklet for proper sequence of pages and questions
      2. Read all instructions carefully
      3. Skip any question which seems too difficult; return to it after all other questions have been answered
      4. Apportion your time properly; do not spend too much time on any single question or group of questions

5. Note and underline key words – *all, most, fewest, least, best, worst, same, opposite,* etc.
6. Pay particular attention to negatives
7. Note unusual option, e.g., unduly long, short, complex, different or similar in content to the body of the question
8. Observe the use of "hedging" words – *probably, may, most likely,* etc.
9. Make sure that your answer is put next to the same number as the question
10. Do not second-guess unless you have good reason to believe the second answer is definitely more correct
11. Cross out original answer if you decide another answer is more accurate; do not erase until you are ready to hand your paper in
12. Answer all questions; guess unless instructed otherwise
13. Leave time for review

  b. Essay questions
1. Read each question carefully
2. Determine exactly what is wanted. Underline key words or phrases.
3. Decide on outline or paragraph answer
4. Include many different points and elements unless asked to develop any one or two points or elements
5. Show impartiality by giving pros and cons unless directed to select one side only
6. Make and write down any assumptions you find necessary to answer the questions
7. Watch your English, grammar, punctuation and choice of words
8. Time your answers; don't crowd material

8) Answering the essay question

Most essay questions can be answered by framing the specific response around several key words or ideas. Here are a few such key words or ideas:

M's: manpower, materials, methods, money, management
P's: purpose, program, policy, plan, procedure, practice, problems, pitfalls, personnel, public relations

  a. Six basic steps in handling problems:
1. Preliminary plan and background development
2. Collect information, data and facts
3. Analyze and interpret information, data and facts
4. Analyze and develop solutions as well as make recommendations
5. Prepare report and sell recommendations
6. Install recommendations and follow up effectiveness

  b. Pitfalls to avoid
1. *Taking things for granted* – A statement of the situation does not necessarily imply that each of the elements is necessarily true; for example, a complaint may be invalid and biased so that all that can be taken for granted is that a complaint has been registered

2. *Considering only one side of a situation* – Wherever possible, indicate several alternatives and then point out the reasons you selected the best one
3. *Failing to indicate follow up* – Whenever your answer indicates action on your part, make certain that you will take proper follow-up action to see how successful your recommendations, procedures or actions turn out to be
4. *Taking too long in answering any single question* – Remember to time your answers properly

IX. AFTER THE TEST

Scoring procedures differ in detail among civil service jurisdictions although the general principles are the same. Whether the papers are hand-scored or graded by machine we have described, they are nearly always graded by number. That is, the person who marks the paper knows only the number – never the name – of the applicant. Not until all the papers have been graded will they be matched with names. If other tests, such as training and experience or oral interview ratings have been given, scores will be combined. Different parts of the examination usually have different weights. For example, the written test might count 60 percent of the final grade, and a rating of training and experience 40 percent. In many jurisdictions, veterans will have a certain number of points added to their grades.

After the final grade has been determined, the names are placed in grade order and an eligible list is established. There are various methods for resolving ties between those who get the same final grade – probably the most common is to place first the name of the person whose application was received first. Job offers are made from the eligible list in the order the names appear on it. You will be notified of your grade and your rank as soon as all these computations have been made. This will be done as rapidly as possible.

People who are found to meet the requirements in the announcement are called "eligibles." Their names are put on a list of eligible candidates. An eligible's chances of getting a job depend on how high he stands on this list and how fast agencies are filling jobs from the list.

When a job is to be filled from a list of eligibles, the agency asks for the names of people on the list of eligibles for that job. When the civil service commission receives this request, it sends to the agency the names of the three people highest on this list. Or, if the job to be filled has specialized requirements, the office sends the agency the names of the top three persons who meet these requirements from the general list.

The appointing officer makes a choice from among the three people whose names were sent to him. If the selected person accepts the appointment, the names of the others are put back on the list to be considered for future openings.

That is the rule in hiring from all kinds of eligible lists, whether they are for typist, carpenter, chemist, or something else. For every vacancy, the appointing officer has his choice of any one of the top three eligibles on the list. This explains why the person whose name is on top of the list sometimes does not get an appointment when some of the persons lower on the list do. If the appointing officer chooses the second or third eligible, the No. 1 eligible does not get a job at once, but stays on the list until he is appointed or the list is terminated.

X. HOW TO PASS THE INTERVIEW TEST

The examination for which you applied requires an oral interview test. You have already taken the written test and you are now being called for the interview test – the final part of the formal examination.

You may think that it is not possible to prepare for an interview test and that there are no procedures to follow during an interview. Our purpose is to point out some things you can do in advance that will help you and some good rules to follow and pitfalls to avoid while you are being interviewed.

What is an interview supposed to test?

The written examination is designed to test the technical knowledge and competence of the candidate; the oral is designed to evaluate intangible qualities, not readily measured otherwise, and to establish a list showing the relative fitness of each candidate – as measured against his competitors – for the position sought. Scoring is not on the basis of "right" and "wrong," but on a sliding scale of values ranging from "not passable" to "outstanding." As a matter of fact, it is possible to achieve a relatively low score without a single "incorrect" answer because of evident weakness in the qualities being measured.

Occasionally, an examination may consist entirely of an oral test – either an individual or a group oral. In such cases, information is sought concerning the technical knowledges and abilities of the candidate, since there has been no written examination for this purpose. More commonly, however, an oral test is used to supplement a written examination.

Who conducts interviews?

The composition of oral boards varies among different jurisdictions. In nearly all, a representative of the personnel department serves as chairman. One of the members of the board may be a representative of the department in which the candidate would work. In some cases, "outside experts" are used, and, frequently, a businessman or some other representative of the general public is asked to serve. Labor and management or other special groups may be represented. The aim is to secure the services of experts in the appropriate field.

However the board is composed, it is a good idea (and not at all improper or unethical) to ascertain in advance of the interview who the members are and what groups they represent. When you are introduced to them, you will have some idea of their backgrounds and interests, and at least you will not stutter and stammer over their names.

What should be done before the interview?

While knowledge about the board members is useful and takes some of the surprise element out of the interview, there is other preparation which is more substantive. It *is* possible to prepare for an oral interview – in several ways:

1) Keep a copy of your application and review it carefully before the interview

This may be the only document before the oral board, and the starting point of the interview. Know what education and experience you have listed there, and the sequence and dates of all of it. Sometimes the board will ask you to review the highlights of your experience for them; you should not have to hem and haw doing it.

2) Study the class specification and the examination announcement

Usually, the oral board has one or both of these to guide them. The qualities, characteristics or knowledges required by the position sought are stated in these documents. They offer valuable clues as to the nature of the oral interview. For example, if the job involves supervisory responsibilities, the announcement will usually indicate that knowledge of modern supervisory methods and the qualifications of the candidate as a supervisor will be tested. If so, you can expect such questions, frequently in the form of a hypothetical situation which you are expected to solve. NEVER go into an oral without knowledge of the duties and responsibilities of the job you seek.

3) Think through each qualification required

Try to visualize the kind of questions you would ask if you were a board member. How well could you answer them? Try especially to appraise your own knowledge and background in each area, *measured against the job sought*, and identify any areas in which you are weak. Be critical and realistic – do not flatter yourself.

4) Do some general reading in areas in which you feel you may be weak

For example, if the job involves supervision and your past experience has NOT, some general reading in supervisory methods and practices, particularly in the field of human relations, might be useful. Do NOT study agency procedures or detailed manuals. The oral board will be testing your understanding and capacity, not your memory.

5) Get a good night's sleep and watch your general health and mental attitude

You will want a clear head at the interview. Take care of a cold or any other minor ailment, and of course, no hangovers.

What should be done on the day of the interview?

Now comes the day of the interview itself. Give yourself plenty of time to get there. Plan to arrive somewhat ahead of the scheduled time, particularly if your appointment is in the fore part of the day. If a previous candidate fails to appear, the board might be ready for you a bit early. By early afternoon an oral board is almost invariably behind schedule if there are many candidates, and you may have to wait. Take along a book or magazine to read, or your application to review, but leave any extraneous material in the waiting room when you go in for your interview. In any event, relax and compose yourself.

The matter of dress is important. The board is forming impressions about you – from your experience, your manners, your attitude, and your appearance. Give your personal appearance careful attention. Dress your best, but not your flashiest. Choose conservative, appropriate clothing, and be sure it is immaculate. This is a business interview, and your appearance should indicate that you regard it as such. Besides, being well groomed and properly dressed will help boost your confidence.

Sooner or later, someone will call your name and escort you into the interview room. *This is it.* From here on you are on your own. It is too late for any more preparation. But remember, you asked for this opportunity to prove your fitness, and you are here because your request was granted.

What happens when you go in?

The usual sequence of events will be as follows: The clerk (who is often the board stenographer) will introduce you to the chairman of the oral board, who will introduce you to the other members of the board. Acknowledge the introductions before you sit down. Do not be surprised if you find a microphone facing you or a stenotypist sitting by. Oral interviews are usually recorded in the event of an appeal or other review.

Usually the chairman of the board will open the interview by reviewing the highlights of your education and work experience from your application – primarily for the benefit of the other members of the board, as well as to get the material into the record. Do not interrupt or comment unless there is an error or significant misinterpretation; if that is the case, do not hesitate. But do not quibble about insignificant matters. Also, he will usually ask you some question about your education, experience or your present job – partly to get you to start talking and to establish the interviewing "rapport." He may start the actual questioning, or turn it over to one of the other members. Frequently, each member undertakes the questioning on a particular area, one in which he is perhaps most competent, so you can expect each member to participate in the examination. Because time is limited, you may also expect some rather abrupt switches in the direction the questioning takes, so do not be upset by it. Normally, a board member will not pursue a single line of questioning unless he discovers a particular strength or weakness.

After each member has participated, the chairman will usually ask whether any member has any further questions, then will ask you if you have anything you wish to add. Unless you are expecting this question, it may floor you. Worse, it may start you off on an extended, extemporaneous speech. The board is not usually seeking more information. The question is principally to offer you a last opportunity to present further qualifications or to indicate that you have nothing to add. So, if you feel that a significant qualification or characteristic has been overlooked, it is proper to point it out in a sentence or so. Do not compliment the board on the thoroughness of their examination – they have been sketchy, and you know it. If you wish, merely say, "No thank you, I have nothing further to add." This is a point where you can "talk yourself out" of a good impression or fail to present an important bit of information. Remember, *you close the interview yourself*.

The chairman will then say, "That is all, Mr. _____, thank you." Do not be startled; the interview is over, and quicker than you think. Thank him, gather your belongings and take your leave. Save your sigh of relief for the other side of the door.

How to put your best foot forward

Throughout this entire process, you may feel that the board individually and collectively is trying to pierce your defenses, seek out your hidden weaknesses and embarrass and confuse you. Actually, this is not true. They are obliged to make an appraisal of your qualifications for the job you are seeking, and they want to see you in your best light. Remember, they must interview all candidates and a non-cooperative candidate may become a failure in spite of their best efforts to bring out his qualifications. Here are 15 suggestions that will help you:

1) Be natural – Keep your attitude confident, not cocky

If you are not confident that you can do the job, do not expect the board to be. Do not apologize for your weaknesses, try to bring out your strong points. The board is interested in a positive, not negative, presentation. Cockiness will antagonize any board member and make him wonder if you are covering up a weakness by a false show of strength.

2) Get comfortable, but don't lounge or sprawl

Sit erectly but not stiffly. A careless posture may lead the board to conclude that you are careless in other things, or at least that you are not impressed by the importance of the occasion. Either conclusion is natural, even if incorrect. Do not fuss with your clothing, a pencil or an ashtray. Your hands may occasionally be useful to emphasize a point; do not let them become a point of distraction.

3) Do not wisecrack or make small talk

This is a serious situation, and your attitude should show that you consider it as such. Further, the time of the board is limited – they do not want to waste it, and neither should you.

4) Do not exaggerate your experience or abilities

In the first place, from information in the application or other interviews and sources, the board may know more about you than you think. Secondly, you probably will not get away with it. An experienced board is rather adept at spotting such a situation, so do not take the chance.

5) If you know a board member, do not make a point of it, yet do not hide it

Certainly you are not fooling him, and probably not the other members of the board. Do not try to take advantage of your acquaintanceship – it will probably do you little good.

6) Do not dominate the interview

Let the board do that. They will give you the clues – do not assume that you have to do all the talking. Realize that the board has a number of questions to ask you, and do not try to take up all the interview time by showing off your extensive knowledge of the answer to the first one.

7) Be attentive

You only have 20 minutes or so, and you should keep your attention at its sharpest throughout. When a member is addressing a problem or question to you, give him your undivided attention. Address your reply principally to him, but do not exclude the other board members.

8) Do not interrupt

A board member may be stating a problem for you to analyze. He will ask you a question when the time comes. Let him state the problem, and wait for the question.

9) Make sure you understand the question

Do not try to answer until you are sure what the question is. If it is not clear, restate it in your own words or ask the board member to clarify it for you. However, do not haggle about minor elements.

10) Reply promptly but not hastily

A common entry on oral board rating sheets is "candidate responded readily," or "candidate hesitated in replies." Respond as promptly and quickly as you can, but do not jump to a hasty, ill-considered answer.

11) Do not be peremptory in your answers

A brief answer is proper – but do not fire your answer back. That is a losing game from your point of view. The board member can probably ask questions much faster than you can answer them.

12) Do not try to create the answer you think the board member wants

He is interested in what kind of mind you have and how it works – not in playing games. Furthermore, he can usually spot this practice and will actually grade you down on it.

13) Do not switch sides in your reply merely to agree with a board member

Frequently, a member will take a contrary position merely to draw you out and to see if you are willing and able to defend your point of view. Do not start a debate, yet do not surrender a good position. If a position is worth taking, it is worth defending.

14) Do not be afraid to admit an error in judgment if you are shown to be wrong

The board knows that you are forced to reply without any opportunity for careful consideration. Your answer may be demonstrably wrong. If so, admit it and get on with the interview.

15) Do not dwell at length on your present job

The opening question may relate to your present assignment. Answer the question but do not go into an extended discussion. You are being examined for a *new* job, not your present one. As a matter of fact, try to phrase ALL your answers in terms of the job for which you are being examined.

Basis of Rating

Probably you will forget most of these "do's" and "don'ts" when you walk into the oral interview room. Even remembering them all will not ensure you a passing grade. Perhaps you did not have the qualifications in the first place. But remembering them will help you to put your best foot forward, without treading on the toes of the board members.

Rumor and popular opinion to the contrary notwithstanding, an oral board wants you to make the best appearance possible. They know you are under pressure – but they also want to see how you respond to it as a guide to what your reaction would be under the pressures of the job you seek. They will be influenced by the degree of poise you display, the personal traits you show and the manner in which you respond.

ABOUT THIS BOOK

This book contains tests divided into Examination Sections. Go through each test, answering every question in the margin. We have also attached a sample answer sheet at the back of the book that can be removed and used. At the end of each test look at the answer key and check your answers. On the ones you got wrong, look at the right answer choice and learn. Do not fill in the answers first. Do not memorize the questions and answers, but understand the answer and principles involved. On your test, the questions will likely be different from the samples. Questions are changed and new ones added. If you understand these past questions you should have success with any changes that arise. Tests may consist of several types of questions. We have additional books on each subject should more study be advisable or necessary for you. Finally, the more you study, the better prepared you will be. This book is intended to be the last thing you study before you walk into the examination room. Prior study of relevant texts is also recommended. NLC publishes some of these in our Fundamental Series. Knowledge and good sense are important factors in passing your exam. Good luck also helps. So now study this Passbook, absorb the material contained within and take that knowledge into the examination. Then do your best to pass that exam.

EXAMINATION SECTION

EXAMINATION SECTION
TEST 1

DIRECTIONS: Each question or incomplete statement is followed by several suggested answers or completions. Select the one that BEST answers the question or completes the statement. *PRINT THE LETTER OF THE CORRECT ANSWER IN THE SPACE AT THE RIGHT.*

Questions 1-6.

DIRECTIONS: Questions 1 through 6 are to be answered on the basis of the following passage.

    A long time ago there lived a great shah. He ordered to build a beautiful palace which had many wonderful things in it. Among other curiosities in the palace, there was a hall, where all the walls, the ceiling, the door, and even the floor were made of mirrors. The mirrors were so clear and smooth that visitors didn't understand at once that there was a mirror in front of them; so accurately the mirrors would reflect the objects. Moreover, the walls of this hall were made in a way that they created an extraordinary increased echo.
    Once, a dog ran into the hall and froze in surprise that in the middle of the hall a whole pack of dogs surrounded him from all sides, from above and below. Just in case, the dog bared his teeth and all the reflections responded to him in the same way. Frightened, the dog frantically barked; the echo imitated the bark and increased it many times. The dog barked even harder and the echo was keeping up. The dog tossed from one side to another, biting the air; his reflections also tossed around snapping their teeth.
    In the morning, the guards found the miserable dog, lifeless and surrounded by a million reflections of lifeless dogs. There was nobody in the hall that would make any harm to the dog. The dog died by fighting his own reflections.
    The world doesn't bring good and evil on its own. Everything that is happening around us is the reflection of our own thoughts feelings, wishes, and actions. The world is a big mirror.

1. What is the main idea of the above reading passage?   1._____
   A. Reflection breeds reflection.
   B. Dogs like their territory.
   C. Our life is a reflection of our thoughts.
   D. A house with lots of mirrors drives evil.

2. What is the MOST appropriate meaning for the word *reflection* according to this passage?   2._____
   A. Mirror image   B. Thinking   C. Echo   D. Reproduction

3. What is the MOST appropriate topic sentence of this passage?   3._____
   A. Attitude towards life is what matters
   B. Dogs
   C. Shah and his mirror house
   D. Fight your reflections

4. What does "surrounded by a million reflections of lifeless dogs" mean in the above passage?
   A. There were millions of dogs around the miserable dog.
   B. The miserable dog's reflection was seen in all the mirrors of the hall in the palace.
   C. The dog is so powerful that he was exhibited by millions of reflections.
   D. The dog fought with his reflections.

4.____

5. What does "frantically" mean?
   A. Wildly
   B. Calmly
   C. Tranquilly
   D. Unperturbedly

5.____

6. The MOST appropriate summary sentence for this passage is:
   A. Dogs don't like to be countered by other dogs
   B. The dog died by fighting his own reflections
   C. Our thoughts are responsible for what we encounter in our life.
   D. The Shad had a beautiful palace that proved to be a disaster for the dog.

6.____

Questions 7-10.

DIRECTIONS: Questions 7 through 10 are to be answered on the basis of the following graph which indicates how a group of students walk during a month of school.

Student Name	Number of Steps Traveled		Step Distance		Total Distance
Suzie Q.	134	x	0.5 m	=	67.0 m
Jim D.	121	x	0.8 m	=	96.8 m
Frank L.	218	x	130.8 m	=	130.8 m
Sally B.	243	x	0.4 m	=	97.2 m
			GROUP TOTAL:		391.8 m

7. Which of the following students have a great step distance?
   A. Sally B.   B. Suzie Q.   C. Frank L.   D. Jim D.

7.____

8. Which of the following students have traveled more number of steps?
   A. Sally B.   B. Suzie Q.   C. Frank L.   D. Jim D.

8.____

9. Based on the above table, which of the following is the formula for finding the distance?
   A. No. of steps traveled – Step distance
   B. No. of steps traveled x Step distance
   C. No. of steps traveled x Step distance – 1
   D. No. of steps traveled x Step distance +1

9.____

10. The combined effort of the students leads to the total traveled distance of
    A. 390 m   B. 130.8 m   C. 392 m   D. 67 m

10.____

11. Which sentence is in the past tense?
    A. Tammy came home and completed her homework.
    B. Hannah is Dalya's new friend.
    C. Ray might become a doctor.
    D. All of the parents are waiting to see the principal in relation with yesterday's incident.

12. Choose the BEST word to complete the following sentence:
    The girl who lives next door _____ some interesting art pieces in her room.
    A. have   B. has   C. will have   D. are

13. Which of the following is NOT a complete sentence?
    A. The boys playing the baseball game need to improve
    B. He plays football with great passion
    C. In conclusion, I feel that the whole idea behind learning from peers
    D. She is a dancer, but she prefers singing over dancing

14. Which word is spelled INCORRECTLY?
    A. Credential   B. Beleiving
    C. Reverberation   D. Jeopardy

15. Which word is spelled CORRECTLY?
    A. ChildKraft   B. Childcraft   C. Child craft   D. Child kraft

16. How many milliliters are in 1 cubic centimeter?
    A. 1   B. 100   C. 10,000   D. 1,000

17. What is the remainder when 73 is divided by 9?
    A. 8   B. 9   C. 0   D. 1

18. Shelly is selling her 4-year-old car for $15,000. She is selling it for $6,000 less, as she has to sell it as soon as possible. What is the actual price of the car?
    A. $16,000   B. $9,000   C. $20,000   D. $21,000

19. What is 45% written as a fraction?
    A. 0.45   B. $^{45}/_{10}$ C. $^{4}/_{100} + ^{5}/_{100}$ D. $^{45}/_{100}$

20. 0.5 could also be written as
    A. $^{6}/_{20}$ B. $^{5}/_{100}$
    C. ½   D. All of the above

21. John is sending his son to a school that is 6 miles away. His son uses a carpooling facility for 60% of the distance. John drives his son for the remaining _____ miles.
    A. 3.1   B. 2.4   C. 4.1   D. 4.7

22. _____ is the actual purchased price of a toy, if the shopkeeper has sold it for a profit of $4.70. The toy was then sold to the end customer for a rate of $17.50.
    A. $22.20   B. $20.70   C. $8.30   D. $12.80

23. Dave sold 84 m of rug. Each piece of the carpet is 2 m. Each piece of the carpet was sold at the rate of $4.00. What is the total price paid by the buyer?
    A. $42   B. $168   C. $116   D. $72

24. Mrs. Higgins is a teacher of a Pre-K classroom. Her class has two students who have difficulty reading words. She asked her teaching assistant to help them. Which is the BEST approach?
    A. Give them a talking dictionary
    B. Read books for them
    C. Teach phonics and use sight words for them
    D. Any of the above

25. Mrs. Preethra, a teaching assistant, is asked to supervise a small group of students while they take an assessment. Which of the following is the MOST appropriate expected action of a teaching assistant in this case?
    A. See if the students are taking the test.
    B. Give hints for students to arrive at the correct answers.
    C. Read questions for the students if they need it, ensure that they don't talk with each other, and ensure that they answer all of the questions.
    D. Ensure that they don't talk to each other.

KEY (CORRECT ANSWERS)

1.	C	11.	A
2.	B	12.	B
3.	A	13.	C
4.	B	14.	B
5.	A	15.	C
6.	C	16.	A
7.	D	17.	D
8.	A	18.	D
9.	B	19.	D
10.	C	20.	C

21.	B
22.	D
23.	B
24.	C
25.	C

TEST 2

DIRECTIONS: Each question or incomplete statement is followed by several suggested answers or completions. Select the one that BEST answers the question or completes the statement. *PRINT THE LETTER OF THE CORRECT ANSWER IN THE SPACE AT THE RIGHT.*

Questions 1-6.

DIRECTIONS: Questions 1 through 6 are to be answered on the basis of the following passage.

Different Strokes for Little Folks: Carol Ann Tomlinson on "Differentiated Instruction"
Professor Carol Ann Tomlinson understands the challenge of providing appropriate learning experiences for all students. Once a classroom teacher who had to simultaneously meet the needs of kids struggling to read at grade level and those who were ready for Harvard, she turned to differentiated instruction.

Is Differentiation the Answer to the Tracking Debate?
Max Fischer is taking steps to transform his classroom into the differentiated model Carol Ann Tomlinson describes, but he is confronting some roadblocks along the way. How different, he wonders, will his classroom might look like a year from now...

Your Students: No Two Are Alike
Educator Brenda Dyck reflects on how she focuses the first two weeks of instruction on helping students become familiar with their learning strengths. Surveys and activities help students learn which intelligences they favor. These beginning-of-the-year activities will be revisited throughout the school year.

Readiness Differentiation: Daring to Get Back on My Bike
Max Fischer compares his first steps at creating a differentiated classroom to learning to ride a bike. Differentiating without drawing attention to students' ability levels has been the biggest challenge.

1. What is the MAIN idea of the above reading passage? 1.____
   A. Differentiated instruction
   B. No two students are alike
   C. Students' ability levels are a challenge
   D. Providing an appropriate learning experience for all students

2. What does the third paragraph discuss about in particular? 2.____
   A. The importance of revisiting beginning-of-the-year activities
   B. The importance of creating a differentiated classroom
   C. Reflection is important for a teacher
   D. Focusing on helping students to identify their learning strengths

3. What is the MOST appropriate topic sentence of this passage? 3._____
   A. Differentiating instruction
   B. Identifying learning strengths
   C. Learning to ride a bike vs. differentiated classroom
   D. Tackling challenges in a differentiated classroom

4. What does *differentiated instruction* NOT mean? 4._____
   A. Preparing different types of assessment sheets for different students
   B. Teacher anticipating and responding to a variety of students
   C. Modifying instruction based on students' needs
   D. Modifying teaching strategies based on students' needs

5. What does *No Two Alike* mean in the above passage? 5._____
   A. No two teachers are the same.
   B. No two teaching strategies are the same.
   C. No two students are the same
   D. No two activities are the same.

6. The MOST appropriate meaning for the word *transform* in this passage is 6._____
   A. renovate   B. modernize   C. update   D. change

Questions 7-10.

DIRECTIONS: Questions 7 through 10 are to be answered on the basis of the following graph.

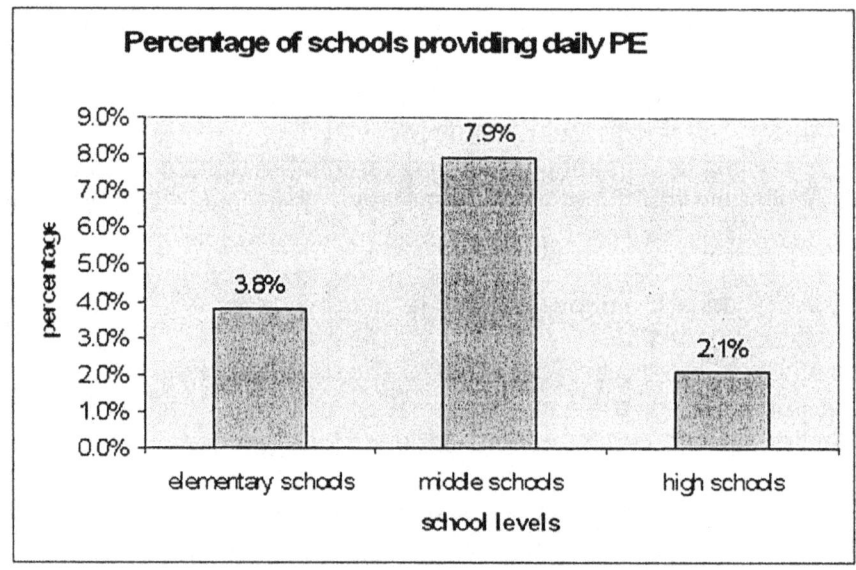

A graph of the percent of schools offering daily physical activity

7. _____ schools provide more physical activity as per the above graph. 7._____
   A. Elementary   B. Middle
   C. High   D. All of the above

8. High schools provide less than _____% of physical activity. 8._____
   A. 1 B. 2 C. 4 D. 0

9. Which of the following statements could be inferred from reading the above graph? 9._____
   A. Elementary and high schools offer very less levels of physical education.
   B. Middle schools offer more physical education than high and elementary schools.
   C. Middle schools offer physical education a lot, but lesser than elementary education.
   D. High schools offer less levels of physical education, as high school students do more physical education at home.

10. What is the total percentage of physical education activities offered by all the elementary, middle, and high schools discussed in the graph? 10._____
    A. 7.9% B. 13.8% C. 12.8% D. 14.8%

11. Which sentence is in the present tense? 11._____
    A. Ian reflected on his actions.
    B. Leora and Maya are discussing their project.
    C. Ben went to his brother's play.
    D. Max might come to the party tomorrow.

12. Choose the BEST word to complete the following sentence: 12._____
    The boy _____ the most interesting character in this play.
    A. plays B. played C. play D. would play

13. Which of the following is NOT a complete sentence? 13._____
    A. Making good rapport with students is essential
    B. He is a very good student of mine
    C. Firstly, the significance of students attending school regularly
    D. She is coming to my home tomorrow

14. Which word is spelled INCORRECTLY? 14._____
    A. Patiense B. Bewildered C. Reverence D. Invincible

15. Which word is spelled CORRECTLY? 15._____
    A. Kindergarten   B. Kinder garten
    C. Kinderkarten   D. Kindergarden

16. How many milliliters are in 3 liters? 16._____
    A. 1,000 B. 100 C. 300 D. 3,000

17. What is the remainder when 56 is divided by 7? 17._____
    A. 8 B. 9 C. 0 D. 1

18. Raymond got a hutch for $76 during a Thanksgiving sale. He sold it after 2 years for $44. What is the cost price of the hutch in this case?
    A. $76 B. $44 C. $32 D. $120

19. What is 70% written as?
    A. $7/10$ B. $70/100$ C. 0.07 D. 0.07

20. $30/100$ could also be written as
    A. $6/20$
    B. $3/100$
    C. 0.3
    D. None of the above

21. John is sending his son to a music school that is 14 miles away. His son uses a carpooling facility for 70% of the distance. John's son uses carpooling for _____ miles.
    A. 9.8 B. 4.1 C. 11.1 D. 2.7

22. _____ is the actual purchase price of a toy if the shopkeeper has sold it for a profit of $6.20. The toy was then sold to the end customer for a rate of $14.50.
    A. $8.20 B. $20.70 C. $8.30 D. $21.70

23. Dave sold 24 m of carpet. Each piece of the carpet is 3 m. Each piece of the carpet was sold at the rate of $3. What is the TOTAL price paid by the buyer?
    A. $24 B. $34 C. $9 D. $72

24. Lisa is a teacher of a Pre-K classroom. She is teaching the concept of addition to her students. One of her students, Evan, finds it difficult to understand addition. She asked her teaching assistant to help Evan. Which is the BEST approach?
    A. Use a calculator and teach how to do addition
    B. Use math manipulatives and help Evan learn about it
    C. Give additional worksheets to Evan
    D. Any of the above

25. Which of the following is the MOST appropriate role of a teaching assistant?
    A. Substitute classes
    B. Take care of the afterschool program at school
    C. Assist the teacher in executing her class program
    D. All of the above

KEY (CORRECT ANSWERS)

1.	A		11.	B
2.	D		12.	A
3.	A		13.	C
4.	A		14.	A
5.	C		15.	A
6.	D		16.	D
7.	C		17.	C
8.	C		18.	A
9.	B		19.	D
10.	B		20.	A

21. A
22. C
23. A
24. B
25. C

TEST 3

DIRECTIONS: Each question or incomplete statement is followed by several suggested answers or completions. Select the one that BEST answers the question or completes the statement. *PRINT THE LETTER OF THE CORRECT ANSWER IN THE SPACE AT THE RIGHT.*

1. Which sentence is in the future tense? 1.____
    A. Maya went home last night.
    B. Eli will be playing the role of Jesus in the Christmas play.
    C. Eden loves to each spaghetti.
    D. William wants to be a football player in the future.

2. Choose the BEST word to complete the following sentence: 2.____
   Richie does not _____ to play guitar.
    A. needed   B. like   C. need   D. likes

3. Which word is NOT spelled correctly? 3.____
    A. Scintillating   B. Elegant   C. Efficeint   D. Evident

4. Which word is spelled INCORRECTLY? 4.____
    A. Comittee   B. Tomorrow   C. Succession   D. Precision

Questions 5-9.

DIRECTIONS: In answering Questions 5 through 9, read the sentence and indicate which part is INCORRECT.

5. Asking for clarifications when you are not clear about something is the 5.____
   properly course of action.
    A. Correct as is   B. you are not clear
    C. for clarifications   D. properly

6. Lazor, a school of its kind: has to be recognized for its service to the students. 6.____
    A. a school   B. of its kind:
    C. has to be   D. Correct as is

7. He would not enroll his child in that afterschool program, if he knew only 7.____
   about the teachers' rebuking approach.
    A. rebuking approach   B. would not
    C. he knew only   D. Correct as is

8. I don't want too and he can't make me do it as well. 8.____
    A. too   B. Correct as is
    C. make me   D. as well

9. Gaby is in a preschool program currently. She will be admitted in a kindergarten program next year.
   A. Correct as is
   B. in a
   C. currently
   D. will be

9.____

Questions 10-14.

DIRECTIONS: In answering Questions 10 through 14, complete the sentences using appropriate pronouns and modifiers.

10. _____ is the only one way to tackle this situation.
    A. There
    B. Their
    C. Here
    D. Heir

10.____

11. _____ is a bird.
    A. He
    B. She
    C. It's
    D. Its'

11.____

12. Make sure to always do your _____ in every work that you do.
    A. better
    B. best
    C. good
    D. part

12.____

13. What if _____ are late for the movie?
    A. their
    B. they
    C. she
    D. he

13.____

14. This vacation is _____ than the last year vacation.
    A. more exciting than
    B. most exciting than
    C. exciting than
    D. exciting

14.____

Questions 15-19.

DIRECTIONS: Questions 15 through 19 are to be answered on the basis of the following passage.

How To Make Iced Tea

Iced tea is easy to make. However, if the basic steps in making this famous drink are not followed, then it is nothing but unsweetened powder. Four simple steps should be performed to create this wonderful concoction.

Firstly, select the flavor that satisfies your taste buds. There is a wide range of different brands in the market selling a wide variety of ready-to-make iced tea packets, from mango, lemon, peach and apple.

Second, make sure your kitchen has the necessary equipment for concocting the drink. Get a two-quart pitcher. It may be glass or plastic, but the former is better as it allows the liquid to shine through, thus making it attractive to everyone. Also get a long spoon, sugar, a measuring cup, water, and an ice cube tray full of ice. When all the requirements have been met, the mixing process can begin.

The third step is all a matter of combining everything together. Then pour the powdered contents of the packet into the pitcher. With the measuring cup, measure the amount of sugar you want to add according to your liking, and then pour it in. Add the cold water till the pitcher is filled within two inches of the top. Use the long spoon to stir the mixture. Stir in a clockwise direction until all the powder has dissolved. Then taste the drink. If it is not sweet enough, add more sugar to it until you are satisfied with the taste. After achieving the desired taste, rinse off the equipment – spoon, measuring cup – and shelve them for future use.

Finally, sit back relax and enjoy your drink. To do this, obtain a glass from the shelf, add ice and then fill the glass with the iced tea.

15. What would be the BEST introductory sentence for this passage?
    A. East or west, ice tea is the best.
    B. Ice tea in four simple steps
    C. Ice tea is one of the most refreshing beverages made by man
    D. Any of the above

16. The first step deals with
    A. making a concoction
    B. mixing
    C. rinsing
    D. choosing the flavor of your taste

17. According to this passage, what pitcher is recommended for making a concoction?
    A. Plastic   B. Glass   C. Ceramic   D. Stainless steel

18. Which of the following is the synonym of concoction?
    A. Mixture   B. Blend   C. Composite   D. Combination

19. What is the sequence followed in this passage?
    A. Choosing a flavor, making a concoction, mixing and tasting
    B. Tasting the flavor, making a concoction, mixing and choosing a flavor
    C. Making a concoction, mixing, tasting, and choosing a flavor
    D. Making a concoction, mixing, choosing a flavor, and tasting

20. How many grams are in 1 pound?
    A. 1,000   B. 100   C. 453.592   D. 450.592

21. How many liters equal 1 gallon?
    A. 1   B. 4   C. 5   D. 3

22. Convert 100°F to Celsius.
    A. 37.778   B. 32.78   C. 32.111   D. 132.78

23. Convert 0.5% into a fraction.
    A. $2/4$ B. $1/3$ C. $1/5$ D. $3/2$

24. Alexandra is 5 years younger than her brother. But her brother is twice as old as their younger brother, Tom. Alexandra is 6 years old. How old is the younger brother, Tom?

    A. 6.5   B. 5.5   C. 4.5   D. 6

24._____

25. Jason wanted his teaching assistant to teach the class instead of him as he wants to relax. He asks his teaching assistant to do so. What is the BEST course of action you would recommend to the teaching assistant?

    A. Take it up happily.
    B. Start teaching and slowly gain an upper hand over Jason.
    C. Refuse it and threaten to inform the school management.
    D. Ask for a reason and help Jason understand the role of a teaching assistant.

25._____

KEY (CORRECT ANSWERS)

1.	B	11.	C
2.	B	12.	B
3.	C	13.	B
4.	A	14.	A
5.	D	15.	C
6.	B	16.	D
7.	C	17.	B
8.	A	18.	A
9.	A	19.	A
10.	A	20.	C

21.	B
22.	A
23.	A
24.	B
25.	D

TEST 4

DIRECTIONS: Each question or incomplete statement is followed by several suggested answers or completions. Select the one that BEST answers the question or completes the statement. *PRINT THE LETTER OF THE CORRECT ANSWER IN THE SPACE AT THE RIGHT.*

1. Which sentence is in the past present tense?   1.____
   A. I had written the story before my teacher proofchecked it.
   B. I have written a novel.
   C. He spoke with my mom yesterday.
   D. We are waiting for the match to begin.

2. Which sentence is in the future perfect tense?   2.____
   A. Dave is going to complete the course.
   B. Jason loves to play guitar.
   C. I shall have completed the course during the summer vacation.
   D. I went to Ken's home yesterday.

3. Which of the following is spelled INCORRECTLY?   3.____
   A. Recortation   B. Recreation   C. Reckoning   D. Reincarnation

4. Which of the following is spelled INCORRECTLY?   4.____
   A. Sanctum   B. Ilustration   C. Achievement   D. Compilation

Questions 5-10.

DIRECTIONS: Questions 5 through 10 are to be answered on the basis of the following passage.

Many of us interested in efforts at educational reform have focused on the learner or student, be she a young child in preschool or an adult bent on acquiring a new skill. It is clarifying to have such a focus and, indeed, any efforts at reform are doomed to fail unless they concentrate on the properties and potentials of the individual learner. My own work on multiple intelligences has partaken of this general focus; colleagues and I have sought to foster a range of intellectual strengths in our students.

But after several years of active involvement in efforts at educational reform, I am convinced that success depends upon the active involvement of at least four factors:

Assessment: Unless one is able to assess the learning that takes place in different domains, and by different cognitive processes, even superior curricular innovations are destined to remain unutilized. In this country, assessment drives instruction. We must devise procedures and instruments which are "intelligent-fair" and which allow us to look directly at the kinds of learning in which we are interested.

Curriculum: Far too much of what is taught today is included primarily for historical reasons. Even teachers, not to mention students, often cannot explain why a certain topic needs to be covered in school. We need to reconfigure curricula so that they focus on skills, knowledge, and above all, understandings that are truly desirable in our country today. And we need to adapt those curricular as much as possible to the particular learning styles and strengths of students.

2 (#4)

Teacher Education: While most teacher education institutions make an honest effort to produce teaching candidates of high quality, these institutions have not been at the forefront of efforts at educational improvement. Too often they are weighted down by students of indifference quality and by excessive – and often counterproductive – requirements which surround training and certification. We need to attract stronger individuals into teaching, improve conditions so that they will remain in teaching, and use our master teachers to help train the next generation of students and teachers.

Community Participation: In the past, Americans have been content to place most educational burdens on the schools. This is no longer a viable option. The increasing cognitive demands of schooling, the severe problems in our society today, and the need for support of students which extends well beyond the 9-3 period each day, all make it essential that other individuals and institutions contribute to the educational process. In addition to support from family members and other mentoring adults, such institutions as business, the professions, and especially museums, need to be involved much more intimately in the educational process.

5. What does *partaken* mean in this passage? 5.____
    A. Joined B. Contributed C. Clubbed D. Separated

6. Reconfiguration of curriculum is discussed under which of the following? 6.____
    A. Assessment
    B. Teacher Education
    C. Community Participation
    D. None of the above

7. What does "intelligence-fair" mean in this passage? 7.____
    A. Intelligence is fair.
    B. It is fair to be intelligent.
    C. Devising procedures that are compatible with intelligence.
    D. Devising procedures that will stimulate intelligence.

8. "Americans have been content to place most educational burdens on the schools." According to this passage, this is a statement of the 8.____
    A. present B. past C. future D. ever living

9. What does *community participation* mean? 9.____
    A. Participation of the community
    B. Support for students from the community to continue their learning process beyond 9-3
    C. Suppor6t for students from the community to ensure that the school is doing its job
    D. Support for students from the community to ensure that the teachers are doing their job

10. What does this passage discuss about in detail? 10.____
    A. The need to address different intelligent styles
    B. The need to have better working conditions for teachers
    C. The museum's participation in education
    D. Businesses' participation in education

11. _____ is the BEST person to do this job?
    A. What
    B. Whose
    C. Who
    D. Any of the above

Questions 12-16.

DIRECTIONS: In answering Questions 12 through 16, read the sentence and indicate which part is INCORRECT.

12. What grammatical advice would you give the student about the sentence beginning "I love tomato sauce but you can use another kind"?
    A. The sentence is perfect as it is.
    B. The sentence needs a comma after sauce.
    C. The sentence needs a semicolon after sauce.
    D. The sentence does not make any sense. Consider revising it.

13. The policemen went to the spot to collect as many as information as they could.
    A. Correct as is
    B. as many as
    C. as they could
    D. to the spot

14. I felt badly when my sister lost her job.
    A. badly
    B. my sister
    C. felt
    D. lost her

15. If you don't feel well, go and lay down.
    A. If you
    B. don't
    C. lay down
    D. feel well

16. The company feels proud to have served our clients for the past 70 years.
    A. have
    B. served
    C. feels proud
    D. none of the above

17. What is the antonym for the word *resourcefulness*?
    A. Inventiveness
    B. Creativity
    C. Originality
    D. Scarcity

18. 1 quart is equal to _____ gallons.
    A. 0.25
    B. 0.4
    C. 1
    D. 0.75

19. Ryan is celebrating his 4th birthday. His sister will be celebrating her 12th birthday this year. His brother is younger than his sister, but his sister is twice older than Ryan's brother. How old is Ryan's brother?
    A. 8
    B. 24
    C. 6
    D. 10

Questions 20-24.

DIRECTIONS: Questions 20 through 24 are to be answered on the basis of the following graph.

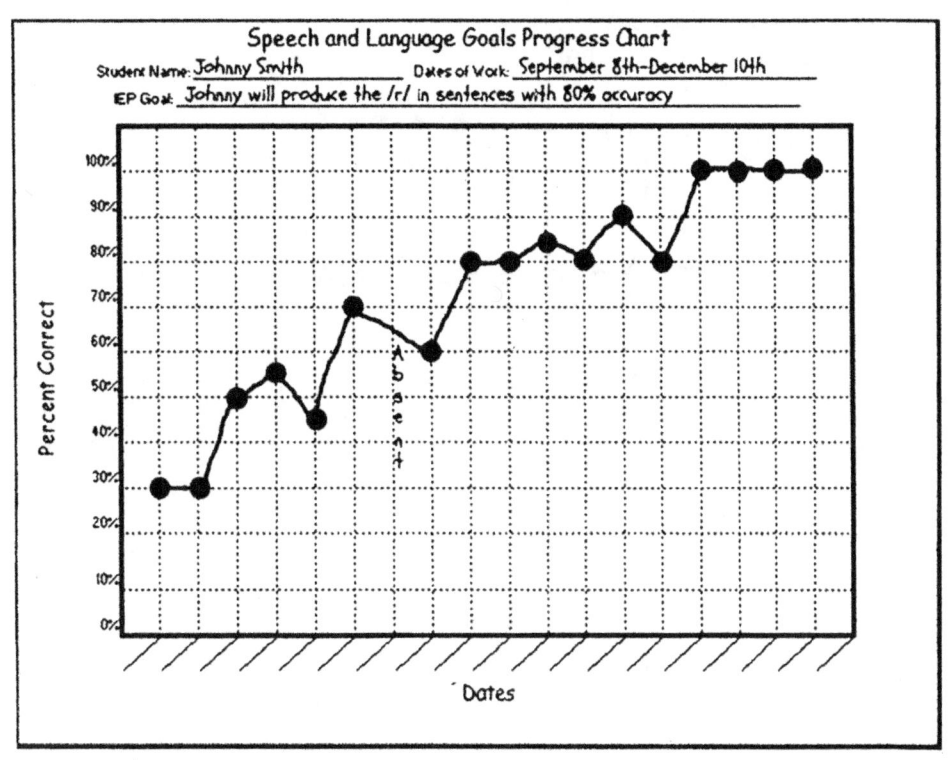

20. The goal is set for _____% accuracy.
    A. 20 B. 45 C. 56 D. 80

21. What percent accuracy did Johnny Smith achieve?
    A. 100 B. 90 C. 80 D. 70

22. What has happened to Johnny Smith's scores over the period of the last four assessments?
    A. It dropped
    B. It increased
    C. It remained constant
    D. None of the above

23. What has happened to John's progress in the beginning?
    A. It dropped
    B. It increased
    C. It varied
    D. None of the above

24. Based on the above graph, what hypothesis could you frame on the impact of absenteeism?
    A. Did not impact
    B. Increased the performance
    C. Decreased the performance
    D. None of the above

25. Mr. Gill's classroom is always noisy. What inference could you draw from it?   25._____
    A. He has poor classroom management skills.
    B. It is a statement; it needs investigation.
    C. His class is full of activities.
    D. His students are misbehaved.

KEY (CORRECT ANSWERS)

1.	A	11.	C
2.	C	12.	B
3.	A	13.	B
4.	B	14.	A
5.	B	15.	C
6.	A	16.	B
7.	C	17.	D
8.	B	18.	A
9.	B	19.	C
10.	A	20.	D

21. A
22. C
23. C
24. C
25. B

EXAMINATION SECTION
TEST 1

DIRECTIONS: Each question or incomplete statement is followed by several suggested answers or completions. Select the one that BEST answers the question or completes the statement. *PRINT THE LETTER OF THE CORRECT ANSWER IN THE SPACE AT THE RIGHT.*

Questions 1-3.

DIRECTIONS: Questions 1 through 3 are to be answered on the basis of the following passage.

When you look at a large factory, you probably do not think about the trees growing in the park. But green plans are a special kind of factory all their own. Using nothing more than water and sunlight green plants have the unique ability to produce their own food. At the same time, they also make it possible for other living things to exist.

All of this work is done by their leaves. Special cells in the leaves absorb energy from sunlight. This light energy reacts with water that the plant has absorbed from the ground and splits the water into two chemicals. One chemical, oxygen, is released into the air. The other chemical, hydrogen, helps produce sugars that enable the plant to grow new stems, leaves, blossoms, and seeds.

By making their own food, plants accomplish several things. They keep themselves alive. They grow the seeds needed to reproduce. They produce the pollen that enables other plants of their kind to reproduce. Meanwhile, the oxygen released into the air makes it possible for other living things to survive.

Human beings have created factories that make wonderful products for us to use and enjoy. But the "living factories" that nature has created produce something even more special—life.

1. Read the sentence below, taken from the first paragraph of the passage: 1.____
   Using nothing more than water and sunlight, green plants have the unique ability to produce their own food.
   Select the word that has the opposite meaning of the word unique as it is used in the above sentence.
   A. interesting   B. distinctive   C. common   D. unusual

2. Which sentence BEST expresses the main idea of the passage?   2.____
   A. Most of the living things on Earth depend upon green plants.
   B. Green plants are a very special kind of living factory.
   C. Leaves do the most important work for green plants.
   D. Human factories and nature's factories have a lot in common.

3. According to the passage, what happens FIRST when sunlight falls on plant leaves?
   A. The plant produces new stems, leaves, and blossoms.
   B. Special cells in the leaves absorb energy in the sun's rays.
   C. Sugars in the leaves are released that feed the plant.
   D. The leaves absorb water from the ground.

4. The pie chart shown at the right shows the monthly expenses for a company. Which of the following is the BEST approximation of the percentage of expenses spent on raw materials?
   A. 15%
   B. 25%
   C. 33%
   D. Insurance

5. In which sentence is the CORRECT verb form used?
   A. Mathematics continue to be a difficult subject for many high school students.
   B. All of the runners is expected to do well in the race.
   C. Which of the seniors have been selected as class president?
   D. The film consists primarily of interviews with world-famous scientists.

6. Which sentence is constructed CORRECTLY?
   A. All of the students in the class did his part to make the play a big success.
   B. Ms. Jones is one of those teachers who are always trying to make her classes more interesting.
   C. Last year, Ms. Jones encouraged the students in her drama class to produce one-act plays.
   D. Ms. Jones hopes the auditorium will have their own stage lights next year.

7. Which sentence is punctuated INCORRECTLY?
   A. According to the curriculum guidelines, students need to learn about the working world.
   B. Working with local businesses is valuable; it provides an interesting and rewarding experience.
   C. Farmers and merchants, as well as health workers, are involved in the program.
   D. Students get actual working experience; while also attending classes.

8. Which underlined word in the sentence below is spelled CORRECTLY?
   The realisation that they were facing an outbreak of typhoid was an ominous development with potentially ghastly consaquences.
   A. realisation   B. ominnous   C. ghastly   D. consaquences

9. 0.07 is equal to
    A. 7/100   B. 1/7   C. 7/10   D. 10/7

10. Select the number that is missing in the following problem: 1,806 - = 358.
    A. 1,448   B. 1,756   C. 2,164   D. 2,774

11. Which number is a multiple of 7?
    A. 27   B. 48   C. 52   D. 63

12. What is 4% of 400?
    A. 16   B. 64   C. 100   D. 160

KEY (CORRECT ANSWERS)

1. C   7. D
2. B   8. C
3. B   9. A
4. C   10. A
5. D   11. D
6. C   12. A

EXAMINATION SECTION
TEST 1

SAMPLE WRITING SKILLS TEST

DIRECTIONS: In the passage that follows, certain words and phrases are underlined and numbered. Below each paragraph, you will find alternatives for each underlined part. You are to choose the one that BEST expresses the idea, makes the statement appropriate for standard written English, or is worded most consistently with the style and tone of the passage as a whole. If you think the original version is best, choose "NO CHANGE." You will also find questions about a section of the passage, or about the passage as a whole. For each question in the test, choose the alternative you consider best and print the letter of the correct answer in the space at the right. Read each passage through once before you begin to answer the questions that accompany it. You cannot determine some answers without reading several sentences beyond the phrase in question. Be sure that you have read far enough ahead each time you choose an alternative.

The following paragraphs may or may not be in the most logical order. Each paragraph is numbered in brackets, and Question 11 will ask you to choose the sequence of paragraph numbers that is in the most logical order.

[1]

In the end, everyone gives up jogging. Some find that their strenuous efforts to earn a living <u>drains</u> away the energy necessary for running. Others <u>suffering from</u> defeat by the
          1   2
hazards of the course, which can range from hard pavement to muddy tracks and from smog to sleet and snow. <u>Person's can also</u> simply collapse in their sneakers. My experience <u>having
                            3   4
been different,</u> however; I had a revelation.
        4

1.   A.   NO CHANGE   B.   drain   1.____
    C.   has drained   D.   is draining

2.   A.   NO CHANGE   B.   suffered   2.____
    C.   suffer   D.   suffering with

3.   A.   NO CHANGE   B.   Still others   3.____
    C.   One may also   D.   It's also possible to

4.   A.   NO CHANGE   B.   being different,   4.____
    C.   was a difference,   D.   was different,

[2]

It happened two summers ago up at Lake Tom, where I was vacationing with friends. I had been accustomed to running fairly regularly, but that whole week I decided to be lazy. I sailed, basked in the sun, and <u>ate wonderful:</u> lobster, steak, corn on the cob, baked potatoes,
5
and ice cream. By the fourth day of this routine I had to face the <u>truth which</u> my body was
6
slowly changing to dough.

5. A. NO CHANGE   B. ate wonderfully: 5.____
    C. eating wonderful: D. eat wonderful:

6. A. NO CHANGE   B. truth about   6.____
    C. truth: D. truth, which

[3]

So, filled with worthy ambition, I tied on my favorite pair of running shoes and loped out to the main road in search of a five-mile route. <u>Out of curiosity, I turned onto Lockout Hill Road</u>
7
and soon discovered how the road had come by its name. I was chugging, at a painfully slow rate, up one of the <u>longest, steepest</u> inclines in the region. Perched at the faraway top of the hill
8
was a solitary house, and only a desire to get a closer look at the place kept me going.

7. A. NO CHANGE   7.____
    B. Out of curiosity, Lookout Hill Road was turned onto
    C. Having become curious, Lookout Hill Road was the road I turned onto
    D. Lookout Hill Road, having become curious, was the route I turned onto -

8. A. NO CHANGE   B. longest, steepest,   8.____
    C. steepest longest,   D. longest and steepest

[4]

I was exhausted when, gasping and bedraggled, I reached the crest of the hill. There I found a native New Englander rocking tranquilly on the front porch of the <u>house, which was painted.</u> "Mister," I panted, "you sure live on a big hill!"
9

9. A. NO CHANGE B. house (painted).
    C. house, and it was painted. D. house.

[5]

He studied me closely for a moment and then responded, "Yep, and I've got the good sense not to run up it." That night I tied the <u>laces of my running</u> shoes around a rock and pitched them into Lake Tom.
                                                    10

10. A. NO CHANGE B. laces, of my running
    C. laces of my running, D. laces; of my running

Questions 11-12.

DIRECTIONS: Questions 11 and 12 pose questions about the essay as a whole.

11. Choose the sequence of paragraph numbers that will make the essay's structure MOST logical.
    A. NO CHANGE B. 1, 4, 5, 2, 3
    C. 1, 5, 4, 3, 2 D. 4, 5, 1, 2, 3

12. Is the use of direct quotation in the essay appropriate?
    A. No, because the essay is an explanation of why the writer gave up jogging.
    B. No, because more physical detail would be better in a descriptive essay.
    C. Yes, because the story is enlivened by dialogue.
    D. Yes, because the essay persuades readers to talk about running.

KEY (CORRECT ANSWERS)

1. B	6. C	11. A
2. C	7. A	12. C
3. B	8. A	
4. D	9. D	
5. B	10. A	

TEST 2

SAMPLE READING SKILLS TEST

DIRECTIONS: The passage below is followed by eight (8) questions. After reading the passage, choose the BEST answer to each question and print the letter of the correct answer in the space at the right. You may look back at the passage as often as you wish.

The Industrial Revolution got under way first in England. This is a historical fact of the utmost significance, for it explains in large part England's primary role in world affairs in the nineteenth century. Consequently, the question of why the Industrial Revolution began where it did is of much more than academic interest.

The problem may be simplified by eliminating those countries that could not, for one reason or another, have generated the Industrial Revolution. Italy at one time had been an economic leader but had dropped behind with the Discoveries and the shift of the main trade routes from the Mediterranean to the Atlantic. Spain had been economically predominant in the sixteenth century but had then lost out to the northwestern states for various reasons already noted. Holland had enjoyed her Golden Age in the seventeenth century, but she lacked the raw materials, labor resources, and water power necessary for machine production. The various countries of Central and Eastern Europe had been little affected by the Commercial Revolution and hence did not develop the technical skills, the trade markets, and the capital reserves needed for industrialization.

This leaves only France and Britain as possible leaders, and of the two, England had certain advantages that enabled her to forge far ahead of her rival. In commerce, for example, the two countries were about equal in 1763, or, if anything, France was somewhat in the lead. But France had a population three times that of England. France also lost ground in foreign trade when she was driven out of Canada and India in 1763. Furthermore, the blockade of the British fleet during the Revolutionary and Napoleonic Wars reduced French commerce to about half its 1788 value, and the loss was not restored until 1825.

Another important advantage enjoyed by Britain is that she had taken an early lead in the basic coal and iron industries. Because the forest reserves were being depleted, Britain early began using coal for fuel and for smelting iron. By the time of the French Revolution in 1789, Britain was producing about 10 million tons of coal per year, while France was producing 700,000 tons. A contemporary poet sensed the significance of this unlimited source of power for English industry when he wrote,

> England's a perfect World! has
>   Indies too!
> Correct your Maps! New-castle
>   is Peru.

England also pioneered in the development of the blast furnace, which, in contrast to the old forges, could mass-produce iron. In 1780 Britain's iron output had been a third that of France; by 1840, it was three times more. All this meant that Britain was pushing ahead in the production of goods of mass consumption for which there was a large and steady demand, whereas France specialized more in luxury commodities of limited and fluctuating demand. Perhaps, Voltaire had this in mind when he wrote in 1735, "In truth we are the whipped cream of Europe"

1. The word *forge*, as it is used in the third paragraph, means   1.____
   A. make use of the blast furnace
   B. alter in order to deceive
   C. move forward steadily
   D. produce wrought iron

2. In comparing the economic development of England and France, the passage shows that: 2.____
   A. England and France were essentially equals until the middle of the nineteenth century
   B. France modeled itself on the examples of Italy and Spain, while England modeled itself on the example of Holland
   C. England gained most of its capital reserves from the spoils of war, while France gained its capital reserves from trade
   D. England began on an equal base with France in the middle of the eighteenth century, but pulled far ahead by the middle of the nineteenth century

3. What reason does the author give for discussing several countries besides England and France?   3.____
   A. Enriching the information provided in the passage
   B. Balancing the passage in the interest of fairness
   C. Simplifying the problem confronted in the passage
   D. Eliminating countries whose Golden Age was yet to come

4. The passage suggests that generating the first Industrial Revolution required which of the following?   4.____
   I. Raw materials
   II. Technical skills
   III. A large population

   The CORRECT answer is:
   A. I only
   B. III only
   C. I and II only
   D. II and III only

5. The author asserts that England's primary role in world affairs in the nineteenth century can be explained in large part by   5.____
   A. the Industrial Revolution getting under way in England first
   B. England's overwhelming naval power
   C. the decline of Italy, Spain, Holland, and Central and Eastern Europe
   D. England's unlimited source of power to fuel its industry

3 (#2)

6. The passage suggests that one indication of a country's success in industrializing was a(n)
   A. educational system that could produce a steady supply of skilled workers
   B. ability to satisfy a large market for necessary, rather than luxury, goods
   C. a forest reserve that could be rapidly and efficiently replenished
   D. a fluctuating demand for luxury, rather than necessary, goods

7. According to the passage, France was compared to whipped cream by
   A. an unnamed contemporary poet   B. Voltaire
   C. Napoleon   D. L.S. Stavrianos

8. The MAIN idea of the passage is that
   A. certain conditions gave England an advantage over other countries in industrializing
   B. with its conquest of Canada in 1763, England controlled the raw materials necessary for industrialization
   C. the English preferred quantity in their goods, while the French demanded quality
   D. England's primary position in international affairs gave it the wealth and influence necessary for industrialization

KEY (CORRECT ANSWERS)

1.	C	6.	B
2.	D	7.	B
3.	C	8.	A
4.	C		
5.	A		

TEST 3

SAMPLE NUMERICAL SKILLS TEST

DIRECTIONS: Solve each problem, choose the correct answer, and print the letter of the correct answer in the space at the right. For some questions, the fifth choice for an answer will be "Not Given." Whenever none of the first four possible answers is correct, choose "Not Given" as your answer.

Do not linger over problems that take too much time. Solve as many as you can; then return to the others in the time you have left.

1. $0.05 + 0.30 =$
   A. 0.08
   B. 0.305
   C. 0.35
   D. 0.38
   E. Not Given

   1.____

2. $0.35 \div 5 =$
   A. 0.07
   B. 0.70
   C. 1.75
   D. 7.00
   E. Not Given

   2.____

3. On a road map with a scale of ¼ inch per 10 miles, the highway from Waukee to Winterset is 1 3/8 inches long. How many miles long is this highway?
   A. 44
   B. 55
   C. 65
   D. 70
   E. 90

   3.____

4. The price of gasoline has increased by 5% during the past month. If the price per gallon a month ago was $1.20, what is the current price per gallon?
   A. $1.24
   B. $1.25
   C. $1.26
   D. $2.70
   E. $1.80

   4.____

5. $-2|3 - 4 - 5| =$
   A. -12
   B. -8
   C. 8
   D. 12
   E. 24

   5.____

6. Which of the following fractions is equivalent to 0.05?
   A. 1/5
   B. 1/20
   C. 1/25
   D. 1/50
   E. 1/200

   6.____

KEY (CORRECT ANSWERS)

1. C
2. A
3. B
4. C
5. A
6. B

TEST 4

SAMPLE ELEMENTARY ALGEBRA TEST

DIRECTIONS: Solve each problem, choose the correct answer, and then print the letter of the correct answer in the space at the right. For some questions, the fifth choice for an answer will be "Not Given." Whenever none of the first four possible answers is correct, choose "Not Given" as your answer.

Do not linger over problems that take too much time. Solve as many as you can; then return to the others in the time you have left.

1. If $5 \times 10^n = 0.005$, then n =
   A. -5   B. -3   C. -2   D. 2   E. 3

   1.____

2. If x = 3, then $x^2 - 2x + 1$ =
   A. 16   B. 4   C. 1   D. -11   E. -14

   2.____

3. Which of the following gives $6a^2b^3 - 3a^2b$ in factored form?
   A. $3a^2b(2b^2)$ B. $3a^2(2b^2-1)$ C. $3ab(2ab^2-1)$
   D. $3a^2b(2b^2-1)$ E. $a^2b(6b^2-1)$

   3.____

4. For all x ≠ 0 and y ≠ 0, $\dfrac{(3x^{-2}y^3)^2}{xy}$ =
   A. $9x^3y^8$ B. $9y^4/x$ C. $9y^4/x^2$ D. $9y^5/x^5$ E. $9y^7/x^5$

   4.____

KEY (CORRECT ANSWERS)

1. B
2. A
3. D
4. D

TEST 5

SAMPLE INTERMEDIATE ALGEBRA TEST

DIRECTIONS: Solve each problem, choose the correct answer, and then print the letter of the correct answer in the space at the right. Do not linger over problems that take too much time. Solve as many as you can; then return to the others in the time you have left.

1. What are the real values of x that are solutions for the inequality $|x-2| \leq 6$? 1.____
   A. $-8 \leq x \leq -4$ B. $-8 \leq x \leq 4$ C. $-8 \leq x \leq 8$
   D. $-4 \leq x \leq 4$ E. $-4 \leq x \leq 8$

2. If $3x - 2 = 2y$ and $y = 3z + 5$, which of the following is equal to x? 2.____
   A. $z + 2$ B. $z + 7/3$ C. $z + 5$ D. $2z + 4$ E. $3z + 7$

3. What is the distance between the points with (x,y) coordinates (3,-2) and (-3,-1)? 3.____
   A. $\sqrt{7}$ B. $\sqrt{37}$ C. $\sqrt{11}$ D. 3   E. 7

KEY (CORRECT ANSWERS)

1. E
2. D
3. B

TEST 6

SAMPLE COLLEGE ALGEBRA TEST

DIRECTIONS: Solve each problem, choose the correct answer, and then print the letter of the correct answer in the space at the right. Do not linger over problems that take too much time. Solve as many as you can; then return to the others in the time you have left.

1. $\log 8 + \log 2 =$ 1.____
   A. $\log 4$ B. $\log 10$ C. $\log 16$
   D. $\log 64$ E. $\log 256$

2. If $f(x) = x^2 - 2$, then $f(a+2) =$ 2.____
   A. $a^2 + 4a + 4$ B. $a^2 + 4a + 2$ C. $a^2 + 4a$
   D. $a^2 + 2$ E. a^2

3. For $0° < x < 90°$, how many solutions are there for the equation $2 \sin x - \cos x$? 3.____
   A. 0   B. 1   C. 2   D. 3   E. 4

KEY (CORRECT ANSWERS)

1. C
2. B
3. B

TEST 7

SAMPLE GEOMETRY TEST

DIRECTIONS: Solve each problem, choose the correct answer, and then print the letter of the correct answer in the space at the right. Do not linger over problems that take too much time. Solve as many as you can; then return to the others in the time you have left.

1. If the diameter of a circle is 6 units long, what is the area of the circle, in square units? 1.____
   A. 36π B. 24π C. 12π D. 9π E. 3π

2. In $\triangle ABC$, the lengths of $\overline{AB}$ and $\overline{BC}$ each equal 13 centimeters. If the perimeter of $\triangle ABC$ is 36 centimeters, what is the area, in square centimeters, of $\triangle ABC$? 2.____
   A. 10 B. 30 C. 60 D. 62 E. 65

3. How many tiles are needed to tile the floor of a closet measuring 6 feet by 4 feet if each tile is a square with sides 8 inches long? 3.____
   A. 18 B. 24 C. 30 D. 54 E. 192

KEY (CORRECT ANSWERS)

1. D
2. C
3. D

EXAMINATION SECTION
TEST 1

DIRECTIONS: Each question or incomplete statement is followed by several suggested answers or completions. Select the one that BEST answers the question or completes the statement. *PRINT THE LETTER OF THE CORRECT ANSWER IN THE SPACE AT THE RIGHT.*

Questions 1-22.

DIRECTIONS: Read through each group of words. Indicate in the space at the right the letter of the misspelled word.

1. A. miniature   B. recession   1.____
    C. accommodate   D. supress

2. A. mortgage   B. illogical   2.____
    C. fasinate   D. pronounce

3. A. calendar   B. heros   3.____
    C. ecstasy   D. librarian

4. A. initiative   B. extraordinary   4.____
    C. villian   D. exaggerate

5. A. absence   B. sense   5.____
    C. dosn't   D. height

6. A. curiosity   B. ninety   6.____
    C. truely   D. grammar

7. A. amateur   B. definate   7.____
    C. meant   D. changeable

8. A. excellent   B. studioes   8.____
    C. achievement   D. weird

9. A. goverment   B. description   9.____
    C. sergeant   D. desirable

10. A. proceed   B. anxious   10.____
    C. neice   D. precede

11. A. environment   B. omitted   11.____
    C. apparant   D. misconstrue

12. A. comparative   B. hindrance   12.____
    C. benefited   D. unamimous

13. A. embarrass B. recommend
     C. desciple   D. argument

14. A. sophomore B. suprintendent
     C. concievable D. disastrous

15. A. agressive B. questionnaire
     C. occurred   D. rhythm

16. A. peaceable B. conscientious
     C. redicule   D. deterrent

17. A. mischievous B. writing
     C. competition D. athletics

18. A. auxiliary B. synonymous
     C. maneuver   D. repitition

19. A. existence B. optomistic
     C. acquitted D. tragedy

20. A. hypocrisy B. parrallel
     C. exhilaration D. prevalent

21. A. convalesence B. infallible
     C. destitute D. grotesque

22. A. magnanimity B. asassination
     C. incorrigible D. pestilence

Questions 23-40.

DIRECTIONS: In Questions 23 through 40, one sentence fragment contains an error in punctuation or capitalization. Indicate the letter of the INCORRECT sentence fragment and place it in the space at the right.

23. A. Despite a year's work
     B. in a well-equipped laboratory
     C. my Uncle failed to complete his research
     D. now he will never graduate.

24. A. Gene, if you are going to sleep
     B. all afternoon I will enter
     C. that ladies' golf tournament
     D. sponsored by the Chamber of Commerce.

3 (#1)

25. A. Seeing the cat slink toward the barn,
    B. the farmer's wife jumped off the
    C. ladder picked up a broom, and began
    D. shouting at the top of her voice.

25.____

26. A. Extending over southeast Idaho and
    B. northwest Wyoming, the Tetons
    C. are noted for their height; however the
    D. highest peak is actually under 14,000 feet.

26.____

27. A. "Sarah, can you recall the name
    B. of the English queen
    C. who supposedly said, 'We are not
    D. amused?"

27.____

28. A. My aunt's graduation present to me
    B. cost, I imagine more than she could
    C. actually afford. It's a
    D. Swiss watch with numerous features.

28.____

29. A. On the left are examples of buildings
    B. from the Classical Period; two temples
    C. one of which was dedicated to Zeus; the
    D. Agora, a marketplace; and a large arch.

29.____

30. A. Tired of sonic booms, the people who
    B. live near Springfield's Municipal Airport
    C. formed an anti noise organization
    D. with the amusing name of Sound Off.

30.____

31. A. "Joe, Mrs. Sweeney said, "your family
    B. arrives Sunday. Since you'll be in
    C. the Labor Day parade, we could ask Mr.
    D. Krohn, who has a big car, to meet them."

31.____

32. A. The plumber emerged from the basement and
    B. said, "Mr. Cohen I found the trouble in
    C. your water heater. Could you move those
    D. Schwinn bikes out of my way?"

32.____

33. A. The President walked slowly to the
    B. podium, bowed to Edward Everett Hale
    C. the other speaker, and began his formal address:
    D. "Fourscore and seven years ago...."

33.____

34. A. Mr. Fontana, I hope, will arrive before
    B. the beginning of the ceremonies; however,
    C. if his plane is delayed, I have a substitute
    D. speaker who can be here at a moments' notice.

34.____

35. A. Gladys wedding dress, a satin creation,
     B. lay crumpled on the floor; her veil,
     C. torn and streaked, lay nearby. "Jilted!"
     D. shrieked Gladys. She was clearly annoyed.

36. A. Although it is poor grammar, the word
     B. hopefully has become television's newest
     C. pet expression; I hope (to use the correct
     D. form) that it will soon pass from favor.

37. A.   Plaza Apartment Hotel
     B.   103 Tower road
     C.   Hampstead, Iowa 52025
     D.   March 13, 2021

38. A. Circulation Department
     B. British History Illustrated
     C. 3000 Walnut Street
     D. Boulder Colorado 80302

39. A. Dear Sirs:
     B. Last spring I ordered a subscription to your
     C. magazine. I had read and enjoyed the May
     D. issue containing the article titled "kings."

40. A. I have not however, received a
     B. single issue. Will you check this?
     C. Sincerely,
     D. Maria Herrera

Questions 41-70.

DIRECTIONS: Questions 41 through 70 represent common grammatical concerns: subject-verb agreement, appropriate use of pronouns, and appropriate use of verbs. Read each sentence and indicate the letter of the grammatically CORRECT answer in the space at the right.

41. THE REIVERS, one of William Faulkner's last works, _____ made into a movie starring Steve McQueen.
    A. has been   B. have been   C. are being   D. were

42. He _____ on the ground, his eyes fastened on an ant slowly pushing a morsel of food toward the ant hill.
    A. layed   B. laid   C. had laid   D. lay

43. Nobody in the tri-cities _____ to admit that a flood could be disastrous.
    A. are willing   B. have been willing
    C. is willing   D. were willing

44. "_____," the senator asked, "have you convinced to run against the incumbent?"
    A. Who   B. Whom   C. Whomever   D. Womsoever

45. Of all the psychology courses that I took, Statistics 101 _____ the most demanding.
    A. was   B. are   C. is   D. were

46. Neither the conductor nor the orchestra members _____ the music to be applauded so enthusiastically.
    A. were expecting
    B. was expecting
    C. is expected
    D. has been expecting

47. The requirements for admission to the Lettermen's Club _____ posted outside the athletic director's office for months.
    A. was   B. was being   C. has been   D. have been

48. Please give me a list of the people _____ to compete in the kayak race.
    A. whom you think have planned
    B. who you think has planned
    C. who you think is planning
    D. who you think are planning

49. I saw Eloise and Abelard earlier today; _____ were riding around in a fancy 1956 MG.
    A. she and him   B. her and him   C. she and he   D. her and he

50. If you _____ the trunk in the attic, I'll unpack it later today.
    A. can sit
    B. are able to sit
    C. can set
    D. have sat

51. _____ all of the flour been used, or may I borrow three cups?
    A. Have   B. Has   C. Is   D. Could

52. In exasperation, the cycle shop's owner suggested that _____ there too long.
    A. us boys were
    B. we boys were
    C. us boys had been
    D. we boys had been

53. Idleness as well as money _____ the root of all evil.
    A. have been
    B. were to have been
    C. is
    D. are

54. Only the string players from the quartet—Gregory, Isaac, _____—remained after the concert to answer questions.
    A. him, and I
    B. he, and I
    C. him, and me
    D. he, and me

55. Of all the antiques that _____ for sale, Gertrude chose to buy a stupid glass thimble.
    A. was
    B. is
    C. would have
    D. were

56. The detective snapped, "Don't confuse me with theories about _____ you believe committed the crime!"
    A. who   B. whom   C. whomever   D. which

57. _____ when we first called, we might have avoided our present predicament.
    A. The plumber's coming
    B. If the plumber would have come
    C. If the plumber had come
    D. If the plumber was to have come

58. We thought the sun _____ in the north until we discovered that our compass was defective.
    A. had rose
    B. had risen
    C. had rised
    D. had raised

59. Each play of Shakespeare's _____ more than _____ share of memorable characters.
    A. contain its
    B. contains; its
    C. contains; it's
    D. contain; their

60. Our English teacher suggested to _____ seniors that either Tolstoy or Dickens _____ the outstanding novelist of the nineteenth century.
    A. we; was considered
    B. we; were considered
    C. us; was considered
    D. us; were considered

61. Sherlock Holmes, together with his great friend and companion Dr. Watson, _____ to aid the woman _____ had stumbled into the room.
    A. has agreed; who
    B. have agreed; whom
    C. has agreed; whom
    D. have agreed; who

62. Several of the deer _____ when they spotted my backpack _____ open in the meadow.
    A. was frightened; laying
    B. were frightened; lying
    C. were frightened; laying
    D. was frightened; lying

63. After the Scholarship Committee announces _____ selection, hysterics often _____.
    A. it's; occur
    B. its; occur
    C. their; occur
    D. their; occurs

64. I _____ the key on the table last night so you and _____ could find it.
    A. layed; her
    B. lay; she
    C. laid; she
    D. laid; her

65. Some of the antelope _____ wandered away from the meadow where the rancher _____ the block of salt.
    A. has; sat
    B. has; set
    C. have; had set
    D. has; sets

66. Macaroni and cheese _____ best to us (that is, to Andy and _____) when Mother adds extra cheddar cheese.
    A. tastes; I
    B. tastes; me
    C. taste; me
    D. taste; I

67. Frank said, "It must have been _____ called the phone company."
    A. she who
    B. she whom
    C. her who
    D. her whom

68. The herd _____ moving restlessly at every bolt of lightning; it was either Ted or _____ who saw the beginning of the stampede.
    A. was; me
    B. were; I
    C. was; I
    D. have been; me

69. The foreman _____ his lateness by saying that his alarm clock _____ until six minutes before eight.
    A. explains; had not rang
    B. explained; has not rung
    C. has explained; rung
    D. explained; hadn't rung

70. Of all the coaches, Ms. Cox is the only one who _____ that Sherry dives more gracefully than _____.
    A. is always saying; I
    B. is always saying; me
    C. are always saying; I
    D. were always saying; me

Questions 71-90.

DIRECTIONS: Choose the word in Questions 71 through 90 that is MOST opposite in meaning to the italicized word.

71. *fact*
    A. statistic
    B. statement
    C. incredible
    D. conjecture

72. *stiff*
    A. fastidious
    B. babble
    C. supple
    D. apprehensive

73. *blunt*
    A. concise
    B. tactful
    C. artistic
    D. humble

74. *foreign*
    A. pertinent
    B. comely
    C. strange
    D. scrupulous

75. *anger*
    A. infer
    B. pacify
    C. taint
    D. revile

76. *frank*
    A. earnest
    B. reticent
    C. post
    D. expensive

77. *secure*
    A. precarious   B. acquire   C. moderate   D. frenzied

78. *petty*
    A. harmonious   B. careful
    C. forthright   D. momentous

79. *concede*
    A. dispute   B. reciprocate
    C. subvert   D. propagate

80. *benefit*
    A. liquidation   B. bazaar
    C. detriment   D. profit

81. *capricious*
    A. preposterous   B. constant
    C. diabolical   D. careless

82. *boisterous*
    A. devious   B. valiant   C. girlish   D. taciturn

83. *harmony*
    A. congruence   B. discord   C. chagrin   D. melody

84. *laudable*
    A. auspicious   B. despicable
    C. acclaimed   D. doubtful

85. *adherent*
    A. partisan   B. stoic   C. renegade   D. recluse

86. *exuberant*
    A. frail   B. corpulent   C. austere   D. bigot

87. *spurn*
    A. accede   B. flail   C. efface   D. annihilate

88. *spontaneous*
    A. hapless   B. corrosive
    C. intentional   D. willful

89. *disparage*
    A. abolish   B. exude   C. incriminate   D. extol

90. *timorous*
    A. succinct   B. chaste   C. audacious   D. insouciant

KEY (CORRECT ANSWERS)

1.	D	21.	A	41.	A	61.	A	81.	B
2.	C	22.	B	42.	D	62.		82.	D
3.	B	23.	C	43.	C	63.	B	83.	B
4.	C	24.	B	44.	B	64.	C	84.	B
5.	C	25.	C	45.	A	65.	C	85.	C
6.	C	26.	C	46.	A	66.	B	86.	C
7.	B	27.	D	47.	D	67.	A	87.	A
8.	B	28.	B	48.	A	68.	C	88.	C
9.	A	29.	B	49.	C	69.	D	89.	D
10.	C	30.	C	50.	C	70.	A	90.	C
11.	C	31.	A	51.	B	71.	D		
12.	D	32.	B	52.	D	72.	C		
13.	C	33.	B	53.	C	73.	B		
14.	C	34.	D	54.	B	74.	A		
15.	A	35.	A	55.	D	75.	B		
16.	C	36.	B	56.	B	76.	B		
17.	A	37.	B	57.	C	77.	A		
18.	D	38.	D	58.	B	78.	D		
19.	B	39.	D	59.	B	79.	A		
20.	B	40.	A	60.	C	80.	C		

EXAMINATION SECTION
TEST 1

DIRECTIONS: Each question or incomplete statement is followed by several suggested answers or completions. Select the one that BEST answers the question or completes the statement. *PRINT THE LETTER OF THE CORRECT ANSWER IN THE SPACE AT THE RIGHT.*

Questions 1-16.

DIRECTIONS: Each sentence below has one or two blanks, each blank indicating that something has been omitted. Beneath the sentence are five words or sets of words labeled A through E. Choose the word or set of words that, when inserted in the sentence, BEST fits the meaning of the sentence as a whole.

Example:
Medieval kingdoms did not become constitutional republics overnight; on the contrary, the change was _____.
  A. unpopular   B. unexpected
  C. advantageous   D. sufficient
  E. gradual

The CORRECT answer is E.

1. The audience responded enthusiastically to Wynton Marsalis' performance of Duke Ellington's music; some of the pieces were interrupted by _____.
  A. melodies   B. interpretations   C. insinuations
  D. assertions   E. applause

2. People often learn more effectively when studying in groups, and many report that they enjoy these cooperative ventures more than _____ sessions.
  A. temporary   B. solitary   C. collective
  D. unscheduled   E. curtailed

3. Although Russians rank this poet among their _____ authors, his works have not been _____ in translation.
  A. strangest; understood   B. greatest; appreciated
  C. wittiest; neglected   D. dullest; enjoyed
  E. firmest; altered

4. The annual summer _____ of the ice sheet covering that part of the sea provides _____ for marine creatures because it releases into the water the algae community that had been trapped in the ice.
  A. drifting; warmth   B. growth; fodder
  C. thinning; light   D. shifting; space
  E. melting; food

5. Lead in paint and in gasoline has been found to be such an environmental hazard that its use is now
   A. condoned   B. insufficient   C. restricted
   D. rampant   E. unmonitored

6. Astronomy is no longer _____ the shortcomings of human vision; it now benefits from instruments that can see throughout a much broader spectrum.
   A. independent of   B. ambivalent toward
   C. limited by   D. knowledgeable about
   E. fixated on

7. The introductory essay was a(n) _____ effort in that each of the three editors wrote the portion concerning her own field of expertise.
   A. collaborative   B. disagreeable   C. indisputable
   D. enduring   E. unrealistic

8. Texas author Larry McMurtry suggests that those who _____ the moral character of cowboys have been seduced by the idea that a rugged, _____ way of life is less corrupting than the life cities have to offer.
   A. understand; reprobate   B. slander; unfettered
   C. ignore; sinister   D. romanticize; political
   E. idealize; rural

9. Margaret Mead studied ways that some non-Western societies deal effectively with certain human experiences and suggested that such strategies might offer remedies for _____ in American responses to similar events.
   A. ideals   B. assumptions   C. idiosyncrasies
   D. shortcomings   E. improvisations

10. Goya's success as a painter for the Spanish court was _____, for the royal family continued to give him its patronage while he produced art that was widely interpreted as an indictment of monarchical rule.
    A. paradoxical   B. quixotic   C. auspicious
    D. exemplary   E. unfulfilled

11. A short-term pessimist but a long-term optimist, she predicts _____ transition from an epoch of competition to one of _____.
    A. an instantaneous; leisure   B. a retrograde; affluence
    C. an insidious; terror   D. a turbulent; fraternity
    E. a beneficent; militarism

12. The _____ the conflict unleashed in the nation's people have made it impossible for them, even decades later, to discuss the subject with _____.
    A. passions; equanimity   B. fears; trepidation
    C. hatreds; anger   D. visions; honor
    E. emotions; hesitation

13. The _____ of the service sector in our country disturbs many who believe that service industries are of less _____ than manufacturing in promoting economic well-being.
    A. productivity; versatility
    B. balance; volatility
    C. burgeoning; value
    D. contribution; interest
    E. decline; significance

14. The award-winning design of this solar-heated house has an _____ value over and above the _____ value it possesses due to the rise in the price of fossil fuels.
    A. accessible; unwarranted
    B. ostentatious; superficial
    C. ephemeral; ecological
    D. ornamental; artistic
    E. aesthetic; pragmatic

15. Giant pandas tend to move _____; they have little need for speed.
    A. implacably
    B. spontaneously
    C. dexterously
    D. deliberately
    E. resoundingly

16. Helga gave orders in such a _____ way that it was clear the expected people to obey her immediately.
    A. peremptory
    B. timorous
    C. garrulous
    D. facetious
    E. redundant

Questions 17-22.

DIRECTIONS: Questions 17 through 22 are to be answered on the basis of the following passage, which is adapted from a survey of two hundred years of Hispanic theater in the Southwest.

The majority of the plays produced in the Hispanic theater in the southwestern United States during the early decades of the twentieth century were examples of the plays typically produced in the major cities of Mexico and Spain. Playwrights and impresarios did not hesitate to deal with controversial material. Many of their plays dealt
(5) with the historical and current circumstances of Hispanic people in the Southwest, but always with the seriousness and propriety.
    Also produced, however, were *revistas*. The *revistas* was a genre that specialized in piquant political satire and commentary: it was a forum for articulating grievances, for poking fun at the governments of both Mexico and the United States, for satirically
(10) considering the Mexican Revolution, and for contrasting Mexican-American culture with Mexican culture. This social and political commentary was carried out despite the fact that both audiences and performers were mostly immigrants who felt themselves liable to deportation or repatriation.
    It should be emphasized that, from the beginning of the Hispanic theater in the
(15) Southwest, the relationship of performers and theaters with the community was close. The Hispanic theater served to reinforce the sense of community by bringing all Spanish speakers together in a cultural act: the preservation and support of the language and art of Mexican people and other Hispanic people in the face of the threat of domination from Anglo-American culture. Theater, more than any other art form, became essential to
(20) promoting ethnic and national identification and to solidifying the colony of expatriates.

Thus, in addition to its artistic functions within the expatriate Mexican community, theater took on specific social functions that were not widely assumed by theaters in Mexico and Spain.

(25) The professional theater houses became temples of culture where the Hispanic community as a whole, regardless of social class, religion, or region of origin, could gather and, in the words of a theater critic writing in 1930, *keep the lamp of our culture lighted.* In 1916 a drama critic for San Antonio's LA PRENSA underlined the social and nationalistic functions of the theater: *Attending the artistic performances at the Teatro Juarez can be considered a patriotic deed which assists in cultural solidarity in support*
(30) *of a modest group of Mexican actors who are fighting for their livelihood in a foreign land and who introduce us to the most precious jewels of contemporary theater in our native tongue that is, the sweet and sonorous language of Cervantes.* Thus, the Hispanic theater became an institution in the Southwest for the preservation of the Hispanic culture and the Spanish language of the dominant Anglo-American society.

17. The passage is PRIMARILY concerned with the
    A. differences among various kinds of plays produced in the Southwest
    B. social and political function of the Hispanic theater in the Southwest
    C. relationship between Mexican theater and the theater of the Southwest
    D. celebration of theater as an important art form
    E. political views of Hispanic actors and playwrights

18. The author gives the MOST emphasis to which of the following aspects of the Hispanic theater?
    The
    A. theater's superiority to other art forms
    B. importance of satirical plays
    C. theater's difference from theater in Mexico and Spain
    D. economic situation of actors and producers
    E. theater's role in building a sense of community

19. Which of the following BEST describes the author's attitude toward those who participated in performances of *revistas*?
    A. Criticism of their lack of seriousness
    B. Mild criticism of their attitude toward government
    C. Admiration for the understatement of their political commentary
    D. Admiration for the subtlety of their art
    E. Respect for their determination

20. By quoting LA PRENSA's drama critic (lines 28-32), the author of the passage PRIMARILY intends to
    A. demonstrate the financial plight of expatriate actors
    B. show appreciation for great artistic performances
    C. praise the translation done for the Hispanic theater
    D. draw attention to the influence of Cervantes
    E. emphasize the role of theater in establishing cultural unity

21. Which of the following can be inferred from the remarks of LA PRENSA's drama critic about the performances at the Teatro Juarez (lines 28-32)? The
    A. actors were not willing to boast about their talents
    B. critic recently had seen a play that dealt with matters of wealth and poverty
    C. language used in the productions did not meet the critic's approval
    D. actors were in a precarious economic situation
    E. performance was taking place during a time of intense military conflict

21.____

22. In the final statement in the passage, the author suggests that
    A. only professional theatrical institutions can preserve Hispanic culture
    B. only the theater can preserve culture in a foreign environment
    C. Hispanic people used the theater as an instrument of economic opportunity
    D. preserving Hispanic culture was important in a non-Hispanic political environment
    E. theater was the least understood of all southwestern art forms

22.____

Questions 23-29.

DIRECTIONS: Questions 23 through 29 are to be answered on the basis of the following passages, which discuss the relationship between people and technology in modern society.

Passage 1

Anti-technologists treat technology as something that has escaped from human control. In the face of today's excruciatingly complex problems, it is understandable that many people agree with them. When people engage in technological activities, these activities appear to have consequences, not only physical but also intellectual,
(5) psychological, and cultural. Thus, anti-technologists argue, technology is deterministic. It causes other things to happen. Someone invents the automobile, for example, and it changes the way people think as well as the way they act. It changes their living patterns, their values, and their expectations in ways that were not anticipated when the automobile was first introduced. Some of the changes appear to be not only
(10) unanticipated but undesired. Nobody wanted traffic jams, accidents, and pollution. Therefore, technological advance seems to be independent of human direction. But sober thought reveals that technology is not an independent force, much less a thing, but one of the types of activities in which people engage.

The anti-technologists discount completely the integrity and intelligence of the
(15) ordinary person. Indeed, pity and disdain for the individual citizen are essential aspects of anti-technology. One of its dogmas is that technological society forces people to consume things that they do not really desire. How can we respond to this falsehood? One might observe that the consumers who buy cars and electric can openers could, if they chose, buy oboes and oil paints, sailboats, and hiking boots, chess sets and
(20) recordings of Mozart. Or, could they not help purchase a kidney machine that would save their neighbor's life? If people are vulgar, foolish, and selfish in their choice of purchases, is it not the worst sort of excuse to blame this on technological society?

Indeed, wouldn't people prefer being called vulgar to being told that they have no will with which to make choices of their own?

Passage 2

(25) A happy technologist once asserted that everyone lampoons modern technology but no one is prepared to give up his or her refrigerator. In the United States there is a general perception that life-style, or the way in which one lives, is a matter of individual choice, at least for a vast majority. Disregarding economic means for a moment, people think that one can choose to lead either a bohemian life-style or a conventional one. But is one truly free to choose to have a refrigerator or not? Is it a simple matter of life-style choice or do other institutional arrangements of society impinge with demands of their
(30) own?
A refrigerator (including freezer) performs several functions. It stores food (a necessity) and cools drinks or produces ice for cooling drinks (a comfort or luxury). The latter category is not an essential function. The desirability of cold beer, for example, is culturally or socially induced; other cultures find warm beer more desirable, so people in
(35) those societies do not need a refrigerator to perform this particular function. Consider another society in which it is possible for people to purchase their perishable food on a daily basis in markets or small shops, easily accessible and within walking distance of their homes. This option is not available to many people in the United States. The supermarket as a social institution, not within walking distance of most people, has its
(40) own imperatives. One buys for a week of eating, not for a day, so storage in a refrigerator becomes essential to living. It is a necessity induced by a life-style over which individuals have little control. To chide individuals for recalcitrance or perversity for their unwillingness to give up their refrigerators is to misjudge profoundly the nature of contemporary technology and its induced social change. It is irrelevant to the
(45) argument whether or not a supermarket/refrigerator society has advantages over the other.
The only question is, do individuals have autonomy to choose freely one or the other?

23. In Passage 1, the author's attitude toward anti-technologists is BEST described as
    A. sympathetic   B. indifferent   C. amused
    D. fearful   E. critical

24. In line 12, *sober* MOST NEARLY means
    A. plain and uncomplicated   B. not intoxicated
    C. sensible   D. unimaginative
    E. alert

25. The author uses the word *dogmas* (line 16) to refer to what he considers to be
    A. religious truths   B. logical premises
    C. prophetic ideas   D. unassailable doctrines
    E. groundless assumptions

26. The author of Passage 2 argues that in much of the United States a refrigerator is an
    A. appliance that has both essential and culturally determined functions
    B. example of modern technology that allows individuals to pursue different life-styles
    C. invention that only recently has become affordable
    D. entity that is independent of a social institution such as the supermarket
    E. illustration of the mindless materialism of modern society

27. What would be the likely response of the author of Passage 2 to the discussion of cars in lines 8-13 of Passage 1?
    A. Consumers have a wide variety of cars from which to choose.
    B. Consumers in some areas must rely on cars for transportation.
    C. Consumers tend to perceive cars as a means of recreation.
    D. Cars are not as essential as refrigerators or medical equipment in most societies.
    E. Cars as possessions are overvalued in modern society.

28. Which BEST describes an assumption about people held by the authors of Passages 1 and 2?
    A. People themselves are to blame for problems in modern society.
    B. People should not be judged too hastily about the choices they make.
    C. The author of Passage 1 views people as reasonable, whereas the author of Passage 2 views the as unreasonable.
    D. The author of Passage 1 views people as altruistic, whereas the author of Passage 2 views them as selfish.
    E. The author of Passage 1 views all people as essentially honest, whereas the author of Passage 2 thinks that only a few are.

29. The author of Passage 1 and the author of Passage 2 DISAGREE most strongly about the
    A. value of particular products of modern technology
    B. seriousness of problems associated with modern technology
    C. availability of consumer goods in a modern technological society
    D. control that people have over the uses and effects of technology
    E. type of life-style enjoyed by the majority of people in a modern technological society

Questions 30-41.

DIRECTIONS: Each question below consists of a related pair of words or phrases, followed by five pairs of words or phrases labeled A through E. Select the pair that BEST expresses a relationship similar to that expressed in the original pair.

   Example: CRUMB : BREAD
   A. ounce : unit   B. splinter : wood
   C. water : bucket   D. twine : rope
   E. cream : butter
The CORRECT answer is B.

30. WRITE : SCRIBBLE
    A. hear : mumble   B. draw : doodle   C. study : concentrate
    D. plan : design   E. read : learn

31. MICROSCOPE : SMALL
    A. kilometer : metric   B. thermometer : hot
    C. telescope : distant   D. stethoscope : loud
    E. calculator : fast

32. CALLIGRAPHER : PAPER
    A. plumber : wrench   B. potter : kiln
    C. prospector : ore   D. painter : canvas
    E. printer : ink

33. WHIFF : NOSE
    A. applause : hands   B. lick : cat
    C. pout : lips   D. spark : fire
    E. glimpse : eyes

34. MANUAL : INSTRUCTIONS
    A. timetable : railroads   B. food : utensils
    C. bibliography : sources   D. magazine : subscriptions
    E. radio : listeners

35. ITINERARY : TRIP
    A. schedule : table   B. agenda : meeting
    C. amendment : document   D. diary : experience
    E. memorandum : record

36. ACROBAT : TRAPEZE
    A. boxer : ring   B. actor : role
    C. swimmer : lap   D. animal : cage
    E. vaulter : pole

37. MISNOMER : NAME
    A. error : mishap   B. variability
    C. exception : rule   D. misconception : idea
    E. misdeed : apology

38. RECONCILE : HARMONY
    A. cure : health   B. disturb : tranquility
    C. perform : entertainment   D. forecast : weather

39. PARABLE : ILLUSTRATIVE
    A. newspaper : daily   B. joke : amusing
    C. cliche : creative   D. lecture : spoken
    E. film : exposed

40. RAMBLE : DIGRESSIVE   40._____
    A. warn : protected   B. prattle : foolish
    C. praise : incorrect   D. whisper : audible
    E. babble : intelligible

41. LURK : FURTIVE   41._____
    A. threaten : menacing   B. accuse : guilty
    C. misrepresent : understated D. respect : contemptuous
    E. spy : informative

Questions 42-52.

DIRECTIONS: Questions 42 through 52 are to be answered on the basis of the following passage. Scientists are often considered to be objective, but we are reminded in this passage that scientists are just as much products of their own cultural prejudices as are other people. For example, despite the efforts of early anatomists to represent the body accurately, early anatomical reproductions reflected the stereotypes of the eighteenth and nineteenth centuries: that physical and intellectual strength defined masculinity and motherhood defined femininity.

    In 1734 anatomist Bernard Albinus produced an illustration of the male human skeleton that would serve as the model for anatomical illustration for more than 75 years. Albinus consciously sought to capture the details not of a particular body but of a universal and ideal type. Though Albinus' fame rested on his reputation for accuracy, at
(5) every step along the way he sacrificed objectivity to the ideal. Having made precise measurements of his subject and transferred them exactly to paper, Albinus then eliminated anatomical details from his drawing that would have destroyed its symmetry.
    Having produced the perfect drawing of the male, Albinus lamented, *we lack a female skeleton*. And numerous drawings of female skeletons were made in subsequent
(10) years. But, although these drawings purported too represent the female skeleton, they differed greatly from one another.
    Marie Thiroux d'Arconville's rendering of a distinctively female skeleton, published in 1759, captured the imagination of physicians for more than half a century. This illustration—one of the very few drawn by a woman anatomist—might also be called the
(15) most *sexist* portrayal of a female skeleton. Thiroux d'Arconville exaggerated, almost to the point of caricature, those parts of the body that were emerging as sites of political debate: the skull as a mark of intelligence and the pelvis as a measure of womanliness. She depicted the female skull (incorrectly) as smaller in proportion to the body than the man's. She also focused attention on the pelvis by exaggerating the narrowness of the
(20) ribs so that the pelvis appeared excessively large. It would seem that either Thiroux d'Arconville intended to emphasize narrow ribs and wide hips as a mark of femininity or she chose for her model a woman who had worn a corset throughout her life. As early as 1741, anatomist J.B. Winslow had noted that regular use of the corset deforms the ribs.
(25)   In 1796 the German anatomist Samuel Thomas von Soemmerring produced a rival female skeleton. He had spent years perfecting the illustration; when it was finished, he considered it to be of such *completeness* and *exactitude* that it made a perfect mate for the great Albinus male. As a model he selected the skeleton of a twenty-year-old

woman who had borne a child. For proportions, he checked his drawing against
(30) classical statues of Venus. Von Soemmerring intended his skeleton to represent not an individual woman but (as a later commentator put it) *the most beautiful* woman as was imagined to exist in life.

Although Thiroux d'Arconville and von Soemmerring drew their female skeletons from nature and considered their work *exact*, great debate erupted over the precise
(35) features of the female skeleton. In contrast to Thiroux d'Arconville, von Soemmerring portrayed the skull of the female (correctly) as larger in proportion to the body than that of the male. He drew the ribs smaller in proportion to the hips than the man's, but not remarkably so.

Despite (or perhaps because of) its exaggerations, the Thiroux d'Arconville skeleton
(40) became the favored drawing. Von Soemmerring's skeleton, by contrast, was attacked for its *inaccuracies*. Edinburgh physician John Barclay criticized von Soemmerring in particular for showing the incorrect proportion of the ribs to the hips; he argued that the female rib cage is much smaller than that shown by von Soemmerring because women's restricted life-style required that they breathe less vigorously. Barclay concluded that
(45) von Soemmerring was an artist, but no anatomist.

Rejecting Thiroux d'Arconville's insistence that the female skull was smaller in proportion to the body than the male skull, von Soemmerring pointed out that women's skulls are actually heavier than men's, relative to total body weight (1:6 for women, 1:8 to 1:10 for men).
(50) Von Soemmerring's view was castigated, for it seemed to counter the idea that men were the more intelligent and creative of the species. In subsequent years, however, anatomists had to concede the truth of von Soemmerring's depiction of the female skull. Yet they did not conclude that women's large skulls were loaded with heavy, high-powered brains. Rather than a mark of intelligence, women's large skulls were
(55) dismissed as a sign of incomplete development. John Barclay, for example, used the proportionally larger size of the female skull to support that physiologically women resemble children, whose skulls are also large relative to their body size.

42. The PRIMARY focus of the passage is on
    A. the effects of Albinus' pioneering work in human anatomy
    B. the influence of social ideas or scientific thinking
    C. conflicting definitions of the ideal male skeleton
    D. the changes in cultural values brought about by the study of anatomy
    E. how similar the male and female skeletons really are

43. According to the passage, Albinus misrepresented certain bone structures in order to
    A. enhance individual variations in the models he used
    B. make structural details more readily visible
    C. make the skeleton conform to his idea of aesthetic perfection
    D. surpass all previous anatomists in exactness
    E. emphasize differences between male and female skeletons

44. In line 10, *the* is underlined in order to indicate that
    A. artistic tastes were changing rapidly during this period
    B. the author is referring to a particular and very important drawing of a woman
    C. there was a great deal of similarity among the drawings mentioned
    D. the drawings were exact representations of the particular models used
    E. each artist intended the drawing to represent an ideal, universal woman

44.____

45. The passage supports which of the following statements about Thiroux d'Arconville's drawing?
    It
    A. reflected physicians' superior knowledge of anatomy
    B. set a new standard for precision of detail
    C. was more reliable than drawings by male artists
    D. conformed to prevailing views about femininity
    E. was free of the inaccuracies of the classical era

45.____

46. The author MOST likely gives a description of von Soermmerring's human model (lines 35-38) in order to suggest that
    A. motherhood and youth were thought to be characteristics of the ideal woman
    B. Winslow's idea that corsets could be harmful was probably based on inadequate evidence
    C. no ordinary woman's skeleton could measure up to the classical idea of beauty
    D. von Soemmerring's powers of observation were superior to those of his critics
    E. von Soemmerring's ideas about skull size were affected by the youthfulness of his model

36.____

47. In line 34, *erupted* MOST NEARLY means
    A. ejected   B. overflowed
    C. increased   D. broke out
    E. became uncontrollable

47.____

48. The author uses the parenthetical phrase *or perhaps because of* in line 39 in order to suggest that
    A. Thiroux d'Arconville's contemporaries tended to share her prejudices
    B. exaggerated drawings are often more useful for conveying fine details
    C. artistic tastes of the eighteenth century regarded exaggeration as beautiful
    D. the author is uncertain about the causes of the drawing's popularity
    E. Thiroux d'Arconville was never fully understood by either the artists or the scientists of her day

48.____

49. The passage implies that von Soemmerring's chief reason for drawing the female skull proportionally larger than the male skull was his wish to
    A. reflect actual physical evidence
    B. correct the distortions in Albinus' work
    C. disprove Barclay's ideas
    D. suggest that women were more intelligent than men
    E. create an aesthetically pleasing work of art

50. The discussion in lines 42-44 about the size of the female rib cage CHIEFLY serves to
    A. show that scientists were concerned with both aesthetics and facts
    B. lead the reader to realize that neither Thiroux d'Arconville's nor von Soemmerring's drawings were entirely accurate
    C. indicate the bias held by most scientists of the period by citing a representative view
    D. contrast with the remarks about female beauty made by the *later commentator* (line 31)
    E. present evidence in support of von Soemmerring's position in the debate

51. Barclay's appraisal of von Soemmerring (lines 43-45) was intended to
    A. praise his skill as a draftsman
    B. emphasize the beauty of his drawing
    C. criticize the excessive embellishment of his drawing
    D. cast doubt on the scientific accuracy of his drawing
    E. suggest that creativity is an important factor in science

52. In line 52, *concede* MOST NEARLY means
    A. acknowledge   B. compromise   C. renounce
    D. disclose   E. surrender

Questions 53-60.

DIRECTIONS: Questions 53 through 60 are too be answered on the basis of the following passage, which is adapted from an American writer's memoir of his childhood.

My father taught me skills and manners: he taught me to shoot, to drive fast, to read respectfully, too handle a boat, and to distinguish between good jazz music and bad. His codes were not novel, but they were rigid. A gentleman was a stickler for precision; life was no more than an inventory of small choices that together formed a man's
(5)   character, entire.
        He looked, and spoke, straight at you. He could stare down anyone. To me everything about him seemed outsized. Doing a school report on the Easter Islanders I found in an encyclopedia pictures of their huge sculptures, and there he was, massive head and nose, nothing subtle or delicate. He was in fact (and how diminishing those
(10)   words, *in fact*, look to me now) an inch or two above six feet, full-bodied, a man who lumbered from here to there with deliberation. When I was a child I noticed that people were respectful of the cubic feet my father occupied; later I understood that I had confused respect with resentment.

I remember his shoes, so meticulously selected and cared for and used, thin-soled,
(15) with cracked uppers, older than I was or could ever be, shining dully and from the
depths. Just a pair of shoes?
   No: I knew before I knew any other complicated thing that for my father there was
nothing he possessed that I was *just* something. His pocket watch was not *just* a
timepiece, it was a miraculous instrument. It struck the hour unassertively, like a silver
(20) tine touched to a crystal glass, no hurry, you might like to know it's noon.
   He despised black leather, said black shoes reminded him of black attache cases, of
bankers, lawyers, look-before-you-leapers anxious not to offend their clients. He owned
nothing black except his umbrella. His umbrella doubled as a shooting stick, and one
afternoon at soccer game he was sitting on it when a man asked him what he would do
(25) if it rained, sit wet or stand dry? I laughed. My father laughed also, but tightly, and he
did not reply; nor did we ever again use this quixotic contraption. He took things, *things*,
seriously.
   When I was a boy, he introduced me, with ceremony, to a couple of family treasures:
my great-grandfather's medical degree from Leyden and, set in blue-velvet cavities in a
(30) worn leather case, my grandfather's surgical instruments. These totems are gone now,
lost during one or another last-minute, dark-of-night escape from a house where the rent
was seven months overdue. Recently I bought a set of compasses and dividers solely
because, snuggled in their own blue-velvet nests, they returned me to evenings when I
sat beside my father and he showed me the probes and scalpels. I would examine a
(35) piece, then return it to its place, and promise never to touch it without supervision. I was
warned that microbes deadly beyond imagining still lurked on the blades, but there was
no need to scare me away from them. I had never seen things so mysterious, cold, or
menacing.

53. The passage portrays the father as a man who is PRIMARILY   53.____
    A. exuberant
    B. malicious
    C. long-winded
    D. complex and preoccupied with appearances
    E. generous and thoughtful toward others

54. The list of skills in the first sentence indicates the father's   54.____
    A. self-discipline   B. lack of subtlety   C. impatience
    D. practicality   E. versatility

55. The author mentions the Easter Island statues (lines 6-10) in order to   55.____
    emphasis his father's apparent
    A. indifference   B. energy   C. massiveness
    D. good looks   E. stodginess

56. Black leather (lines 21-23) represents which of the following for the father?   56.____
    A. Reckless pursuit of goals   B. Extraordinary self-discipline
    C. Unabashed greed   D. Excessive caution
    E. Admirably good manners

57. The incident at the soccer game (lines 24-26) shows that the father
    A. was too depressed to be able to enjoy jokes
    B. was unreasonably fearful of strangers
    C. was extremely sensitive to the judgment of others
    D. was able to compromise when necessary
    E. had an unpredictable and violent temper

58. The passage does all of the following to establish the father's character EXCEPT
    A. describe him physically
    B. quote his words directly
    C. recount the son's youthful attitude toward him
    D. show him interacting with others
    E. comment on his likes and dislikes

59. The writer emphasizes an aspect of his father's character that is in ironic contrast to his outsized and obtrusive appearance, which had *nothing subtle* or *delicate* (line 14) about it.
    This trait of his personality would be
    A. crude sense of humor
    B. animosity towards bankers and lawyers
    C. attention to detail exemplified by his meticulously selected shoes and his musically precise pocket watch
    D. the respect he inspired because of his formidable size
    E. a sentimental attachment to family heirlooms

60. The style and tone of this passage may be described as being predominantly
    A. humorous and sarcastic
    B. poetic and metaphorical
    C. descriptive, reminiscent and nostalgic
    D. factual and pedantic
    E. sharply satiric

KEY (CORRECT ANSWERS)

1. E	11. D	21. D	31. C	41. A	51. D
2. B	12. A	22. D	32. D	42. B	52. A
3. B	13. C	23. E	33. E	43. C	53. D
4. E	14. E	24. C	34. C	44. E	54. E
5. C	15. D	25. E	35. B	45. D	55. C
6. C	16. A	26. A	36. E	46. A	56. D
7. A	17. B	27. B	37. D	47. D	57. C
8. E	18. E	28. B	38. A	48. A	58. B
9. D	19. E	29. D	39. B	49. A	59. C
10. A	20. E	30. B	40. B	50. C	60. C

EXAMINATION SECTION
TEST 1

DIRECTIONS: Each question or incomplete statement is followed by several suggested answers or completions. Select the one that BEST answers the question or completes the statement. *PRINT THE LETTER OF THE CORRECT ANSWER IN THE SPACE AT THE RIGHT.*

1. Which of the following basic listening skills is prerequisite to the others? 1.____

    A. Identifying stated main ideas
    B. Making generalizations
    C. Drawing conclusions
    D. Comparing different points of view

2. Which of the following factors is the MOST important indication of a child's readiness for reading? 2.____

    A. Motor development
    B. Maturational age
    C. Physical development
    D. Chronological age

Questions 3-4.

DIRECTIONS: Read the passage below from MYTHOLOGY, and then answer Questions 3 and 4.

   The first written record of Greece is the ILIAD. Greek mythology begins with Homer, generally believed to be not earlier than a thousand years before Christ. The ILIAD is, or contains, the oldest Greek literature; and it is written in a rich and subtle and beautiful language which must have had behind it centuries when men were striving to express themselves with clarity and beauty, an indisputable proof of civilization. The tales of Greek mythology do not throw any clear light upon what early mankind was like - a matter, it would seem, of more importance to us, who are their descendants intellectually, artistically, and politically, too. Nothing we learn about them is alien to ourselves.

3. Which line from the passage is a statement of fact? 3.____

    A. The tales of Greek mythology do not throw any clear light upon what early mankind was like.
    B. Nothing we learn about them is alien to ourselves.
    C. It is written in a rich and subtle and beautiful language which must have had behind it centuries when men were striving to express themselves with clarity and beauty.
    D. The ILIAD is, or contains, the oldest Greek literature.

4. The author's point of view toward the subject of this passage is one of 4.____

    A. humorous indulgence
    B. respect and admiration
    C. tongue-in-cheek flattery
    D. longing and nostalgia

5. Which of the following sentences is capitalized CORRECTLY? 5.____

    A. My aunt told Uncle Leon about the documentary she saw at the Biograph Theater.
    B. In the Southern Hemisphere, the first day of winter is in June.

C. The Riveras plan to spend their vacation in California at Yosemite national Park.
D. Gloria's room had an Eastern exposure, and the sun woke her up at dawn.

6. Which sentence demonstrates proper pronoun-antecedent agreement?

   A. The council of officials has announced his decision.
   B. All public parks will close its gates at 5:00 P.M.
   C. All wardens must report to her stations by 5:15 P.M.
   D. Workers in public parks must display their identification cards.

7. Which of the following is a compound sentence?

   A. Sonya painted the sign, and *I* did the lettering.
   B. Without a dictionary, I couldn't check my spelling.
   C. No one noticed the mistakes until this morning.
   D. Of twelve words on the sign, three were misspelled.

8. What number is represented above?

   A. 136   B. 316   C. 361   D. 631

9. Marcy is practicing for a track meet. Each day she runs around a quarter-mile track two and one-half times. How many miles does she run in five days?
   _____ miles.

   A. 5/8   B. 1 1/4   C. 3 1/8   D. 12 1/2

10. Everything in a hardware store is being sold at 20 percent off the regular price. Mark bought a garden hose regularly priced at $12.95 and a wheelbarrow regularly priced at $23.95.
    What operations are needed to calculate how much Mark had to pay?

    A. Divide 0.20 by $23.95 and add $12.95
    B. Add $12.95 and $23.95 and multiply the sum by 0.8
    C. Multiply $23.95 by 0.20 and add $12.95
    D. Subtract $12.95 from $23.95 and multiply by 0.2

11. How many lines of symmetry does an equilateral triangle have?

    A. One   B. Two   C. Three   D. Four

12. Humans are responsible for the extinction of other species PRIMARILY through   12.____

    A. environmental pollution
    B. experimental hybridization
    C. hunting and poaching
    D. habitat destruction

13. Replacement of a cold air mass by a warm air mass is usually FIRST indicated by the   13.____
    formation of which cloud type?

    A. Cirrus
    C. Cumulus
    B. Cumulonimbus
    D. Stratus

14. Edward is writing a brief report on specific examples of extreme weather conditions in the   14.____
    United States. Which of the following pieces of information would be MOST relevant to
    his report?

    A. A hurricane is defined as a storm in which winds blow at greater than 74 miles per
       hour near the storm center.
    B. The highest temperature ever recorded was in Libya in 1922; it was 136 degrees
       Fahrenheit.
    C. In the Texas panhandle, snowfall averages about 2 feet each year.
    D. The greatest rainfall ever recorded in 1 minute was 1.23 inches; it occurred in
       Unionville, Maryland.

15. In the United States, all citizens have the responsibility to   15.____

    A. petition the government
    B. exercise freedom of religion
    C. serve on juries
    D. determine the rate of income tax

16.   16.____

    According to the map above, Bombay, India, is located at APPROXIMATELY which longitude and latitude?
    Longitude _____; latitude _____.

    A. 73° E; 19° N
    C. 73° E; 21° N
    B. 21° N; 73° E
    D. 19° N; 73° E

17. The Monroe Doctrine was intended to

    A. promote commercial relations with the Concert of Europe
    B. protect American sailors from involuntary service
    C. prevent European expansion in Latin America
    D. open the southeastern United States to settlement

18. Which of the following activities would be MOST helpful for a sixth grader in developing his or her individual response to art?

    A. Matching artistic techniques to artworks
    B. Participating in a critique of various artworks
    C. Matching artists to their works
    D. Learning terminology associated with art criticism

KEY (CORRECT ANSWERS)

1.	A	11.	C
2.	B	12.	D
3.	D	13.	A
4.	B	14.	D
5.	A	15.	C
6.	D	16.	A
7.	A	17.	C
8.	B	18.	B
9.	C		
10.	B		

TEST 2

DIRECTIONS: Each question or incomplete statement is followed by several suggested answers or completions. Select the one that BEST answers the question or completes the statement. *PRINT THE LETTER OF THE CORRECT ANSWER IN THE SPACE AT THE RIGHT.*

1. At the early elementary level, which of the following activities would be MOST appropriate for developing fine-motor skills? 1.____

   A. Tying shoelaces
   B. Pushing a swing
   C. Throwing a ball
   D. Skipping rope

2. When educationally disadvantaged students enter school, the problems they face are MOST often a function of 2.____

   A. traumatic childhood incidents
   B. an inability to think clearly in solving problems
   C. overemphasis on achievement
   D. a lack of exposure to positive, varied experiences

3. Which of the following criteria is MOST important in determining whether a given learning opportunity is appropriate for an elementary class? 3.____

   A. Levels of cognitive and psychomotor development among students
   B. Content of available textbooks
   C. Usefulness of the subject matter in life outside the classroom
   D. Testing programs in use at the school

4. Which of the following is MOST important for a teacher to consider when selecting materials for a specific lesson? 4.____

   A. Relationship to learner objectives
   B. Popularity of the material
   C. Relationship to the teacher's personal interests
   D. Publisher of the material

5. Recent data from nationwide standardized tests show that students in the Alpha school district scored below average in mathematics skills. 5.____
Based on these data, which is the MOST appropriate short-term goal for this school district?

   A. Emphasize higher-level skills in mathematics
   B. Assess students' strengths and weaknesses in reading
   C. Improve Alpha's curriculum in reading and mathematics
   D. Compare the Alpha curriculum with those of other districts

6. A class has just read *Jack and the Beanstalk*. 6.____
Which of the following questions would be MOST appropriate for a teacher to ask if the objective of the lesson is to teach interpretive reading skills?

   A. How many times did Jack climb the beanstalk?
   B. Who planted the beanstalk?

C. What did Jack do before he climbed the beanstalk?
D. Why did Jack climb the beanstalk the third time?

7. In the scope and sequence of social studies skills, the emphasis of objectives in the elementary grades tends to follow a progression from

   A. history to politics
   B. self to family to community
   C. culture to economics
   D. world to nation to neighborhood

8. A teacher notes that on a particular multiple-choice test item, about the same number of students chose each of the four responses.
This MOST likely means that the

   A. item was too easy for the students
   B. students did not follow the directions
   C. item had two correct responses
   D. students were guessing at the answer

9. One advantage of essay tests as compared with multiple-choice tests is that essay tests

   A. are more easily standardized
   B. allow for more creative responses
   C. can be completed in a shorter period of time
   D. are easier to score

10. When using a criterion-referenced test, student test scores should be compared with

    A. average statewide scores
    B. scores of other students
    C. a preset standard of mastery
    D. national norms

11. Which of the following should be the FIRST step in teaching material related to a new learning objective?

    A. Assign related readings
    B. Give a preview of new vocabulary
    C. Present the necessary information
    D. Explain the purpose of the lesson

12. A teacher plans to teach students how to locate resources in the school library.
How could the teacher approach this objective using didactic methodology?

    A. Encourage independent exploration to discover how library materials are organized
    B. Have students find materials through a process of trial and error
    C. Teach one skill at a time and provide frequent practice
    D. Give students a self-directed guide to using the library

13. A teacher has passed out reading material with a brief glossary of new words.
The BEST way to ensure that students understand the new words is to assign the students to

    A. circle the new words where they occur in the text
    B. read the material aloud to each other
    C. write sentences using the new words
    D. arrange the new words in alphabetical order

14. Good rapport between students and teachers is MOST likely to occur in classrooms in which

    A. rules are permissive
    B. students determine the pace of instruction
    C. decisions are made democratically
    D. teacher expectations are clear and reasonable

15. Which of the following is the MOST effective way to manage instruction for an elementary class involving students with a wide range of ability?

    A. Divide the class into small groups according to level
    B. Use the same materials for all students to challenge the weaker ones
    C. Assign extra work to those students who are furthest behind
    D. Work directly with the weakest students and ask others to work on their own

16. When applying discipline in an elementary school classroom, it is MOST important for the teacher to be

    A. compassionate
    B. firm and strong
    C. consistent
    D. broad-minded

17. In the school system, a MAJOR function of setting long-range educational goals is to

    A. provide overall direction for the curriculum
    B. make sure parents know what their children are learning
    C. find out what students need to learn
    D. eliminate repetition from one grade to another

18. According to the Family Educational Rights and Privacy Act, also known as the Buckley Amendment, parents have the right to

    A. select the public schools their children will attend
    B. inspect and review their children's educational records
    C. withhold information about their children from school officials
    D. attend classes with their children to monitor progress

KEY (CORRECT ANSWERS)

1.	A	11.	D
2.	D	12.	C
3.	A	13.	C
4.	A	14.	D
5.	A	15.	A
6.	D	16.	C
7.	B	17.	A
8.	D	18.	B
9.	B		
10.	C		

EXAMINATION SECTION
TEST 1

DIRECTIONS: This test is composed of a series of words. Some of them are correctly spelled; some are incorrectly spelled. You are to indicate whether each word is correctly spelled. In the margin next to the question, write 'C' for correct or 'W' for wrong.

1. apointed
2. commission
3. limited
4. arival
5. comunity
6. variety
7. agentcy
8. distrubute
9. hereafter
10. conference
11. salery
12. preveous
13. colusion
14. director
15. essential
16. cilinder
17. astablish
18. quarrel
19. premeum
20. relize
21. gratitude
22. sugestion
23. consinment
24. revenue
25. inferier

26. condem
27. absolutely
28. cancel
29. carreer
30. bullitin
31. oposition
32. ammunition
33. survay
34. energey
35. sundery
36. visinity
37. sheriff
38. pamflet
39. conserning
40. securety
41. necessity
42. expences
43. testomony
44. avalable
45. stating
46. courtesy
47. naturaly
48. apoligy
49. invilid
50. construction

51.	secratary	76.	deploma
52.	duplacate	77.	abundent
53.	gosple	78.	tedious
54.	traffic	79.	dilegent
55.	captian	80.	aquainted
56.	sanatary	81.	resonable
57.	specimen	82.	customery
58.	accommodate	83.	muslin
59.	Sabbath	84.	investagation
60.	consious	85.	temperary
61.	athority	86.	indignant
62.	owing	87.	wretched
63.	emergancy	88.	unusal
64.	opperation	89.	definate
65.	sylable	90.	garrulous
66.	talant	91.	allowence
67.	nourish	92.	appropriate
68.	ignorence	93.	rememberance
69.	behavor	94.	presense
70.	exceedingly	95.	caisson
71.	murmer	96.	appendicitis
72.	signiture	97.	convienient
73.	guardian	98.	occured
74.	interrupt	99.	intuition
75.	congradulate	100.	greatful

KEY (CORRECT ANSWERS)

1. W	21. C	41. C	61. W	81. W
2. C	22. W	42. W	62. C	82. W
3. C	23. W	43. W	63. W	83. C
4. W	24. C	44. W	64. W	84. W
5. W	25. W	45. C	65. W	85. W
6. C	26. W	46. C	66. W	86. C
7. W	27. C	47. W	67. C	87. C
8. W	28. C	48. W	68. W	88. W
9. C	29. W	49. W	69. W	89. W
10. C	30. W	50. C	70. C	90. C
11. W	31. W	51. W	71. W	91. W
12. W	32. C	52. W	72. W	92. C
13. W	33. W	53. W	73. C	93. W
14. C	34. W	54. C	74. C	94. W
15. C	35. W	55. W	75. W	95. C
16. W	36. W	56. W	76. W	96. C
17. W	37. C	57. C	77. W	97. W
18. C	38. W	58. C	78. C	98. W
19. W	39. W	59. C	79. W	99. C
20. W	40. W	60. W	80. W	100. W

TEST 2

DIRECTIONS: This test consists of a series of sentences, each divided into five parts lettered A, B, C, D, and E. You are to look at each and decide which, if any, of the lettered parts have errors in grammar, punctuation or spelling. When you have decided which part(s) are wrong, circle the letters representing them. If a sentence has no errors, write *correct* in the margin.

EXAMPLE
Ain't we / going to the / office / next week / at all.
  (A)   B   C   D   (E)

A has been circled because "ain't" is wrong; E has been circled because "at all" should be followed by a question mark. There is nothing wrong in parts B, C and D, so those letters have not been circled.

1. Where / did you / stop at / on your trip / to Chicago.
    A   B   C   D   E
2. Was it / him / who / got burned / when the boiler bursted?
    A   B   C   D   E
3. The dog laid / sleeping / after chasing John and I / with hardly no / time out.
    A   B   C   D   E
4. I doubt / if Jack / has fewer / than sixteen / baseball bats.
    A   B   C   D   E
5. "It is me," / said Will, / as his mother / answered / his knock.
    A   B   C   D   E
6. If I were / he, / I'd be / sure / of myself.
    A   B   C   D   E
7. I could / of won / if I had stood / in the game / a little longer.
    A   B   C   D   E
8. If John were here / he'd sure / have done / faster work / than Fred.
           A   B   C   D   E
9. I can't hardly / raise my hand / more than / three foot / above the board.
    A   B   C   D   E
10. I sung / until / I was hoarse, / and then drunk / a quart of water.
     A   B   C   D   E
11. Neither money / or fame / would of been / alright as payment / for such a job.
     A   B   C   D   E
12. I don't understand / how anyone / could admire / a person as careless / as her.
     A   B   C   D   E
13. Is it / I / whom / they / are calling?
     A   B   C   D   E
14. I didn't feel / good enough / to attend / the conference / last tuesday.
     A   B   C   D   E
15. I did / pretty good / in history / on last / week's quizzes.
     A   B   C   D   E

16. Her father replied / "I feel / that Carol / is some better / than Mary."
         A   B   C   D   E
17. The rivers raised / ten feet / after the rains / overflowing / their banks.
         A   B   C   D   E
18. I thought / you was through / doing / your work / all ready.
     A   B   C   D   E
19. We O.K.'d / there proposal / that we cooperate / for our / mutual profit.
       A   B   C   D   E
20. The writer / made / an illusion / to his hero's / earlier exploits.
        A   B   C   D   E
21. I don't like / those kind / of peaches; / give me some / of the ripe ones.
       A   B   C   D   E
22. Leave / me go / with John / and she / to the show.
     A   B   C   D   E
23. He is / one of those men / who works / well / and long.
     A   B   C   D   E
24. James said, / "Work, / not words, / is what / is needed."
       A   B   C   D   E
25. None of the books / were / worth reading / more then / once or twice.
           A   B   C   D   E
26. They / nearly were / starved / before they landed / somewheres in Florida.
     A   B   C   D   E
27. She / got hurt / when the dish / busted / in her hands.
     A   B   C   D   E
28. I thought it / was him, / and it sure / looked like him / from this distance.
       A   B   C   D   E
29. Who / do you / think / your / talking about?
     A   B   C   D   E
30. The number / of volunteers / were / seldom ever / enough.
        A   B   C   D   E
31. One issue of bonds / were / distributed / between / three banks.
          A   B   C   D   E
32. There goes / John and Bill, / fighting / like / always.
       A   B   C   D   E
33. Is it / me / who / you wanted / to see?
     A   B   C   D   E
34. I don't see / as good / as Tom, / my friend / can.
       A   B   C   D   E
35. Paul had / promised / to return / the book / in two weeks.
       A   B   C   D   E
36. The man who / everybody likes / is one / who / they can trust.
        A   B   C   D   E
37. He asked / we three, / "where / is the folks / which lived here?"
       A   B   C   D   E
38. I've had / less headaches / since I / went to sleep / earlier.
      A   B   C   D   E
39. The books / laid / in the grass / all day / and got wet.
       A   B   C   D   E
40. You can / leave the house / in an hour / if you feel / good.
      A   B   C   D   E
41. I will / be real glad / to visit you / whenever / you would prefer.
     A   B   C   D   E
42. The bible / is one / of the best books / their / are for serious study.
       A   B   C   D   E
43. Each of / these flowers / look best / in a different / sort of a plot.
      A   B   C   D   E
44. We allways turn / to who / we use to / know, the old friend / is best.
         A   B   C   D   E

3 (#2)

45. Being that / a pipe bust, / we hadn't / hardly / any water.
    A   B   C   D   E

46. He had smoked / their tobacco, / drank their wine / and heard / their tales.
    A   B   C   D   E

47. A man, / who beats his wife, / is considered depraved / by people / nowadays.
    A   B   C   D   E

48. We seldom ever / have to / watch close / in our kind / of a job.
    A   B   C   D   E

49. If it was possible, / we would of / gave him / the workers / which he wanted.
    A   B   C   D   E

50. Neither Jones / nor Smith / are / the men / for that sort of a job.
    A   B   C   D   E

KEY (CORRECT ANSWERS)

#	Ans	#	Ans	#	Ans	#	Ans	#	Ans
1.	CE	11.	BCD	21.	B	31.	BD	41.	BE
2.	BDE	12.	E	22.	AD	32.	AD	42.	DE
3.	ACDE	13.	C	23.	Correct	33.	B	43.	CE
4.	B	14.	BE	24.	Correct	34.	BD	44.	ABD
5.	A	15.	B	25.	BD	35.	Correct	45.	ABCD
6.	Correct	16.	AD	26.	BE	36.	A	46.	Correct
7.	BC	17.	A	27.	BD	37.	BDE	47.	AE
8.	BD	18.	BE	28.	BC	38.	B	48.	ACE
9.	AD	19.	AB	29.	D	39.	B	49.	ABCE
10.	AD	20.	C	30.	CD	40.	E	50.	E

SPELLING

EXAMINATION SECTION

TEST 1

DIRECTIONS: In each of the following tests in this part, select the letter of the one MISSPELLED word in each of the following groups of words. *PRINT THE LETTER OF THE CORRECT ANSWER IN THE SPACE AT THE RIGHT.*

1. A. grateful   B. fundimental   C. census   D. analysis   1.____
2. A. installment   B. retrieve   C. concede   D. dissapear   2.____
3. A. accidentaly   B. dismissal   C. conscientious D. indelible   3.____
4. A. perceive   B. carreer   C. anticipate   D. acquire   4.____
5. A. facillity   B. reimburse   C. assortment   D. guidance   5.____
6. A. plentiful   B. across   C. advantagous   D. similar   6.____
7. A. omission   B. pamphlet   C. guarrantee   D. repel   7.____
8. A. maintenance   B. always   C. liable   D. anouncement   8.____
9. A. exaggerate   B. sieze   C. condemn   D. commit   9.____
10. A. pospone   B. altogether   C. grievance   D. excessive   10.____
11. A. banana   B. trafic   C. spectacle   D. boundary   11.____
12. A. commentator   B. abbreviation C. battaries   D. monastery   12.____
13. A. practically   B. advise   C. pursuade   D. laboratory   13.____
14. A. fatigueing   B. invincible   C. strenuous   D. ceiling   14.____
15. A. propeller   B. reverence   C. piecemeal   D. underneth   15.____
16. A. annonymous   B. envelope   C. transit   D. variable   16.____
17. A. petroleum   B. bigoted   C. meager   D. resistence   17.____

2 (#1)

18. A. permissible B. indictment C. fundemental D. nowadays 18.____
19. A. thief B. bargin C. nuisance D. vacant 19.____
20. A. technique B. vengeance C. aquatic D. heighth 20.____

KEY (CORRECT ANSWERS)

1. B. fundamental
2. D. disappear
3. A. accidentally
4. B. career
5. A. facility

6. C. advantageous
7. C. guarantee
8. D. announcement
9. B. seize
10. A. postpone

11. B. traffic
12. C. batteries
13. C. persuade
14. A. fatiguing
15. D. underneath

16. A. anonymous
17. D. resistance
18. C. fundamental
19. B. bargain
20. D. height

TEST 2

DIRECTIONS: In each of the following tests in this part, select the letter of the one MISSPELLED word in each of the following groups of words. *PRINT THE LETTER OF THE CORRECT ANSWER IN THE SPACE AT THE RIGHT.*

1. A. apparent   B. superintendent   C. relieve   D. calendar   1._____
2. A. foreign   B. negotiate   C. typical   D. disipline   2._____
3. A. posponed   B. argument   C. susceptible   D. deficit   3._____
4. A. preferred   B. column   C. peculiar   D. equiped   4._____
5. A. exaggerate   B. disatisfied   C. repetition   D. already   5._____
6. A. livelihood   B. physician   C. obsticle   D. strategy   6._____
7. A. courageous   B. ommission   C. ridiculous   D. awkward   7._____
8. A. sincerely   B. abundance   C. negligable   D. elementary   8._____
9. A. obsolete   B. mischievous   C. enumerate   D. atheletic   9._____
10. A. fiscel   B. beneficiary   C. concede   D. translate   10._____
11. A. segregate   B. excessivly   C. territory   D. obstacle   11._____
12. A. unnecessary   B. monopolys   C. harmonious   D. privilege   12._____
13. A. sinthetic   B. intellectual   C. gracious   D. archaic   13._____
14. A. beneficial   B. fulfill   C. sarcastic   D. disolve   14._____
15. A. umbrella   B. sentimental   C. ineffifient   D. psychiatrist   15._____
16. A. noticable   B. knapsack   C. librarian   D. meant   16._____
17. A. conference   B. upheaval   C. vulger   D. odor   17._____
18. A. surmount   B. pentagon   C. calorie   D. inumerable   18._____
19. A. classifiable   B. moisturize   C. monitor   D. assesment   19._____
20. A. thermastat   B. corrupting   C. approach   D. thinness   20._____

KEY (CORRECT ANSWERS)

1. C. relieve
2. D. discipline
3. A. postponed
4. D. equipped
5. B. dissatisfied

6. C. obstacle
7. B. omission
8. C. negligible
9. D. athletic
10. A. fiscal

11. B. excessively
12. B. monopolies
13. A. synthetic
14. D. dissolve
15. C. inefficient

16. A. noticeable
17. C. vulgar
18. D. innumerable
19. D. assessment
20. A. thermostat

TEST 3

DIRECTIONS: In each of the following tests in this part, select the letter of the one MISSPELLED word in each of the following groups of words. *PRINT THE LETTER OF THE CORRECT ANSWER IN THE SPACE AT THE RIGHT.*

1. A. typical B. descend C. summarize D. continuel 1._____
2. A. courageous B. recomend C. omission D. eliminate 2._____
3. A. compliment B. illuminate C. auxilary D. installation 3._____
4. A. preliminary B. aquainted C. syllable D. analysis 4._____
5. A. accustomed B. negligible C. interupted D. bulletin 5._____
6. A. summoned B. managment C. mechanism D. sequence 6._____
7. A. commitee B. surprise C. noticeable D. emphasize 7._____
8. A. occurrance B. likely C. accumulate D. grievance 8._____
9. A. obstacle B. particuliar C. baggage D. fascinating 9._____
10. A. innumerable B. seize C. applicant D. dictionery 10._____
11. A. monkeys B. rigid C. unnatural D. roomate 11._____
12. A. surveying B. figurative C. famous D. curiosety 12._____
13. A. rodeo B. inconcievable C. calendar D. magnificence 13._____
14. A. handicaped B. glacier C. defiance D. emperor 14._____
15. A. schedule B. scrawl C. seclusion D. sissors 15._____
16. A. tissues B. tomatos C. tyrants D. tragedies 16._____
17. A. casette B. graceful C. penicillin D. probably 17._____
18. A. gnawed B. microphone C. clinicle D. batch 18._____
19. A. amateur B. altitude C. laborer D. expence 19._____
20. A. mandate B. flexable C. despise D. verify 20._____

KEY (CORRECT ANSWERS)

1. D. continual
2. B. recommend
3. C. auxiliary
4. B. acquainted
5. C. interrupted

6. B. management
7. A. committee
8. A. occurrence
9. B. particular
10. D. dictionary

11. D. roommate
12. D. curiosity
13. B. inconceivable
14. A. handicapped
15. D. scissors

16. B. tomatoes
17. A. cassette
18. C. clinical
19. D. expense
20. B. flexible

TEST 4

DIRECTIONS: In each of the following tests in this part, select the letter of the one MISSPELLED word in each of the following groups of words. *PRINT THE LETTER OF THE CORRECT ANSWER IN THE SPACE AT THE RIGHT.*

1. A. primery B. mechanic C. referred D. admissible 1.____
2. A. cessation B. beleif C. aggressive D. allowance 2.____
3. A. leisure B. authentic C. familiar D. contemtable 3.____
4. A. volume B. forty C. dilemma D. seldum 4.____
5. A. discrepancy B. aquisition C. exorbitant D. lenient 5.____
6. A. simultanous B. penetrate C. revision D. conspicuous 6.____
7. A. ilegible B. gracious C. profitable D. obedience 7.____
8. A. manufacturer B. authorize C. compelling D. pecular 8.____
9. A. anxious B. rehearsal C. handicaped D. tendency 9.____
10. A. meticulous B. accompaning C. initiative D. shelves 10.____
11. A. hammaring B. insecticide C. capacity D. illogical 11.____
12. A. budget B. luminous C. aviation D. lunchon 12.____
13. A. moniter B. bachelor C. pleasurable D. omitted 13.____
14. A. monstrous B. transistor C. narrative D. anziety 14.____
15. A. engagement B. judical C. pasteurize D. tried 15.____
16. A. fundimental B. innovation C. perpendicular D. extravagant 16.____
17. A. bookkeeper B. brutality C. gymnaseum D. cemetery 17.____
18. A. sturdily B. pretentious C. gourmet D. enterance 18.____
19. A. resturant B. tyranny C. kindergarten D. ancestry 19.____
20. A. benefit B. possess C. speciman D. noticing 20.____

KEY (CORRECT ANSWERS)

1. A. primary
2. B. belief
3. D. contemptible
4. D. seldom
5. B. acquisition

6. A. simultaneous
7. A. illegible
8. D. peculiar
9. C. handicapped
10. B. accompanying

11. A. hammering
12. D. luncheon
13. A. monitor
14. D. anxiety
15. B. judicial

16. A. fundamental
17. C. gymnasium
18. D. entrance
19. A. restaurant
20. C. specimen

TEST 5

DIRECTIONS: In each of the following tests in this part, select the letter of the one MISSPELLED word in each of the following groups of words. *PRINT THE LETTER OF THE CORRECT ANSWER IN THE SPACE AT THE RIGHT.*

1. A. arguing B. correspondance C. forfeit D. dissension 1.____
2. A. occasion B. description C. prejudice D. elegible 2.____
3. A. accomodate B. initiative C. changeable D. enroll 3.____
4. A. temporary B. insistent C. benificial D. separate 4.____
5. A. achieve B. dissappoint C. unanimous D. judgment 5.____
6. A. procede B. publicly C. sincerity D. successful 6.____
7. A. deceive B. goverment C. preferable D. repetitive 7.____
8. A. emphasis B. skillful C. advisible D. optimistic 8.____
9. A. tendency B. rescind C. crucial D. noticable 9.____
10. A. privelege B. abbreviate C. simplify D. divisible 10.____
11. A. irresistible B. varius C. mutual D. refrigerator 11.____
12. A. amateur B. distinguish C. rehearsal D. poision 12.____
13. A. biased B. ommission C. precious D. coordinate 13.____
14. A. calculated B. enthusiasm C. sincerely D. parashute 14.____
15. A. sentry B. materials C. incredable D. budget 15.____
16. A. chocolate B. instrument C. volcanoe D. shoulder 16.____
17. A. ancestry B. obscure C. intention D. ninty 17.____
18. A. artical B. bracelet C. beggar D. hopeful 18.____
19. A. tournament B. sponsor C. perpendiclar D. dissolve 19.____
20. A. yeild B. physician C. greasiest D. admitting 20.____

KEY (CORRECT ANSWERS)

1. B. correspondence
2. D. eligible
3. A. accommodate
4. C. beneficial
5. B. disappoint

6. A. proceed
7. B. government
8. C. advisable
9. D. noticeable
10. A. privilege

11. B. various
12. D. poison
13. B. omission
14. D. parachute
15. C. incredible

16. C. volcano
17. D. ninety
18. A. article
19. C. perpendicular
20. A. yield

TEST 6

DIRECTIONS: In each of the following tests in this part, select the letter of the one MISSPELLED word in each of the following groups of words. *PRINT THE LETTER OF THE CORRECT ANSWER IN THE SPACE AT THE RIGHT.*

1. A. achievment   B. maintenance   C. questionnaire   D. all are correct   1.____
2. A. prevelant   B. pronunciation C. separate   D. all are correct   2.____
3. A. permissible   B. relevant   C. seize   D. all are correct   3.____
4. A. corroborate   B. desparate   C. eighth   D. all are correct   4.____
5. A. exceed   B. feasibility   C. psycological   D. all are correct   5.____
6. A. parallel   B. aluminum   C. calendar   D. eigty   6.____
7. A. microbe   B. ancient   C. autograph   D. existance   7.____
8. A. plentiful   B. skillful   C. amoung   D. capsule   8.____
9. A. erupt   B. quanity   C. opinion   D. competent   9.____
10. A. excitement   B. discipline   C. luncheon   D. regreting   10.____
11. A. magazine   B. expository   C. imitation   D. permenent   11.____
12. A. ferosious   B. machinery   C. precise   D. magnificent   12.____
13. A. conceive   B. narritive   C. separation   D. management   13.____
14. A. muscular   B. witholding   C. pickle   D. glacier   14.____
15. A. vehicel   B. mismanage   C. correspondence   D. dissatisfy   15.____
16. A. sentince   B. bulletin   C. notice   D. definition   16.____
17. A. appointment   B. exactly   C. typest   D. light   17.____
18. A. penalty   B. suparvise   C. consider   D. division   18.____
19. A. schedule   B. accurate   C. corect   D. simple   19.____
20. A. suggestion   B. installed   C. proper   D. agincy   20.____

KEY (CORRECT ANSWERS)

1.	A. achievement		11.	D. permanent
2.	B. prevalent		12.	A. ferocious
3.	D. all are correct		13.	B. narrative
4.	B. desperate		14.	B. withholding
5.	C. psychological		15.	A. vehicle
6.	D. eighty		16.	A. sentence
7.	D. existence		17.	C. typist
8.	C. among		18.	B. supervise
9.	B. quantity		19.	C. correct
10.	D. regretting		20.	D. agency

TEST 7

DIRECTIONS: In each of the following tests in this part, select the letter of the one MISSPELLED word in each of the following groups of words. *PRINT THE LETTER OF THE CORRECT ANSWER IN THE SPACE AT THE RIGHT.*

1. A. symtom B. serum B. antiseptic D. aromatic 1.____
2. A. register B. registrar C. purser D. burser 2.____
3. A. athletic B. tragedy C. batallion D. sophomore 3.____
4. A. latent B. godess C. aisle D. whose 4.____
5. A. rhyme B. rhythm C. thime D. thine 5.____
6. A. eighth B. exaggerate C. electoral D. villain 6.____
7. A. statute B. superintendent 7.____
   C. iresistible D. colleague
8. A. sieze B. therefor C. auxiliary D. changeable 8.____
9. A. siege B. knowledge C. lieutenent D. weird 9.____
10. A. acquitted B. polititian C. professor D. conqueror 10.____
11. A. changeable B. chargeable C. salable D. useable 11.____
12. A. promissory B. prisoner C. excellent D. tyrrany 12.____
13. A. conspicuous B. essance C. comparative D. brilliant 13.____
14. A. notefying B. accentuate C. adhesive D. primarily 14.____
15. A. exercise B. sublime C. stuborn D. shameful 15.____
16. A. presume B. transcript C. strech D. wizard 16.____
17. A. specify B. regional C. arbitrary D. segragation 17.____
18. A. requirement B. happiness C. achievement D. gentely 18.____
19. A. endurance B. fusion C. balloon D. enormus 19.____
20. A. luckily B. schedule C. simplicity D. sanwich 20.____

KEY (CORRECT ANSWERS)

1.	A. symptom		11.	D. usable
2.	D. bursar		12.	D. tyranny
3.	C. battalion		13.	B. essence
4.	B. goddess		14.	A. notifying
5.	C. thyme		15.	C. stubborn
6.	C. electoral		16.	C. stretch
7.	C. irresistible		17.	D. segregation
8.	A. seize		18.	D. gently
9.	C. lieutenant		19.	D. enormous
10.	B. politician		20.	D. sandwich

TEST 8

DIRECTIONS: In each of the following tests in this part, select the letter of the one MISSPELLED word in each of the following groups of words. *PRINT THE LETTER OF THE CORRECT ANSWER IN THE SPACE AT THE RIGHT.*

1. A. maintain B. maintainance C. sustain D. sustenance 1.____
2. A. portend B. portentious C. pretend D. pretentious 2.____
3. A. prophesize B. prophesies C. farinaceous D. spaceous 3.____
4. A. choose B. chose C. choosen D. chasten 4.____
5. A. censure B. censorious C. pleasure D. pleasurable 5.____
6. A. cover B. coverage C. adder D. adage 6.____
7. A. balloon B. diregible C. direct D. descent 7.____
8. A. whemsy B. crazy C. flimsy D. lazy 8.____
9. A. derision B. pretention C. sustention D. contention 9.____
10. A. question B. questionaire C. legion D. legionary 10.____
11. A. chattle B. cattle C. dismantle D. kindle 11.____
12. A. canal B. cannel C. chanel D. colonel 12.____
13. A. hemorrage B. storage C. manage D. foliage 13.____
14. A. surgeon B. sturgeon C. luncheon D. stancheon 14.____
15. A. diploma B. commission C. dependent D. luminious 15.____
16. A. likelihood B. blizzard C. machanical D. suppress 16.____
17. A. commercial B. releif C. disposal D. endeavor 17.____
18. A. operate B. bronco C. excaping D. grammar 18.____
19. A. orchard B. collar C. embarass D. distant 19.____
20. A. sincerly B. possessive C. weighed D. waist 20.____

KEY (CORRECT ANSWERS)

1. B. maintenance
2. B. portentous
3. D. spacious
4. C. chosen
5. D. pleasurable

6. D. adage
7. B. dirigible
8. A. whimsy
9. B. pretension
10. B. questionnaire

11. A. chattel
12. C. channel
13. A. hemorrhage
14. D. stanchion
15. D. luminous

16. C. mechanical
17. B. relief
18. C. escaping
19. C. embarrass
20. A. sincerely

TEST 9

DIRECTIONS: In each of the following tests in this part, select the letter of the one MISSPELLED word in each of the following groups of words. *PRINT THE LETTER OF THE CORRECT ANSWER IN THE SPACE AT THE RIGHT.*

1. A. statute B. stationary C. staturesque D. stature 1.____
2. A. practicible B. practical C. particle D. reticule 2.____
3. A. plague B. plaque C. ague D. aigrete 3.____
4. A. theology B. idealogy C. psychology D. philology 4.____
5. A. dilema B. stamina C. feminine D. strychnine 5.____
6. A. deceit B. benefit C. grieve D. hienous 6.____
7. A. commensurable B. measurable C. duteable D. salable 7.____
8. A. homogeneous B. heterogeneous C. advantageous D. religeous 8.____
9. A. criticize B. dramatise C. exorcise D. exercise 9.____
10. A. ridiculous B. comparable C. merciful D. cotten 10.____
11. A. antebiotic B. stitches C. pitiful D. sneaky 11.____
12. A. amendment B. candadate C. accountable D. recommendation 12.____
13. A. avocado B. recruit C. tripping D. probally 13.____
14. A. calendar B. desirable C. familar D. vacuum 14.____
15. A. deteriorate B. elligible C. liable D. missile 15.____
16. A. amateur B. competent C. mischeivous D. occasion 16.____
17. A. friendliness B. saleries C. cruelty D. ammunition 17.____
18. A. wholesome B. cieling C. stupidity D. eligible 18.____
19. A. comptroller B. traveled C. accede D. procede 19.____
20. A. Britain B. Brittainica C. conductor D. vendor 20.____

KEY (CORRECT ANSWERS)

1. C. statuesque
2. A. practicable
3. D. aigrette
4. B. ideology
5. A. dilemma

6. D. heinous
7. C. dutiable
8. D. religious
9. B. dramatize
10. D. cotton

11. A. antibiotic
12. B. candidate
13. D. probably
14. C. familiar
15. B. eligible

16. C. mischievous
17. B. salaries
18. B. ceiling
19. D. proceed
20. B. Brittanica

TEST 10

DIRECTIONS: In each of the following tests in this part, select the letter of the one MISSPELLED word in each of the following groups of words. *PRINT THE LETTER OF THE CORRECT ANSWER IN THE SPACE AT THE RIGHT.*

1. A. lengthen B. region C. gases D. inspecter 1._____
2. A. imediately B. forbidden C. complimentary D. aeronautics 2._____
3. A. continuous B. paralel C. opposite D. definite 3._____
4. A. Antarctic B. Wednesday C. Febuary D. Hungary 4._____
5. A. transmission B. exposure C. pistol D. customery 5._____
6. A. juvinile B. martyr C. deceive D. collaborate 6._____
7. A. unnecessary B. repetitive C. cancellation D. airey 7._____
8. A. transit B. availible C. objection D. galaxy 8._____
9. A. ineffective B. believeable C. arrangement D. aggravate 9._____
10. A. possession B. progress C. reception D. predjudice 10._____
11. A. congradulate B. percolate C. major D. leisure 11._____
12. A. convenience B. privilige C. emerge D. immerse 12._____
13. A. erasable B. inflammable C. audable D. laudable 13._____
14. A. final B. fines C. finis D. Finish 14._____
15. A. emitted B. representative C. discipline D. insistance 15._____
16. A. diphthong B. rarified C. library D. recommend 16._____
17. A. compel B. belligerent C. successful D. sergeant 17._____
18. A. dispatch B. dispise C. dispose D. dispute 18._____
19. A. administrator B. adviser C. diner D. celluler 19._____
20. A. ignite B. ignision C. igneous D. ignited 20._____

KEY (CORRECT ANSWERS)

1. D. inspector
2. A. immediately
3. B. parallel
4. C. February
5. D. customary

6. A. juvenile
7. D. airy
8. B. available
9. B. believable
10. D. prejudice

11. A. congratulate
12. B. privilege
13. C. audible
14. D. Finnish
15. D. insistence

16. B. rarefied
17. D. sergeant
18. B. despise
19. D. cellular
20. B. ignition

TEST 11

DIRECTIONS: In each of the following tests in this part, select the letter of the one MISSPELLED word in each of the following groups of words. *PRINT THE LETTER OF THE CORRECT ANSWER IN THE SPACE AT THE RIGHT.*

1. A. repellent B. secession C. sebaceous D. saxaphone 1.____
2. A. navel B. counteresolution 2.____
   C. marginalia D. perceptible
3. A. Hammerskjold B. Nehru C. U Thamt D. Krushchev 3.____
4. A. perculate B. periwinkle C. perigee D. retrogression 4.____
5. A. buccaneer B. tobacco C. buffalo D. oscilate 5.____
6. A. siege B. wierd C. seize D. cemetery 6.____
7. A. equaled B. bigoted C. benefited D. kaleideoscope 7.____
8. A. blamable B. bullrush C. questionnaire D. irascible 8.____
9. A. tobogganed B. acquiline C. capillary D. cretonne 9.____
10. A. daguerrotype B. elegiacal C. iridescent D. inchoate 10.____
11. A. bayonet B. braggadocio C. corollary D. connoiseur 11.____
12. A. equinoctial B. fusillade C. fricassee D. potpouri 12.____
13. A. octameter B. impressario C. hyetology D. hieroglyphics 13.____
14. A. innanity B. idyllic C. fylfot D. inimical 14.____
15. A. liquefy B. rarefy C. putrify D. sapphire 15.____
16. A. canonical B. stupified C. millennium D. memorabilia 16.____
17. A. paraphenalia B. odyssey 17.____
    C. onomatopoeia D. osseous
18. A. peregrinate B. pecadillo C. reptilian D. uxorious 18.____
19. A. pharisaical B. vicissitude C. puissance D. wainright 19.____
20. A. holocaust B. tesselate C. scintilla D. staccato 20.____

KEY (CORRECT ANSWERS)

1. D. saxophone
2. B. counterresolution
3. C. U Thant
4. A. percolate
5. D. oscillate

6. B. weird
7. D. kaleidoscope
8. B. bulrush
9. B. aquiline
10. A. daguerreotype

11. D. connoisseur
12. D. potpourri
13. B. impresario
14. A. inanity
15. C. putrefy

16. B. stupefied
17. A. paraphernalia
18. B. peccadillo
19. D. wainwright
20. B. tessellate

TEST 12

DIRECTIONS: In each of the following tests in this part, select the letter of the one MISSPELLED word in each of the following groups of words. *PRINT THE LETTER OF THE CORRECT ANSWER IN THE SPACE AT THE RIGHT.*

1. A. questionnaire B. gondoleer C. chandelier D. acquiescence 1.____
2. A. surveilance B. surfeit C. vaccinate D. belligerent 2.____
3. A. occassionally B. recurrence C. silhouette D. incessant 3.____
4. A. transferral B. benefical C. descendant D. dependent 4.____
5. A. separately B. flouresence C. deterrent D. parallel 5.____
6. A. acquittal B. enforceable C. counterfeit D. indispensible 6.____
7. A. susceptible B. accelarate C. exhilarate D. accommodation 7.____
8. A. impedimenta B. collateral C. liason D. epistolary 8.____
9. A. inveigle B. panegyric C. reservoir D. manuver 9.____
10. A. synopsis B. paraphernalia C. affidavit D. subpoena 10.____
11. A. grosgrain B. vermilion C. abbatoir D. connoiseur 11.____
12. A. gabardine B. camoflage C. hemorrhage D. contraband 12.____
13. A. opprobrious B. defalcate C. fiduciery D. recommendations 13.____
14. A. nebulous B. necessitate C. impricate D. discrepancy 14.____
15. A. discrete B. condescension C. condign D. condiment 15.____
16. A. cavalier B. effigy C. legitimatly D. misalliance 16.____
17. A. rheumatism B. vaporous C. cannister D. hallucinations 17.____
18. A. paleonthology B. octogenarian C. gradient D. impingement 18.____
19. A. fusilade B. fusilage C. ensilage D. desiccate 19.____
20. A. rationale B. raspberry C. reprobate D. varigated 20.____

KEY (CORRECT ANSWERS)

1. B. gondolier
2. A. surveillance
3. A. occasionally
4. B. beneficial
5. B. fluorescence

6. D. indispensable
7. B. accelerate
8. C. liaison
9. D. maneuver
10. B. paraphernalia

11. D. connoisseur
12. B. camouflage
13. C. fiduciary
14. C. imprecate
15. B. condescension

16. C. legitimately
17. C. canister
18. A. paleontology
19. A. fusillade
20. D. variegated

EXAMINATION SECTION
TEST 1

DIRECTIONS: Each question or incomplete statement is followed by several suggested answers or completions. Select the one that BEST answers the question or completes the statement. *PRINT THE LETTER OF THE CORRECT ANSWER IN THE SPACE AT THE RIGHT.*

Questions 1-10.

DIRECTIONS: Some of the following groups of words make correct, complete sentences. Others contain errors or are not complete sentences. If the group of words makes a correct, complete sentence, indicate 0 (ZERO). If the group of words does not make a correct, complete sentence, indicate the letter of the part which contains the error or which should be changed to make a complete sentence.

1. A. No one
   B. knows
   C. why he came
   D. or where he went.

2. A. What do you
   B. think
   C. is the answer
   D. to the problem?

3. A. What
   B. fun to be
   C. on the
   D. relay team!

4. A. Hope
   B. to win
   C. the next set
   D. of races.

5. A. The class giving
   B. a play
   C. for parents
   D. and friends

6. A. How
   B. exciting
   C. winning
   D. would be!

7. A. Richard
    B. likes
    C. swimming and to water ski
    D. in the summer.

    7.____

8. Charles
    A. has played
    B. football for
    C. three years and
    D. will again next year.

    8.____

9. He likes
    A. all sports the coach
    B. says Charles is the best
    C. all-round athlete
    D. the school has ever had.

    9.____

10. A. Although the weather
    B. is cold,
    C. we can see
    D. signs of nature's reawakening

    10.____

Questions 11-25.

DIRECTIONS: In each sentence below, one or more letters are underlined. Indicate C (CORRECT) or W (WRONG) in the space at the right of each sentence in which the letter or letters underlined are CORRECTLY capitalized.

11. Tom learned much about the sea from <u>c</u>aptain Jones.   11.____

12. Dear <u>s</u>ir: 12.____

13. Will you please send us information about tours through the <u>e</u>ast? I am especially interested in seeing   13.____

14. <u>i</u>ndia and the   14.____

15. <u>T</u>aj <u>M</u>ahal.   15.____

16. Yours <u>v</u>ery <u>s</u>incerely, John Brown   16.____

17. Jeffrey calls his dog <u>F</u>risker.   17.____

18. He bought the dog from a neighbor who lives a black <u>n</u>orth of Jeffrey.   18.____

19. He got the dog last <u>S</u>ummer.   19.____

20. Once we visited the United States <u>s</u>enate.   20.____

3 (#1)

21. Washington Irving wrote "The legend of Sleepy Hollow." 21.____

22. My uncle says that story is one of his favorites. 22.____

23. I shall always remember my drive through the Cumberland Mountains. 23.____

24. "It is early," the guide said, "but we shall be ready to start the tour soon." 24.____

25. "I am glad," Jane replied. "we are very eager to go." 25.____

Questions 26-50.

DIRECTIONS: From the list of choices below, select the punctuation mark which should be used where the parenthesis appear in each sentence. Indicate the letter of the correct answer in the space at the right.

- A. Colon
- B. Comma
- C. Dash
- D. Double quotation marks
- E. Exclamation point
- F. Hyphen
- G. Question mark
- H. Period
- I. Semicolon
- J. Single quotation marks
- K. No punctuation

26. Last night we heard a bird call from the woods near our home(). 26.____

27. We wondered what it could be() 27.____

28. Because we had not heard the call before() we did not recognize it as the song of a whippoorwill. 28.____

29. Are you ready for school now() Nancy? 29.____

30. School does not begin until 8()30. 30.____

31. I want to arrive in time to see Miss Smith() the music teacher. 31.____

32. I should like to join the chorus() but tryouts come during the time when I have band practice. 32.____

33. It is possible() of course() that band practice will be over before the tryouts are. 33.____

34. The snow() covered bushes looked like ghosts huddled together. 34.____

35. On the farm were the following() 35.____

36. cows() pigs() chickens() and geese. 36.____

101

37. The farm is near Lincoln() Nebraska.   37.____

38. On our vacation, we traveled in Minnesota() and Wisconsin() and Michigan.   38.____

39. What interesting experiences we had()   39.____

40. Someone said the world would end on August 7() 1987.   40.____

41. Sammy's bright() happy smile made him popular with everyone.   41.____

42. We appreciate your help; however() it is too late to continue.   42.____

43. Da Vinci() who was famous as a painter() was also a scientist and an inventor.   43.____

44. Please mail the package to 412 Park Avenue() Denver.   44.____

45. Mother said the border was three and three() fourths inches wide.   45.____

46. Miss Swanson() our home economics teacher() has taught us to bake bread.   46.____

47. The Home Economics Club is for everyone() who enjoys cooking or sewing.   47.____

48. The path was steep and rough() nevertheless, we did not turn back.   48.____

49. "Father likes to quote the lines, ()He prayeth best who loveth best,()" said Joanne.   49.____

50. "Do you like poetry()" asked James.   50.____

KEY (CORRECT ANSWERS)

1.	0	11.	W	21.	W	31.	B	41.	B
2.	0	12.	W	22.	C	32.	B	42.	B
3.	B	13.	W	23.	C	33.	B	43.	B
4.	A	14.	W	24.	C	34.	F	44.	B
5.	A	15.	C	25.	W	35.	A	45.	F
6.	0	16.	C	26.	H	36.	B	46.	B
7.	C	17.	C	27.	H	37.	B	47.	K
8.	D	18.	C	28.	B	38.	K	48.	I
9.	A	19.	W	29.	B	39.	E	49.	J
10.	0	20.	W	30.	A	40.	B	50.	G

TEST 2

DIRECTIONS: Each question or incomplete statement is followed by several suggested answers or completions. Select the one that BEST answers the question or completes the statement. *PRINT THE LETTER OF THE CORRECT ANSWER IN THE SPACE AT THE RIGHT.*

Questions 1-10.

DIRECTIONS: In answering Questions 1 through 10, indicate the CORRECT answer.

1. Perhaps the jewelry is
 A. hers B. her's C. hers' 1._____

2. _____ the best musician in our group.
 A. You're B. Your 2._____

3. _____ painting did you think was most pleasing?
 A. Who's B. Whose 3._____

4. The children gave _____ pennies to buy a gift for the sick child.
 A. there B. their C. they're 4._____

5. It is _____ too warm for ice fishing.
 A. all together B. altogether 5.._____

6. _____ going to rain soon.
 A. Its B. It's 6._____

7. The speaker used so many _____ that we found it tiresome to listen to him.
 A. wells B. wells' C. well's 7._____

8. _____ eyes were sparkling happily.
 A. Agneses B. Agne's C. Agnes's 8._____

9. We faced the mountain and called, but only our _____ answered us.
 A. echos B. echoes 9._____

10. Alice likes skiing and skating, _____.
 A. to B. two C. too 10._____

Questions 11-25.

DIRECTIONS: In answering Questions 11 through 25, indicate which choice makes the sentence CORRECT?

11. Paul _____ hardly started to wade when his foot slipped, and he fell into the water.
 A. had B. had not 11._____

12. _____ across a chair was a beautiful Spanish shawl.   12._____

13. The book had been _____ by some careless child.   13._____
    A. teared   B. tore   C. torn

14. The clown _____ a tattered hat.   14._____
    A. weared   B. wore   C. worn

15. Someone had _____ all of the orange juice.   15._____
    A. drinked   B. drank   C. drunk

16. Our dog _____ like music.   16._____
    A. don't   B. doesn't

17. The child had _____ so softly that we were not sure that we had heard him correctly.   17._____
    A. speaked   B. spoke   C. spoken

18. Jim had _____ across the pool twice before I even got started.   18._____
    A. swimmed   B. swam   C. swum

19. The _____ milk   19._____
    A. freezed   B. frozen   C. froze

20. _____ the bottle.   20._____
    A. busted   B. bursted   C. burst

21. _____ are always teasing each other.   21._____
    A. She and Joanne   B. Her and Joanne

22. Where had you _____ the drawings?   22._____
    A. lay   B. laid   C. lain

23. Children were _____ on the stairway.   23._____
    A. sitting   B. setting

24. I have _____ most of the invitations.   24._____
    A. writed   B. wrote   C. written

25. Holding onto a flimsy thread of its web,   25._____
    A. a spider swayed back and forth.
    B. we saw a spider swaying back and forth.

Questions 26-50.

DIRECTIONS: In answering Questions 26 through 50, indicate from the even-numbered items that which makes the sentence correct. Select from the odd-numbered choices that rule which makes the sentence incorrect.

104

3 (#2)

26. John is wittier than 26.____
    A. I B. me C. myself

27. A. Nominative case, predicate pronoun 27.____
    B. Objective case, object of a preposition
    C. Reflexive pronoun, to refer to the speaker
    D. Nominative case, subject of a verb understood

28. No one could catch Jack and 28.____
    A. I B. me C. myself

29. A. Nominative case, predicate pronoun 29.____
    B. Objective case, object of a verb
    C. Objective case, object of a preposition
    D. Reflexive pronoun, to refer to the speaker

30. One of the children _____ an excellent violinist. 30.____
    A. is B. are

31. A. Singular verb, to agree with One 31.____
    B. Singular verb, to agree with violinist
    C. Plural verb, to agree with children

32. Neither Tom nor his brothers _____ able to play yesterday. 32.____
    A. was B. were

33. A. Singular verb, to agree with Tom 33.____
    B. Singular verb, to agree with Neither
    C. Plural verb, to agree with brothers
    D. Plural verb, to agree with a compound subject

34. Either the team members or the coach _____ asked to pick up the trophy. 34.____
    A. was B. were

35. A. Singular verb, to agree with coach 35.____
    B. Singular verb, to agree with team
    C. Plural verb, to agree with members
    D. Plural verb, to agree with a compound object

36. Both of the boys _____ excellent students. 36.____
    A. is B. are

37. A. Singular verb, to agree with Both 37.____
    B. Plural verb, to agree with Both
    C. Plural verb, to agree with boys

38. Everybody at the party _____ having a good time. 38.____
    A. was B. were

39. A. Singular verb, to agree with Everybody
     B. Singular verb, too agree with party
     C. Singular verb, to agree with time
     D. Plural verb, to agree with Everybody

39.____

40. Which of the two dresses do you think is the
     A. prettier   B. prettiest

40.____

41. A. Comparative degree of an adjective
     B. Superlative degree of an adjective
     C. Comparative degree of the adverb

41.____

42. Miss Brown sent Bob and _____ postcards from France.
     A. I   B. me   C. myself

42.____

43. A. Nominative case, predicate pronoun
     B. Objective case, direct object of the verb
     C. Objective case, indirect object of the verb
     D. Reflexive pronoun, to refer to the speaker

43.____

44. Because the gift came from Jerry and _____, we appreciated it very much.
     A. he   B. him

44.____

45. A. Nominative case, predicate pronoun
     B. Objective case, object of the verb
     C. Objective case, object of a preposition

45.____

46. Everyone present had _____ own opinion about the problem.
     A. his   B. their

46.____

47. A. Singular pronoun, to refer to Everyone
     B. Singular pronoun, to refer to problem
     C. Plural pronoun, to refer to Everyone

47.____

48. It is _____ too late to call now.
     A. sure   B. surely

48.____

49. A. Adjective, to modify It
     B. Adverb, to modify is
     C. Adverb, to modify to call

49.____

50. The sunset was _____ beautiful.
     A. real   B. very

50.____

51. A. Adjective, to modify sunset
     B. Adverb, to modify was
     C. Adverb, to modify beautiful

51.____

KEY (CORRECT ANSWERS)

1. A	11. A	21. A	31. A	41. A
2. A	12. A	22. B	32. B	42. B
3. B	13. C	23. A	33. C	43. B
4. B	14. B	24. C	34. A	44. B
5. B	15. C	25. A	35. A	45. C
6. B	16. B	26. A	36. B	46. A
7. A	17. C	27. A	37. B	47. A
8. C	18. C	28. B	38. A	48. B
9. B	19. B	29. B	39. A	49. B
10. C	20. C	30. A	40. A	50. B
				51. C

TEST 3

DIRECTIONS: Each question or incomplete statement is followed by several suggested answers or completions. Select the one that BEST answers the question or completes the statement. *PRINT THE LETTER OF THE CORRECT ANSWER IN THE SPACE AT THE RIGHT.*

Questions 1-14.

DIRECTIONS: In answering Questions 1 through 14, indicate from the even-numbered items that which makes the sentence correct. Select from the odd-numbered choices that rule which makes the sentence incorrect.

1. Velvet feels _____
   A. soft
   B. softly

2. A. Adjective, to modify Velvet
   B. Adverb, to modify feels
   C. Adjective, to modify feels

3. Jane asked _____ rang the doorbell.
   A. who
   B. whom

4. A. Objective case, object of asked
   B. Objective case, object of rang
   C. Nominative case, subject of rang

5. For _____ did you ask when you telephoned the office?
   A. who
   B. whom

6. A. Nominative case, subject of did ask
   B. Objective case, object of the verb
   C. Objective case, object of a preposition

7. _____ can laugh at himself will probably make an agreeable companion.
   A. Whoever
   B. whomever

8. A. Nominative case, subject of will make
   B. Nominative case, subject of can laugh
   C. Objective case, object of can laugh
   D. Objective case, object of will make

9. Father thinks that _____ tries can succeed.
   A. whoever
   B. whomever

10. A. Nominative case, subject of can succeed
    B. Nominative case, subject of tries
    C. Objective case, object of thinks

11. Our government is run by _____ the people elect. 11.____
    A. whoever   B. whomever

12. A. Objective case, object of a preposition 12.____
    B. Objective case, object of elect
    C. Nominative case, predicate nominative

13. The child speaks 13.____
    A. distinct   B. distinctly

14. A. Adverb, to modify speaks 14.____
    B. Adjective, to modify child
    C. Adjective, to modify speaks

Questions 15-24.

DIRECTIONS: Indicate the letter of the part of speech which correctly describes the use of the word, phrase, or clause in the following sentences. Choose the parts of speech from the column at the right.

<u>Parts of Speech</u>

15. Early   A. Adjective   15.____
16. May   B. Adverb   16.____
17. Plains   C. Conjunction   17.____
18. was rising   D. Interjection   18.____
19. of rosy splendor   E. Noun   19.____
20. above   F. Preposition   20.____
21. to be alive and free   G. Pronoun   21.____
22. and   H. Verb   22.____
23. the   23.____
24. we   24.____

Questions 25-34.

DIRECTIONS: Indicate the title of the book which would be alphabetized FIRST among the choices that follow.

25. A. WIND IN THE PINES   B. NIGHT WIND   25.____
    C. IVANHOE   D. KIDNAPED

26. A. VELVET SHOES   B. USES OF COAL   26.____
    C. WONDERLAND   D. YOUNG HEROES

27. A. BUFFALO BILL   B. CARAVAN   27.____
    C. DAYS TO REMEMBER   D. FROM DAWN TO DUSK

28. A. TELEPHONE TALES   B. TELEGRAPHIC CODES   28.____
    C. TEMPEST IN A TEAPOT   D. TELLING SEA TALES

29. A. LEARNING TO SWIM   29.____
    B. THE LAST LEAF
    C. THE SPIDER
    D. THE MAN WITHOUT A COUNTRY

30. A. FOG   B. THE GYPSY   30.____
    C. HOBBIES   D. A PECK OF GOLD

31. A. SKATING   B. SILVER SHIPS   31.____
    C. THE MAN WITH THE MASK   D. TIMBER COUNTRY

32. A. WILD ANIMALS I HAVE KNOWN   32.____
    B. FOOL'S GOLD
    C. THE JESTER
    D. UNCLE JAKE'S ADVENTURES WITH A WILDCAT

33. A. PAUL REVERE'S RIDE   B. PRIVATE ZOO   33.____
    C. LOCHINVAR   D. TOP SECRET

34. A. ONCE UPON A STORYTIME   34.____
    B. HEROES OF PROGRESS
    C. HEART, HEALTH, AND HAPPINESS
    D. HENRIETTA HARVEY'S HAVEN

KEY (CORRECT ANSWERS)

1.	A	11.	B	21.	F	31.	C
2.	A	12.	A	22.	C	32.	B
3.	A	13.	B	23.	A	33.	C
4.	C	14.	A	24.	G	34.	C
5.	B	15.	A	25.	C		
6.	C	16.	E	26.	B		
7.	A	17.	E	27.	A		
8.	B	18.	H	28.	B		
9.	A	19.	F	29.	B		
10.	A	20.	A	30.	A		

EXAMINATION SECTION
TEST 1

DIRECTIONS: Each question or incomplete statement is followed by several suggested answers or completions. Select the one that BEST answers the question or completes the statement. *PRINT THE LETTER OF THE CORRECT ANSWER IN THE SPACE AT THE RIGHT.*

Questions 1-30.

DIRECTIONS: In each of the following sentences, one or more of the punctuation marks are enclosed in brackets. If the punctuation enclosed in brackets is CORRECT, mark C in the space at the right. If any punctuation mark in brackets is NOT the CORRECT mark for the place, mark W in the space at the right.

1. Why was Frederick, the Great[,] called *great*?   1.____

2. A distant whistle sounded[,] and there was a shuffling of feet on the platform.   2.____

3. George turned to the banker[;] the only one of the group he knew.   3.____

4. The road[,] along the river[,] and under the long lines of poplars.   4.____

5. The group of men behind Edward hesitated[;] glanced questioningly at one one another[;] and awkwardly followed his example.   5.____

6. Hoping to find his friend at home[,] Joe knocked on the door.   6.____

7. Dear Sir[,]
Please send the books by express.   7.____

8. My address has been 1342 State Street, Kansas City, Missouri[,] since Christmas.   8.____

9. "You are going with us[?]" asked Jane, as soon as she saw me.   9.____

10. Mrs. Green and her daughter, Miss[.] Eva Green, are members of our party.   10.____

11. On their way they passed a weather[-]beaten, stone house.   11.____

12. Senator Martin, if elected in[,] November, will be in Washington for the next six years.   12.____

13. The freshman had many things to do[;] such as enrolling for classes, unpacking his trunk, and writing home.   13.____

14. Mrs. Carter is a leader in several of the women[']s organizations.   14.____

113

15. We did not tell Clark[,] who the man was.   15._____

16. Steavens, the young stranger[,] noticed the card on the door.   16._____

17. "No, they have not come yet[;] the family is scattered," was the reply.   17._____

18. There were one hundred[-]twelve people at the lecture.   18._____

19. James asked his brother ["]where he had left the car.["]   19._____

20. "Who is the congressman from this district," asked Charles, "if it is not Mr.   20._____
    James[?]"

21. The sailor had a three months['] leave of absence.   21._____

22. "It's a long walk," said Jones. "You ought to take a taxi.["] ["]Our car is not   22._____
    running."

23. It has been three hours['] since the train left.   23._____

24. There were not more than forty[-]two boys in the class.   24._____

25. The woman was beautifully[-]dressed in a light blue velvet gown.   25._____

26. He answered the question[;] then he rose and left the room.   26._____

27. The boy[,] that delivers the Gazette[,] has come to collect his money.   27._____

28. "If Roberts is captain," said James[,] "we shall be happy."   28._____

29. A fast train from Chicago[,] to New York[,] makes the distance in eighteen   29._____
    hours.

30. My mother[,] who has been in Kansas City for a week[,] returned home   30._____
    yesterday.

Questions 31-40.

DIRECTIONS: Questions 31 through 40 refer to capitalization. If the sentence is correct,
              indicate C (CORRECT). If the sentence is incorrect, indicate W (WRONG)).

31. A new junior high school was built in our city.   31._____

32. Ten seniors in Lincoln High School will attend college next fall.   32._____

33. Vermont was the native state of ex-President Coolidge.   33._____

34. The highway we took going north was no. 75.   34._____

35. A good road in the middle west is between Tulsa and Winnipeg.   35.____

36. Five nations were represented in a Disarmament Conference in London in   36.____
    January, 1930.

37. For a number of years Father subscribed to Harper's Magazine.   37.____

38. Yours Sincerely,   38.____
    Mary Orr

39. James Smith from Portland County was elected to the United States Senate.   39.____

40. The president of Lawrence College attended the N.E.A. meeting at   40.____
    Columbus.

Questions 41-50.

DIRECTIONS: In each of the following sentences, one of the lettered words is INCORRECTLY used. Indicate the letter of this word in the space at the right. If you think that a sentence has more than one error, indicate only the one that you think is the WORST.

41. Success (A) is (B) when one (C) accomplishes the task (D) that he undertakes.   41.____

42. Paul has (A) eaten one of the apples which (B) were given to him and has   42.____
    distributed the (C) balance (D) among his friends.

43. Since the (A) taking of the 1980 census, it has been announced (B) that   43.____
    New York City has a million more inhabitants (C) than (D) any city in the United
    States.

44. As (A) most all the students were studying in the library (B) because it was   44.____
    (C) quiet there, only a (D) few heard the fire alarm.

45. (A) due to a mistake of (B) only a (C) few cents, John had (D) already   45.____
    refused to pay the bill.

46. Had we not been (A) present and (B) seen the accident, we could not (C)   46.____
    of explained why the car (D) had turned over.

47. Anyone (A) who has had good training in high school (B) can do (C) well   47.____
    in college if (D) they study sufficiently.

48. After (A) ringing the bell for (B) only a few seconds, the door opened (C)   48.____
    slowly. (D) Who do you think entered?

49. Upon (A) entering the class, the first words heard were, "If (B) your   49.____
    absence was (C) due to illness, (D) all right. You may be excused."

50. The reason there is a junior college in (A) almost every city of fifteen thousand is (B) because there is economy in a (C) student's living at home while he is (D) attending college.

50.____

KEY (CORRECT ANSWERS)

1.	W	11.	C	21.	C	31.	C	41.	B
2.	C	12.	W	22.	W	32.	C	42.	C
3.	W	13.	W	23.	W	33.	C	43.	D
4.	W	14.	C	24.	C	34.	W	44.	A
5.	W	15.	W	25.	W	35.	W	45.	A
6.	C	16.	C	26.	C	36.	C	46.	C
7.	W	17.	C	27.	W	37.	C	47.	D
8.	C	18.	W	28.	C	38.	C	48.	A
9.	C	19.	W	29.	W	39.	C	49.	A
10.	W	20.	C	30.	C	40.	W	50.	B

TEST 2

DIRECTIONS: Each question or incomplete statement is followed by several suggested answers or completions. Select the one that BEST answers the question or completes the statement. *PRINT THE LETTER OF THE CORRECT ANSWER IN THE SPACE AT THE RIGHT.*

Questions 1-20.

DIRECTIONS: In each of the following sentences, one of the lettered words is INCORRECTLY used. Indicate the letter of this word in the space at the right. If you think that a sentence has more than one error, indicate only the one that you think is the WORST.

1. The boys seemed (A) real (B) sure that (C) their school would (D) lose only one game.   1.____

2. There can (A) not but one of (B) us girls go; therefore, he must make a (C) choice between you and (D) me.   2.____

3. Their reason for (A) feeling certain (B) of victory was (C) that they had a center, dependable in every way, (D) and who had been on a winning team for three years.   3.____

4. Soon after (A) enrolling in the class, John learned-he (B) would not pass (C) without he studied three hours (D) a day.   4.____

5. A (A) dark-complected youth entered the office and left B) without (C) my asking (D) who he was.   5.____

6. The (A) principal in our school is (B) quite different (C) than the one (D) whom we met at the Walnut School.   6.____

7. The men (A) effected a settlement and ended (B) all the disputes (C) without calling an officer, (D) which was gratifying to every one.   7.____

8. Neither the debaters (A) or (B) their coach (C) was present at last (D) night's meeting.   8.____

9. People of Asia have such different (A) customs (B) from (C) those we in America have that (D) it is a great curiosity.   9.____

10. We agreed (A) with the plan (B) that the committee (C) was offering (D) us.   10.____

11. The rope became (A) loose and (B) laid on the ground in curved lines (C) as if some one had (D) laid it there.   11.____

12. The principal (A) ought to have known better (B) than to (C) let (D) them boys go.   12.____

117

2 (#2)

13. Our radio has (A) two knobs, the (B) turning of one of (C) which very much (D)   13.____
    effects the tone.

14. The (A) principal reason for our country's (B) demanding passports is (C)   14.____
    that the country may keep out undesirable (D) immigrants.

15. The children were (A) so quiet that (B) some one remarked how (C) like   15.____
    (D) statues they looked.

16. If Miss James (A) accepts the position in Kansas City, the superintendent (B)   16.____
    will (C) leave her have charge (D) of the sixth grade.

17. After (A) examining my surroundings (B) thoroughly, I could not remember (C)   17.____
    of (D) having been there before.

18. Mr. Roe is a teacher, (A) well-liked by his students, (B) and whom (C) his   18.____
    co-workers appreciate, (D) too.

19. Years (A) ago (B) most men thought a great event in (C) their lives was   19.____
    (D) when they rode in an airplane.

20. (A) Because thousands of (B) persons (C) travel by air today is a sign   20.____
    (D) that great progress has been made in the scientific world.

Questions 21-35.

DIRECTIONS: Here are fifteen numbered groups of words. Some of these groups make
              complete sentences; others do not. Indicate C (CORRECT) if the sentence is
              complete; indicate W (WRONG) if the sentence is incomplete.

21. Last night read in a magazine a story of some children being lost in the   21.____
    mountains.

22. A boy, seven years old, and a girl, nine.   22.____

23. They having strolled away from camp where a party of tourists had stopped   23.____
    for the night.

24. There was great excitement among the other members of the party.   24.____

25. Especially was the mother of the children wild with anxiety.   25.____

26. As she knew of many dangers that surrounded her dear ones.   26.____

27. She also imagined many others.   27.____

28. If only for a minute, put yourself in her place.   28.____

3 (#2)

29. Everyone out to find the children, both those who were of their party and those from other camps who heard of the trouble.   29.____

30. What a great commotion there was!   30.____

31. Some calling, others whistling, and the mother crying.   31.____

32. When finally the report came that the children had been found playing beside a brook which they had followed, up a narrow valley.   32.____

33. Then was everyone greatly relieved.   33.____

34. Why should anyone have thought them lost?   34.____

35. Knew all the time where they were and how to get back.   35.____

Questions 36-50.

DIRECTIONS: In each of the following sentences, a word is enclosed in brackets. If this word is the correct word for the place, indicate C (CORRECT). If the word is NOT the correct one, indicate W (WRONG).

36. Had the coach [knew] the rules better, we might have won the game.   36.____

37. Not a voice [raised] in our behalf.   37.____

38. I am certain James would have [spoke] to us.   38.____

39. The man had [shaken] his head in protest.   39.____

40. The boat had tipped over and had [sank] to the bottom   40.____

41. All night long they had [ridden] on the train.   41.____

42. Many beautiful blanket are [woven] by the Indians.   42.____

43. Have the new strawberry plants [grown] as fast as last year's plants?   43.____

44. Long before frost came, the apples were [shook] from the tree.   44.____

45. Was the first prize in the contests [took] by John or Mary?   45.____

46. For a day or two the ships had [lain] there in the harbor.   46.____

47. How many miles had they [driven] that day?   47.____

48. No one know why he [choose] to attend that college.   48.____

4 (#2)

49. George hopes to get the work all [done] before he leaves. 49._____

50. The plank bent low, then [sprang] back quickly. 50._____

KEY (CORRECT ANSWERS)

1.	A	11.	B	21.	W	31.	W	41.	C
2.	A	12.	D	22.	W	32.	W	42.	C
3.	D	13.	D	23.	W	33.	C	43.	C
4.	C	14.	D	24.	C	34.	C	44.	W
5.	A	15.	B	25.	W	35.	W	45.	W
6.	C	16.	C	26.	W	36.	W	46.	C
7.	D	17.	C	27.	C	37.	W	47.	C
8.	A	18.	A	28.	C	38.	W	48.	W
9.	D	19.	D	29.	W	39.	C	49.	C
10.	A	20.	C	30.	C	40.	W	50.	C

TEST 3

DIRECTIONS: Each question or incomplete statement is followed by several suggested answers or completions. Select the one that BEST answers the question or completes the statement. *PRINT THE LETTER OF THE CORRECT ANSWER IN THE SPACE AT THE RIGHT.*

Questions 1-50.

DIRECTIONS: Each of the following sentences marked *a* has a word in brackets. If the word is the correct grammatical form to be used in that place, indicate C (CORRECT). If the form is incorrect, indicate W (WRONG).

Under *b* is a reason for the form of the word to be used in the brackets in *a*. If the reason is the correct one to be applied in this case, indicate C (CORRECT). If the reason is NOT the correct one, indicate W (WRONG).

1. a. Anyone who [likes] to read will enjoy this book.   1._____
2. b. Singular number should be used, to agree with *who*.   2._____
3. a. [Has] either of the girls been in to see you?   3._____
4. b. Plural number should be used, to agree with *girls*.   4._____
5. a. There [have] been many a dollar spent on the new road.   5._____
6. b. Plural number should be used, to agree with *many*.   6._____
7. a. The doctor asked me, who [am] still in high school, if I were going to college.   7._____
8. b. First person should be used, to agree with *who*.   8._____
9. a. A large flock of geese [was] shown in the picture last night.   9._____
10. b. Singular number should be used, to agree with subject *flock*.   10._____
11. a. The banker looked [sharp] at the stranger.   11._____
12. b. Adverb should be used, to modify *looked*.   12._____
13. a. The table feels [roughly], as I run my hand over it.   13._____
14. b. Predicate adjective should be used with *feels*.   14._____
15. a. I can [easily] feel the rough board underneath the cloth.   15._____
16. b. Adverb should be used, to modify verb *feel*.   16._____

2 (#3)

17.	a.	The superintendent left word for John and [I] to report the next day.	17._____
18.	b.	Nominative case should be used, subject of *report*.	18._____
19.	a.	It could not have been [them] whom we saw yesterday.	19._____
20.	b.	Objective case should be used, object of *could have been*.	20._____
21.	a.	My aunt wishes that you and [she] could go to Europe.	21._____
22.	b.	Nominative case should be used, subject of verb *could go*.	22._____
23.	a.	It was announced that James and [myself] ranked high in the music contest.	23._____
24.	b.	Reflexive pronoun should be used, to refer to speaker.	24._____
25.	a.	Did you know all [we] four had our names in last night's paper?	25._____
26.	b.	Nominative case should be used, subject of *had*.	26._____
27.	a.	The teacher had heard of [our] being late.	27._____
28.	b.	Objective case should be used, object of *of*.	28._____
29.	a.	It might have been [I] whom you saw.	29._____
30.	b.	Nominative case should be used, predicate nominative.	30._____
31.	a.	I supposed the girl who was telephoning to be [her].	31._____
32.	b.	Objective case should be used, to agree with *girl*.	32._____
33.	a.	It seems to be [us] who are wrong.	33._____
34.	b.	Nominative case should be used, after *seems to be*.	34._____
35.	a.	Two boys, Mark and [me], were detailed to carry water to the camp kitchen.	35._____
36.	b.	Nominative case should be used, to agree with *boys*.	36._____
37.	a.	No one realized how the coach hoped [to have won] that game.	37._____
38.	b.	Perfect infinitive should be used, to indicate past time.	38._____
39.	a.	I wish I [were] in Boston today.	39._____
40.	b.	Present tense should be used, to agree with *today*.	40._____

3 (#3)

41.	a.	[Having delivered] his oration, the boy left the stage.	41.____
42.	b.	Present participle should be used, to indicate same time as verb *left*.	42.____
43.	a.	The librarian gave the book to [whoever] she thought would appreciate it.	43.____
44.	b.	Objective case should be used, object of *to*.	44.____
45.	a.	The students did not know [whom] the principal would appoint to fill the vacancy.	45.____
46.	b.	Objective case should be used, object of verb *know*.	46.____
47.	a.	Boys especially admire Colonel Johnson, [whom] they consider their ideal.	47.____
48.	b.	Objective case should be used, object of *consider*.	48.____
49.	a.	We are going faster now than [they].	49.____
50.	b.	Objective case should be used, object of *than*.	50.____

KEY (CORRECT ANSWERS)

1.	C	11.	W	21.	C	31.	W	41.	C
2.	C	12.	C	22.	C	32.	W	42.	W
3.	C	13.	W	23.	W	33.	W	43.	W
4.	W	14.	C	24.	W	34.	C	44.	C
5.	C	15.	C	25.	C	35.	W	45.	C
6.	C	16.	C	26.	C	36.	C	46.	C
7.	W	17.	W	27.	C	37.	C	47.	C
8.	C	18.	W	28.	W	38.	C	48.	C
9.	C	19.	W	29.	C	39.	C	49.	C
10.	C	20.	W	30.	C	40.	W	50.	W

SENTENCE COMPLETION
EXAMINATION SECTION
TEST 1

DIRECTIONS: Each question in this part consists of a sentence in which one word is missing; a blank line indicates where the word has been removed from the sentence. Beneath each sentence are five words, one of which is the missing word. You are to select the number of the missing word by deciding which one of the five words BEST fits in with the meaning of the sentence. *PRINT THE LETTER OF THE CORRECT ANSWER IN THE SPACE AT THE RIGHT.*

1. Although they had little interest in the game they were playing, rather than be _____, they played it through to the end.
    - A. inactive
    - B. inimical
    - C. busy
    - D. complacent
    - E. vapid

2. That he was unworried and at peace with the world could be, perhaps, observed from his _____ brow.
    - A. unwrinkled
    - B. wrinkled
    - C. furrowed
    - D. twisted
    - E. askew

3. Among the hundreds of workers in the assembly plant of the factory, one was _____ because of his skill and speed.
    - A. steadfast
    - B. condemned
    - C. consistent
    - D. outstanding
    - E. eager

4. The story of the invention of many of our best known machines is a consistent one: they are the result of a long series of experiments by many people; thus, the Wright Brothers in 1903 _____ the airplane rather than invented it.
    - A. popularized
    - B. regulated
    - C. perfected
    - D. contrived
    - E. developed

5. As soon as the former political exile returned to his native country, he looked up old supporters, particularly those whom he knew to be _____ and whose help he might need.
    - A. potent
    - B. pusillanimous
    - C. attentive
    - D. free
    - E. retired

6. A recent study of the New Deal shows that no other man than the President could have brought together so many _____ interests and combined them into so effective a political organization.
    - A. secret
    - B. interior
    - C. predatory
    - D. harmonious
    - E. conflicting

7. A study of tides presents an interesting _____ in that, while the forces that set them in motion are universal in application, presumably affecting all parts of our world without distinction, the action of tides in particular areas is completely local in nature.
    - A. phenomenon
    - B. maneuver
    - C. paradox
    - D. quality
    - E. spontaneity

8. Many of the facts that are found in the ancient archives constitute _____ that help shed light upon human activities in the past.

    A. facts
    B. reminders
    C. particles
    D. sources
    E. indications

9. It is a regrettable fact that in a caste society which deems manual toil a mark of _____, rarely does the laborer improve his social position or gain political power.

    A. inferiority
    B. consolation
    C. fortitude
    D. hardship
    E. brilliance

10. As a generalization, one can correctly say that crises in history are caused by the re-opening of questions which have been safely _____ for long periods of time.

    A. debated
    B. joined
    C. recondite
    D. settled
    E. unanswered

KEY (CORRECT ANSWERS)

1. A
2. A
3. D
4. C
5. A

6. E
7. C
8. D
9. A
10. A

TEST 2

DIRECTIONS: Each question in this part consists of a sentence in which one word is missing; a blank line indicates where the word has been removed from the sentence. Beneath each sentence are five words, one of which is the missing word. You are to select the number of the missing word by deciding which one of the five words BEST fits in with the meaning of the sentence. *PRINT THE LETTER OF THE CORRECT ANSWER IN THE SPACE AT THE RIGHT.*

1. We can see in retrospect that the high hopes for lasting peace conceived at Versailles in 1919 were _____.   1.____

    A. ingenuous B. transient C. nostalgic
    D. ingenious E. species

2. One of the constructive effects of Nazism was the passage by the U.N. of a resolution to combat _____.   2.____

    A. armaments B. nationalism C. colonialism
    D. genocide E. geriatrics

3. In our prisons, the role of _____ often gains for certain inmates a powerful position among their fellow prisoners.   3.____

    A. informer B. clerk C. warden
    D. trusty E. turnkey

4. It is the _____ liar, experienced in the ways of the world, who finally trips upon some incongruous detail.   4.____

    A. consummate B. incorrigible C. congenital
    D. flagrant E. contemptible

5. Anyone who is called a misogynist can hardly be expected to look upon women with _____ contemptuous eyes.   5.____

    A. more than B. nothing less than C. decidedly
    D. other than E. always

6. Demagogues such as Hitler and Mussolini aroused the masses by appealing to their _____ rather than to their intellect.   6.____

    A. emotions B. reason C. nationalism
    D. conquests E. duty

7. He was in great demand as an entertainer for his _____ abilities: he could sing, dance, tell a joke, or relate a story with equally great skill and facility.   7.____

    A. versatile B. logical C. culinary
    D. histrionic E. creative

8. The wise politician is aware that, next to knowing when to seize an opportunity, it is also important to know when to _____ an advantage.   8.____

    A. develop B. seek C. revise D. proclaim E. forego

127

9. Books on psychology inform us that the best way to break a bad habit is to _____ a new habit in its place.

    A. expel
    B. substitute
    C. conceal
    D. curtail
    E. supplant

10. The author who uses one word where another uses a whole paragraph, should be considered a _____ writer.

    A. successful
    B. grandiloquent
    C. succinct
    D. prolix
    E. experienced

KEYS (CORRECT ANSWERS)

1. A
2. D
3. A
4. A
5. D
6. A
7. A
8. E
9. B
10. C

TEST 3

DIRECTIONS: Each question in this part consists of a sentence in which one word is missing; a blank line indicates where the word has been removed from the sentence. Beneath each sentence are five words, one of which is the missing word. You are to select the number of the missing word by deciding which one of the five words BEST fits in with the meaning of the sentence. *PRINT THE LETTER OF THE CORRECT ANSWER IN THE SPACE AT THE RIGHT.*

1. The prime minister, fleeing from the rebels who had seized the government, sought _____ in the church.

    A. revenge B. mercy C. relief
    D. salvation E. sanctuary

2. It does not take us long to conclude that it is foolish to fight the _____, and that it is far wiser to accept it.

    A. inevitable B. inconsequential C. impossible
    D. choice E. invasion

3. _____ is usually defined as an excessively high rate of interest.

    A. Injustice B. Perjury C. Exorbitant
    D. Embezzlement E. Usury

4. "I ask you, gentlemen of the jury, to find this man guilty since I have _____ the charges brought against him."

    A. documented B. questioned C. revised
    D. selected E. confused

5. Although the critic was a close friend of the producer, he told him that he could not _____ his play.

    A. condemn B. prefer C. congratulate
    D. endorse E. revile

6. Knowledge of human nature and motivation is an important _____ in all areas of endeavor.

    A. object B. incentive C. opportunity
    D. asset E. goal

7. Numbered among the audience were kings, princes, dukes, and even a maharajah, all attempting to _____ one another in the glitter of their habiliments and the number of their escorts.

    A. supersede B. outdo C. guide
    D. vanquish E. equal

8. There seems to be a widespread feeling that peoples who are located below us in respect to latitude are _____ also in respect to intellect and ability.

    A. superior B. melodramatic C. inferior
    D. ulterior E. contemptible

9. This should be considered a(n) _____ rather than the usual occurrence.

   A. coincidence B. specialty C. development
   D. outgrowth E. mirage

10. Those who were considered states' rights aherents in the early part of our history espoused the diminution of the powers of the national government because they had always been _____ of these powers.

    A. solicitous B. advocates C. apprehensive
    D. mindful E. respectful

KEYS (CORRECT ANSWERS)

1. E
2. A
3. E
4. A
5. D

6. D
7. B
8. C
9. A
10. C

TEST 4

DIRECTIONS: Each question in this part consists of a sentence in which one word is missing; a blank line indicates where the word has been removed from the sentence. Beneath each sentence are five words, one of which is the missing word. You are to select the number of the missing word by deciding which one of the five words BEST fits in with the meaning of the sentence. *PRINT THE LETTER OF THE CORRECT ANSWER IN THE SPACE AT THE RIGHT.*

1. The life of the mining camps as portrayed by Bret Harte - boisterous, material, brawling - was in direct _____ to the contemporary Eastern world of conventional morals and staid deportment depicted by other men of letters.

    A. model
    B. parallel
    C. antithesis
    D. relationship
    E. response

2. The agreements were to remain in force for three years and were subject to automatic _____ unless terminated by the parties concerned on one month's notice.

    A. renewal
    B. abrogation
    C. amendment
    D. confiscation
    E. option

3. In a democracy, people are recognized for what they do rather than for their _____.

    A. alacrity
    B. ability
    C. reputation
    D. skill
    E. pedigree

4. Although he had often loudly proclaimed his _____ concerning world affairs, he actually read widely and was usually the best informed person in his circle.

    A. weariness
    B. complacency
    C. condolence
    D. indifference
    E. worry

5. This student holds the _____ record of being the sole failure in his class.

    A. flagrant
    B. unhappy
    C. egregious
    D. dubious
    E. unusual

6. She became enamored _____ the acrobat when she witnessed his act.

    A. of   B. with   C. for   D. by   E. about

7. This will _____ all previous wills.

    A. abrogates
    B. denies
    C. supersedes
    D. prevents
    E. continues

8. In the recent terrible Chicago _____, over ninety children were found dead as a result of the fire.

    A. hurricane
    B. destruction
    C. panic
    D. holocaust
    E. accident

9. I can ascribe no better reason why he shunned society than that he was a _____.

    A. mentor
    B. Centaur
    C. aristocrat
    D. misanthrope
    E. failure

10. One who attempts to learn all the known facts before he comes to a conclusion may most aptly be described as a   10._____

    A. realist   B. philosopher   C. cynic
    D. pessimist   E. skeptic

KEY (CORRECT ANSWERS)

1. C
2. A
3. E
4. D
5. D

6. A
7. C
8. D
9. D
10. E

TEST 5

DIRECTIONS: Each question in this part consists of a sentence in which one word is missing; a blank line indicates where the word has been removed from the sentence. Beneath each sentence are five words, one of which is the missing word. You are to select the number of the missing word by deciding which one of the five words BEST fits in with the meaning of the sentence. *PRINT THE LETTER OF THE CORRECT ANSWER IN THE SPACE AT THE RIGHT.*

1. The judge exercised commendable _____ in dismissing the charge against the prisoner. In spite of the clamor that surrounded the trial, and the heinousness of the offense, the judge could not be swayed to overlook the lack of facts in the case.   1.____

    A. avidity B. meticulousness C. clemency
    D. balance E. querulousness

2. The pianist played the concerto _____, displaying such facility and skill as has rarely been matched in this old auditorium.   2.____

    A. strenuously B. deftly C. passionately
    D. casually E. spiritedly

3. The Tanglewood Symphony Orchestra holds its outdoor concerts far from city turmoil in a _____, bucolic setting.   3.____

    A. spectacular B. atavistic C. serene
    D. chaotic E. catholic

4. Honest satire gives true joy to the thinking man. Thus, the satirist is most _____ when he points out the hypocrisy in human actions.   4.____

    A. elated B. humiliated C. ungainly
    D. repressed E. disdainful

5. She was a(n) _____ who preferred the company of her books to the pleasures of cafe society.   5.____

    A. philanthropist B. stoic C. exhibitionist
    D. extrovert E. introvert

6. So many people are so convinced that people are driven by _____ motives that they cannot believe that anybody is unselfish!   6.____

    A. interior B. ulterior C. unworthy
    D. selfish E. destructive

7. These _____ results were brought about by a chain of fortuitous events.   7.____

    A. unfortunate B. odd C. harmful
    D. haphazard E. propitious

8. The bank teller's _____ of the funds was discovered the following month when the auditors examined the books.   8.____

    A. embezzlement B. burglary C. borrowing
    D. assignment E. theft

133

9. The monks gathered in the _____ for their evening meal. 9._____

    A. lounge   B. auditorium   C. refectory
    D. rectory   E. solarium

10. Local officials usually have the responsibility in each area of determining when the need 10._____
is sufficiently great to _____ withdrawals from the community water supply.

    A. encourage   B. justify   C. discontinue
    D. advocate   E. forbid

KEY (CORRECT ANSWERS)

1. D
2. B
3. C
4. A
5. E

6. B
7. D
8. A
9. C
10. B

PREPARING WRITTEN MATERIALS
EXAMINATION SECTION
TEST 1

DIRECTIONS: Each question or incomplete statement is followed by several suggested answers or completions. Select the one that BEST answers the question or completes the statement. *PRINT THE LETTER OF THE CORRECT ANSWER IN THE SPACE AT THE RIGHT.*

Questions 1-21.

DIRECTIONS: In each of the following sentences, which were taken from students' transcripts, there may be an error. Indicate the appropriate correction in the space at the right. If the sentence is correct as is, indicate this choice. Unnecessary changes will be considered incorrect.

1. In that building there seemed to be representatives of Teachers College, the Veterans Bureau, and the Businessmen's Association.
   A. Teacher's College
   B. Veterans' Bureau
   C. Businessmens Association
   D. Correct as is

   1.____

2. In his travels, he visited St. Paul, San Francisco, Springfield, Ohio, and Washington, D.C.
   A. Ohio and
   B. Saint Paul
   C. Washington, D.C.
   D. Correct as is

   2.____

3. As a result of their purchasing a controlling interest in the syndicate, it was well-known that the Bureau of Labor Statistics' calculations would be unimportant.
   A. of them purchasing
   B. well known
   C. Statistics
   D. Correct as is

   3.____

4. Walter Scott, Jr.'s, attempt to emulate his father's success was doomed to failure.
   A. Junior's,
   B. Scott's, Jr.
   C. Scott, Jr.'s attempt
   D. Correct as is

   4.____

5. About B.C. 250 the Romans invaded Great Britain, and remains of their highly developed civilization can still be seen.
   A. 250 B.C.
   B. Britain and
   C. highly-developed
   D. Correct as is

   5.____

6. The two boss's sons visited the children's department.
   A. bosses
   B. bosses'
   C. childrens'
   D. Correct as is

   6.____

135

7. Miss Amex not only approved the report, but also decided that it needed no revision.
   A. report; but   B. report but   C. report. But   D. Correct as is

8. Here's brain food in a jiffy—economical, too!
   A. economical too!
   B. "brain food"
   C. jiffy-economical
   D. Correct as is

9. She said, "He likes the "Gatsby Look" very much."
   A. said "He
   B. "he
   C. 'Gatsby Look'
   D. Correct as is

10. We anticipate that we will be able to visit them briefly in Los Angeles on Wednesday after a five day visit.
    A. Wednes-   B. 5 day   C. five-day   D. Correct as is

11. She passed all her tests, and, she now has a good position.
    A. tests, and she
    B. past
    C. tests;
    D. Correct as is

12. The billing clerk said, "I will send the bill today"; however, that was a week ago, and it hasn't arrived yet!
    A. today;"   B. today,"   C. ago and   D. Correct as is

13. "She types at more-than-average speed," Miss Smith said, "but I feel that it is a result of marvelous concentration and self control on her part."
    A. more than average
    B. "But
    C. self-control
    D. Correct as is

14. The state of Alaska, the largest state in the union, is also the northernmost state.
    A. Union
    B. Northernmost State
    C. State of Alaska
    D. Correct as is

15. The memoirs of Ex-President Nixon, according to figures, sold more copies than Six Crises, the book he wrote in the '60s.
    A. Six Crises
    B. ex-President
    C. 60s
    D. Correct as is

16. "There are three principal elements, determining the hazard of buildings: the contents hazard, the fire resistance of the structure, and the character of the interior finish," concluded the speaker.
    The one of the following statements that is MOST acceptable is that, in the above passage,
    A. the comma following the word *elements* is incorrect
    B. the colon following the word *buildings* is incorrect
    C. the comma following the word *finish* is incorrect
    D. there is no error in the punctuation of the sentence

17. He spoke on his favorite topic, "Why We Will Win." (How could I stop him?)   17._____
    A. Win".   B. him?).   C. him)?   C. Correct as is

18. "All any insurance policy is, is a contract for services," said my insurance   18._____
    agent, Mr. Newton.
    A. Insurance Policy   B. Insurance Agent
    C. policy is is a   D. Correct as is

19. Inasmuch as the price list has now been up dated, we should sent it to the   19._____
    printer.
    A. In as much   B. updated
    C. pricelist   D. Correct as is

20. We feel that "Our know-how" is responsible for the improvement in technical   20._____
    developments.
    A. "our   B. know how   C. that,   D. Correct as is

21. Did Cortez conquer the Incas? the Aztecs? the South American Indians?   21._____
    A. Incas, the Aztecs, the South American Indians?
    B. Incas; the Aztecs; the South American Indians?
    C. south American Indians?
    D. Correct as is

22. Which one of the following forms for the typed name of the dictator in the closing   22._____
    lines of a letter is generally MOST acceptable in the United States?
    A. (Dr.) James F. Farley   B. Dr. James F. Farley
    C. Me. James J. Farley, Ph.D.   D. James F. Farley

23. The plural of   23._____
    A. turkey is turkies   B. cargo is cargoes
    C. bankruptcy is bankruptcys   D. son-in-law is son-in-laws

24. The abbreviation viz. means MOST NEARLY   24._____
    A. namely   B. for example
    C. the following   D. see

25. In the sentence, *A man in a light-gray suit waited thirty-five minutes in the*   25._____
    ante-room for the all-important document, the word IMPROPERLY hyphenated
    is
    A. light-gray   B. thirty-five   C. ante-room   D. all-important

KEY (CORRECT ANSWERS)

1.	D	11.	A
2.	C	12.	D
3.	B	13.	D
4.	D	14.	A
5.	A	15.	B
6.	B	16.	A
7.	B	17.	D
8.	D	18.	D
9.	C	19.	B
10.	C	20.	A

21. D
22. D
23. B
24. A
25. C

TEST 2

DIRECTIONS: Each question or incomplete statement is followed by several suggested answers or completions. Select the one that BEST answers the question or completes the statement. *PRINT THE LETTER OF THE CORRECT ANSWER IN THE SPACE AT THE RIGHT.*

Questions 1-10.

DIRECTIONS: In each of the following groups of four sentences, one sentence contains an error in sentence structure, grammar, usage, diction, or punctuation. Indicate the INCORRECT sentence.

1. A. The lecture finished, the audience began asking questions. 1.____
   B. Any man who could accomplish that task the world would regard as a hero.
   C. Our respect and admiration are mutual.
   D. George did like his mother told him, despite the importunities of his playmates.

2. A. I cannot but help admiring you for your dedication to your job. 2.____
   B. Because they had insisted upon showing us films of their travels, we have lost many friends whom we once cherished.
   C. I am constrained to admit that your remarks made me feel bad.
   D. My brother having been notified of his acceptance by the university of his choice, my father immediately made plans for a vacation.

3. A. In no other country is freedom of speech and assembly so jealously guarded. 3.____
   B. Being a beatnik, he felt that it would be a betrayal of his cause to wear shoes and socks at the same time.
   C. Riding over the Brooklyn Bridge gave us an opportunity to see the Manhattan skyline.
   D. In 1961, flaunting SEATO, the North Vietnamese crossed the line of demarcation.

4. A. I have enjoyed the study of the Spanish language not only because of its beauty and the opportunity it offers to understand the Hispanic culture but also to make use of it in the business associations I have in South America. 4.____
   B. The opinions he expressed were decidedly different from those he had held in his youth.
   C. Had he actually studied, he certainly would have passed.
   D. A supervisor should be patient, tactful, and firm.

5. A. At this point we were faced with only three alternatives: to push on, to remain where we were, or to return to the village. 5.____
   B. We had no choice but to forgive so venial a sin.
   C. In their new picture, the Warners are flouting tradition.
   D. Photographs taken revealed that 2.5 square miles had been burned.

6. A. He asked whether he might write to his friends.
   B. There are many problems which must be solved before we can be assured of world peace.
   C. Each person with whom I talked expressed his opinion freely.
   D. Holding on to my saddle with all my strength the horse galloped down the road at a terrifying pace.

7. A. After graduating high school, he obtained a position as a runner in Wall Street.
   B. Last night, in a radio address, the President urged us to subscribe to the Red Cross.
   C. In the evening, light spring rain cooled the streets.
   D. "Un-American" is a word which has been used even by those whose sympathies may well have been pro-Nazi.

8. A. It is hard to conceive of their not doing good work.
   B. Who won—you or I?
   C. He having read the speech caused much comment.
   D. Their finishing the work proves that it can be done.

9. A. Our course of study should not be different now than it was five years ago.
   B. I cannot deny myself the pleasure of publicly thanking the mayor for his actions.
   C. The article on "Morale" has appeared in the Times Literary Supplement.
   D. He died of tuberculosis contracted during service with the Allied Forces.

10. A. If it wasn't for a lucky accident, he would still be an office-clerk.
    B. It is evident that teachers need help.
    C. Rolls of postage stamps may be bought at stationery stores.
    D. Addressing machines are used by firms that publish magazines.

11. The one of the following sentences which contains NO error in usage is:
    A. After the robbers left, the proprietor stood tied in his chair for about two hours before help arrived.
    B. In the cellar I found the watchmans' hat and coat.
    C. The persons living in adjacent apartments stated that they had heard no unusual noises.
    D. Neither a knife or any firearms were found in the room.

12. The one of the following sentences which contains NO error in usage is:
    A. The policeman lay a firm hand on the suspect's shoulder.
    B. It is true that neither strength nor agility are the most important requirement for a good patrolman.
    C. Good citizens constantly strive to do more than merely comply the restraints imposed by society.
    D. Twenty years is considered a severe sentence for a felony.

13. Select the sentence containing an adverbial objective.
    A. Concepts can only acquire content when they are connected, however indirectly, with sensible experience.
    B. The cloth was several shades too light to match the skirt which she had discarded.
    C. The Gargantuan Hall of Commons became a tri-daily horror to Kurt, because two youths discerned that he had a beard and courageously told the world about it.
    D. Brooding morbidly over the event, Elsie found herself incapable of engaging in normal activity.

14. Select the sentence containing a verb in the subjunctive mood.
    A. Had he known of the new experiments with penicillin dust for the cure of colds, he might have been tempted to try them in his own office.
    B. I should be very much honored by your visit.
    C. Though he has one of the highest intelligence quotients in his group, he seems far below the average in actual achievement.
    D. Long had I known that he would be the man finally selected for such signal honors.

15. Select the sentence containing one (or more) passive perfect participle(s).
    A. Having been apprised of the consequences of his refusal to answer, the witness finally revealed the source of his information.
    B. To have been placed in such an uncomfortable position was perhaps unfair to a journalist of his reputation.
    C. When deprived of special immunity he had, of course, no alternative but to speak.
    D. Having been obdurate until now, he was reluctant to surrender under this final pressure exerted upon him.

16. Select the sentence containing a predicate nominative.
    A. His dying wish, which he expressed almost with his last breath, was to see that justice was done toward his estranged wife.
    B. So long as we continue to elect our officials in truly democratic fashion, we shall have the power to preserve our liberties.
    C. We could do nothing, at this juncture, but walk the five miles back to camp.
    D. There was the spaniel, wet and cold and miserable, waiting silently at the door.

17. Select the sentence containing exactly TWO adverbs.
    A. The gentlemen advanced with exasperating deliberateness, while his lonely partner waited.
    B. If you are well, will you come early?
    C. I think you have guessed right, though you were rather slow, I must say.
    D. The last hundred years have seen more change than a thousand years of the Roman Empire, than a hundred thousand years of the stone age.

Questions 18-24.

DIRECTIONS: Select the choice describing the error in the sentence.

18. If us seniors do not support school functions, who will? 18.____
    A. Unnecessary shift in tense
    B. Incomplete sentence
    C. Improper case of pronoun
    D. Lack of parallelism

19. The principal has issued regulations which, in my opinion, I think are too harsh. 19.____
    A. Incorrect punctuation
    B. Faulty sentence structure
    C. Misspelling
    D. Redundant expression

20. The freshmens' and sophomores' performances equaled those of the juniors and seniors. 20.____
    A. Ambiguous reference
    B. Incorrect placement of punctuation
    C. Misspelling of past tense
    D. Incomplete comparison

21. Each of them, Anne and her, is an outstanding pianist I can't tell you which one is best. 21.____
    A. Lack of agreement
    B. Improper degree of comparison
    C. Incorrect case of pronoun
    D. Run-on sentence

22. She wears clothes that are more expensive than my other friends. 22.____
    A. Misuse of *than*
    B. Incorrect relative pronoun
    C. Shift in tense
    D. Faulty comparison

23. At the very end of the story it implies that the children's father died tragically. 23.____
    A. Misuse of *implies*
    B. Indefinite use of pronoun
    C. Incorrect spelling
    D. Incorrect possessive

24. At the end of the game both of us, John and me, couldn't scarcely walk because we were so tired. 24.____
    A. Incorrect punctuation
    B. Run-on sentence
    C. Incorrect case of pronoun
    D. Double negative

Questions 25-30.

DIRECTIONS: Questions 25 through 30 consist of a sentence lacking certain needed punctuation. Pick as your answer the description of punctuation which will CORRECTLY complete the sentence.

25. If you take the time to keep up your daily correspondence you will no doubt be most efficient. 25.____
    A. Comma only after *doubt*
    B. Comma only after *correspondence*
    C. Commas after *correspondence*, *will*, and *be*
    D. Commas after *if*, *correspondence*, and *will*

26. Because he did not send the application soon enough he did not receive the up to date copy of the book. 26.____
    A. Commas after *application* and *enough,* and quotation marks *before* up *and after* date
    B. Commas after *application* and *enough,* and hyphens between *to* and *date*
    C. Comma after *enough,* and hyphens between *up* and *to* and between *to* and *date*
    D. Comma after *application,* and quotation marks before *up* and after *date*

27. The coordinator requested from the department the following items a letter each week summarizing progress personal forms and completed applications for tests. 27.____
    A. Commas after *items* and *completed*
    B. Semi-colon after *items* and *progress,* comma after *forms*
    C. Colon after *items,* commas after *progress* and *forms*
    D. Colon after *items,* commas after *forms* and *applications*

28. The supervisor asked Who will attend the conference next month. 28.____
    A. Comma after *asked,* period after *month*
    B. Period after *asked,* question mark after *month*
    C. Comma after *asked,* quotation marks before *Who,* quotation marks after *month,* and question mark after the quotation marks
    D. Comma after *asked,* quotation marks before *Who,* question mark after *month,* and quotation marks after the question mark

29. When the statistics are collected, we will forward the results to you as soon as possible. 29.____
    A. Comma after *you*
    B. Commas after *forward* and *you*
    C. Commas after *collected, results* and *you*
    D. Comma after *collected*

30. The ecology of our environment is concerned with mans pollution of the atmosphere. 30.____
    A. Comma after *ecology*
    B. Apostrophe after *n* and before *s* in *mans*
    C. Commas after *ecology* and *environment*
    D. Apostrophe after *s* in *mans*

KEY (CORRECT ANSWERS)

1.	D	11.	C	21.	B
2.	A	12.	D	22.	D
3.	D	13.	B	23.	B
4.	A	14.	A	24.	D
5.	B	15.	A	25.	B
6.	D	16.	A	26.	C
7.	A	17.	C	27.	C
8.	C	18.	C	28.	D
9.	A	19.	D	29.	D
10.	A	20.	B	30.	B

TEST 3

DIRECTIONS: Each question or incomplete statement is followed by several suggested answers or completions. Select the one that BEST answers the question or completes the statement. *PRINT THE LETTER OF THE CORRECT ANSWER IN THE SPACE AT THE RIGHT.*

Questions 1-6.

DIRECTIONS: From the four choices offered in Questions 1 through 6, select the one which is INCORRECT.

1. A. Before we try to extricate ourselves from this struggle in which we are now engaged in, we must be sure that we are not severing ties of honor and duty.
    B. Besides being an outstanding student, he is also a leader in school government and a trophy-winner in school sports.
    C. If the framers of the Constitution were to return to life for a day, their opinion of our amendments would be interesting.
    D. Since there are three m's in the word, it is frequently misspelled.

    1.____

2. A. It was a college with an excellance beyond question.
    B. The coach will accompany the winners, whomever they may be.
    C. The dean, together with some other faculty members, is planning a conference.
    D. The jury are arguing among themselves.

    2.____

3. A. This box is less nearly square than that one.
    B. Wagner is many persons' choice as the world's greatest composer.
    C. The habits of Copperheads are different from Diamond Backs.
    D. The teacher maintains that the child was insolent.

    3.____

4. A. There was a time when the Far North was unknown territory. Now American soldiers manning radar stations there wave to Boeing jet planes zooming by overhead.
    B. Exodus, the psalms, and Deuteronomy are all books of the Old Testament.
    C. Linda identified her china dishes by marking their bottoms with india ink.
    D. Harry S. Truman, former president of the United States, served as a captain in the American army during World War I.

    4.____

5. A. The sequel of their marriage was a divorce.
    B. We bought our car secondhand.
    C. His whereabouts is unknown.
    D. Jones offered to use his own car, providing the company would pay for gasoline, oil, and repairs,

    5.____

6. A. I read Golding's "Lord of the Flies".
    B. The orator at the civil rights rally thrilled the audience when he said, "I quote Robert Burns's line, 'A man's a man for a' that."
    C. The phrase "producer to consumer" is commonly used by market analysts.
    D. The lawyer shouted, "Is not this evidence illegal?"

Questions 7-9.

DIRECTIONS: In answering Questions 7 through 9, mark the letter A if faulty because of incorrect grammar, mark the letter B if faulty because of incorrect punctuation, mark the letter C if correct.

7. Mr. Brown our accountant, will audit the accounts next week.

8. Give the assignment to whomever is able to do it most efficiently.

9. The supervisor expected either your or I to file these reports.

Questions 10-14.

DIRECTIONS: In each of the following groups of four sentences, one sentence contains an error in sentence structure, grammar, usage, diction, or punctuation. Indicate the INCORRECT sentence.

10. A. The agent asked, "Did you say, 'Never again?'"
    B. Kindly let me know whether you can visit us on the 17th.
    C. "I cannot accept that!" he exploded. "Please show me something else.
    D. Ed, will you please lend me your grass shears for an hour or so.

11. A. Recalcitrant though he may have been, Alexander was willfully destructive.
    B. Everybody should look out for himself.
    C. John is one of those students who usually spends most of his time in the principal's office.
    D. She seems to feel that what is theirs is hers.

12. A. Be he ever so much in the wrong, I'll support the man while deploring his actions.
    B. The schools' lack of interest in consumer education is shortsighted.
    C. I think that Fitzgerald's finest stanza is one which includes the reference to youth's "sweet-scented manuscript.
    D. I never would agree to Anderson having full control of the company's policies.

13. A. We had to walk about five miles before finding a gas station.
    B. The willful sending of a false alarm has, and may, result in homicide.
    C. Please bring that book to me at once.
    D. Neither my sister nor I am interested in bowling.

14. A. He is one of the very few football players who doesn't wear a helmet with a face guard.
    B. But three volunteers appeared at the recruiting office.
    C. Such consideration as you can give us will be appreciated.
    D. When I left them, the group were disagreeing about the proposed legislation.

Question 15.

DIRECTIONS: Question 15 contains two sentences concerning criminal law. The sentences could contain errors in English grammar or usage. A sentence does not contain an error simply because it could be written in a different manner. In answering this question, choose answer
A. if only sentence I is correct
B. if only sentence II is correct
C. if both sentences are correct
D. if neither sentence is correct

15. I. The use of fire or explosives to destroy tangible property is proscribed by the criminal mischief provisions of the Revised Penal Law.
    II. The defendant's taking of a taxicab for the immediate purpose of affecting his escape did not constitute grand larceny.

KEY (CORRECT ANSWERS)

1.	A	6.	A	11.	C
2.	B	7.	B	12.	D
3.	C	8.	A	13.	B
4.	B	9.	A	14.	A
5.	D	10	A	15.	A

WRITTEN ENGLISH EXPRESSION
EXAMINATION SECTION
TEST 1

DIRECTIONS: In each of the sentences below, four portions are underlined and lettered. Read each sentence and decide whether any of the UNDERLINED parts contains an error in spelling, punctuation, or capitalization, or employs grammatical usage which would be inappropriate for carefully written English. If so, note the letter printed under the unacceptable form and indicate this choice in the space at the right. If all four of the underlined portions are acceptable as they stand, select the answer E. (No sentence contains more than ONE unacceptable form.)

1. The revised <u>procedure</u> was <u>quite</u> different <u>than</u> the one which <u>was</u> employed up to that time. <u>No error</u>
         A   B   C   D   E

1.____

2. <u>Blinded</u> by the storm that <u>surrounded</u> him, his plane <u>kept going</u> in <u>circles</u>. <u>No error</u>
    A   B   C   D   E

2.____

3. They <u>should</u> give the book to <u>whoever</u> <u>they</u> think deserves <u>it</u>. <u>No error</u>
         A   B   C   D   E

3.____

4. The <u>government</u> will not consent to your <u>firm</u> <u>sending</u> that package as <u>second class</u> matter. <u>No error</u>
     A   B   C
     D   E

4.____

5. She <u>would have</u> avoided all the trouble <u>that</u> followed if she <u>would have</u> waited ten minutes <u>longer</u>. <u>No error</u>
       A   B   C
               D   E

5.____

6. <u>His</u> poetry, <u>when</u> it was carefully examined, showed <u>characteristics</u> not unlike <u>Wordsworth</u>. <u>No error</u>
  A   B   C
   D   E

6.____

7. <u>In my opinion</u>, based upon long years of research, <u>I think</u> the plan offered by my opponent is <u>unsound</u>, because it is not <u>founded</u> on true facts. <u>No error</u>
     A   B
           C   D   E

7.____

8. The soldiers of <u>Washington's</u> army at Valley Forge <u>were</u> men ragged in 8.____
                        A   B
   <u>appearance</u> but <u>who were</u> noble in character. <u>No error</u>
      C   D   E

9. Rabbits <u>have a distrust</u> of man <u>due to</u> the fact <u>that</u> they are <u>so often</u> shot. 9.____
               A   B   C   D
   <u>No error</u>
     E

10. <u>This</u> is the man <u>who</u> I believe <u>is</u> best <u>qualified</u> for the position. <u>No error</u> 10.____
      A   B   C   D   E

11. Her voice was <u>not only good</u>, but <u>she</u> also very clearly <u>enunciated</u>. 11.____
                    A   B   C   D
    <u>No error</u>
      E

12. <u>Today he</u> is wearing a <u>different</u> suit <u>than</u> the <u>one</u> he wore yesterday. <u>No error</u> 12.____
         A   B   C   D   E

13. Our work <u>is</u> to improve the club; if anybody <u>must</u> resign, let it <u>not</u> be you or <u>I</u>. 13.____
             A   B   C   D
    <u>No error</u>
      E

14. There was so much talking <u>in back of</u> me <u>as</u> I <u>could</u> not <u>enjoy</u> the music. 14.____
                                    A   B   C   D
    <u>No error</u>
      E

15. <u>Being that</u> he is that <u>kind of boy</u>, he cannot be blamed <u>for</u> the mistake. 15.____
        A   B   C   D
    <u>No error</u>
      E

16. <u>The king, having read</u> the speech, <u>he</u> and the <u>queen</u> <u>departed</u>. <u>No error</u> 16.____
             A   B   C   D   E

17. I <u>am</u> <u>so tired</u> I <u>can't</u> <u>scarcely</u> stand. <u>No error</u> 17.____
       A   B   C   D   E

18. We are <u>mailing bills</u> to our customers <u>in Canada</u>, and, <u>being</u> eager to 18.____
                 A   B   C
    clear our books before the new season opens, it is <u>to be hoped</u> they will
                                                                           D
    send their remittances promptly. <u>No error</u>
                                           E

19. I reluctantly acquiesced to the proposal. No error
    A   B   C   D   E

20. It had lain out in the rain all night. No error
    A   B   C   D   E

21. If he would have gone there, he would have seen a marvelous sight.
          A   B   C   D
    No error
    E

22. The climate of Asia Minor is somewhat like Utah. No error
                 A   B   C   D   E

23. If everybody did unto others as they would wish others to do unto them, this
          A   B   C   D
    world would be a paradise. No error
                                E

24. This was the jockey whom I saw was most likely to win the race. No error
    A   B   C   D   E

25. The only food the general demanded was potatoes. No error
        A   B   C   D   E

KEY (CORRECT ANSWERS)

1.	C	11.	C
2.	A	12.	C
3.	B	13.	D
4.	B	14.	B
5.	C	15.	A
6.	D	16.	A
7.	B	17.	C
8.	D	18.	C
9.	B	19.	E
10.	E	20.	E

21. A
22. D
23. D
24. B
25. E

TEST 2

DIRECTIONS: In each of the sentences below, four portions are underlined and lettered. Read each sentence and decide whether any of the UNDERLINED parts contains an error in spelling, punctuation, or capitalization, or employs grammatical usage which would be inappropriate for carefully written English. If so, note the letter printed under the unacceptable form and indicate this choice in the space at the right. If all four of the underlined portions are acceptable as they stand, select the answer E. (No sentence contains more than ONE unacceptable form.)

1. A party <u>like</u> <u>that</u> <u>only</u> <u>comes</u> once a year. <u>No error</u>
         A   B   C   D   E
1.____

2. <u>Our's</u> <u>is</u> <u>a</u> <u>swift moving</u> age. <u>No error</u>
   A   B C   D   E
2.____

3. The <u>healthy</u> climate soon <u>restored</u> him <u>to</u> his <u>accustomed</u> vigor. <u>No error</u>
        A   B   C   D   E
3.____

4. <u>They</u> needed six typists and hoped that <u>only</u> that <u>many</u> <u>would</u> apply for the position. <u>No error</u>
   A   B   C   D
                      E
4.____

5. He <u>interviewed</u> people <u>whom</u> he thought had <u>something</u> <u>to impart</u>. <u>No error</u>
       A   B   C   D   E
5.____

6. <u>Neither</u> of his three sisters <u>is</u> older <u>than</u> <u>he</u>. <u>No error</u>
   A   B   C D   E
6.____

7. <u>Since</u> he is <u>that</u> <u>kind</u> of <u>a</u> boy, he cannot be expected to cooperate with us. <u>No error</u>
   A   B   C   D
          E
7.____

8. <u>When passing</u> <u>through</u> the tunnel, the air pressure <u>affected</u> <u>our</u> years. <u>No error</u>
   A   B   C   D   E
8.____

9. <u>The story having</u> a sad ending, <u>it</u> never <u>achieved</u> popularity <u>among</u> the students. <u>No error</u>
     A   B   C   D
             E
9.____

10. <u>Since</u> we are both hungry, <u>shall</u> we go <u>somewhere</u> for lunch? <u>No error</u>
    A   B   C   D E
10.____

2 (#2)

11. <u>Will</u> you please <u>bring</u> this book <u>down to</u> the library and give it to my friend<u>,</u> who is waiting for it? <u>No error</u>
    A   B   C   D   E

    11.____

12. You <u>may</u> <u>have</u> the book; I <u>am</u> finished <u>with</u> it. <u>No error</u>
       A   B   C   D   E

    12.____

13. I <u>don't</u> know <u>if</u> I <u>should</u> mention <u>it</u> to her or not. <u>No error</u>
      A   B   C   D   E

    13.____

14. Philosophy is not <u>a subject</u> <u>which</u> <u>has to do</u> with philosophers and mathematics <u>only</u>. <u>No error</u>
                           A   B   C   D   E

    14.____

15. The thoughts of the scholar <u>in his library</u> are little different <u>than</u> the old woman who first said, <u>"It's</u> no use crying over spilt milk.<u>"</u> <u>No error</u>
                                A   B   C   D   E

    15.____

16. A complete <u>system</u> of philosophical ideas <u>are</u> <u>implied</u> in many simple <u>utterances.</u> <u>No error</u>
                A   B   C   D   E

    16.____

17. Even <u>if</u> one has never put <u>them</u> into words, <u>his</u> ideas <u>compose</u> a kind of a philosophy. <u>No error</u>
        A   B   C   D   E

    17.____

18. Perhaps it <u>is</u> <u>well enough</u> that most <u>people</u> do not attempt this <u>formulation.</u> <u>No error</u>
         A   B   C   D   E

    18.____

19. <u>Leading their</u> ordered lives, this <u>confused</u> <u>body</u> of ideas and feelings <u>is</u> sufficient. <u>No error</u>
          A   B   C   D   E

    19.____

20. Why <u>should</u> we <u>insist upon</u> <u>them</u> <u>formulating</u> it? <u>No error</u>
           A   B   C   D   E

    20.____

21. <u>Since</u> it includes <u>something</u> of the wisdom of the ages, it is <u>adequate</u> for the <u>purposes</u> of ordinary life. <u>No error</u>
      A   B   C   D   E

    21.____

3 (#2)

22. Therefore, I <u>have sought</u> to make a pattern <u>of mine,</u> <u>and so</u> there were, early
                        A   B   C

    moments of <u>my trying</u> to find out what were the elements with which I had to
                      D

    deal. <u>No error</u>
            E

22.____

23. I <u>wanted</u> <u>to get</u> <u>what</u> knowledge I <u>could</u> about the general structure of the
     A   B   C   D

    universe. <u>No error</u>
                E

23.____

24. I wanted to <u>know</u> <u>if</u> life <u>per se</u> had any meaning or <u>whether</u> I must strive to give
                  A B   C   D

    it one. <u>No error</u>
           E

24.____

25. <u>So,</u> in a <u>desultory</u> way, I <u>began</u> <u>to read</u>. <u>No error</u>
    A   B   C   D   E

25.____

KEY (CORRECT ANSWERS)

1.	C		11.	B
2.	A		12.	C
3.	A		13.	B
4.	C		14.	D
5.	B		15.	B
6.	A		16.	B
7.	D		17.	A
8.	A		18.	C
9.	A		19.	A
10.	E		20.	D

21. E
22. C
23. C
24. B
25. E

WORD MEANING
EXAMINATION SECTION
TEST 1

DIRECTIONS: Each question or incomplete statement is followed by several suggested answers or completions. Select the one that BEST answers the question or completes the statement. *PRINT THE LETTER OF THE CORRECT ANSWER IN THE SPACE AT THE RIGHT.*

1. He implied that he would work overtime if necessary.
   In this sentence, the word *implied* means

   A. denied
   B. explained
   C. guaranteed
   D. hinted

   1.____

2. The bag of the vacuum cleaner was inflated.
   In this sentence, the word *inflated* means

   A. blown up with air
   B. filled with dirt
   C. loose
   D. torn

   2.____

3. Burning material during certain hours is prohibited.
   In this sentence, the word *prohibited* means

   A. allowed   B. forbidden   C. legal   D. required

   3.____

4. He was rejected when he applied for the job. In this sentence, the word *rejected* means

   A. discouraged
   B. put to work
   C. tested
   D. turned down

   4.____

5. The foreman was able to substantiate his need for extra supplies.
   In this sentence, the word *substantiate* means

   A. estimate   B. meet   C. prove   D. reduce

   5.____

6. The new instructions supersede the old ones.
   In this sentence, the word *supersede* means

   A. explain   B. improve   C. include   D. replace

   6.____

7. Shake the broom free of surplus water and hang it up to dry.
   In this sentence, the word *surplus* means

   A. dirty   B. extra   C. rinse   D. soapy

   7.____

8. When a crack is filled, the asphalt must be tamped.
   In this sentence, the word *tamped* means

   A. cured
   B. heated
   C. packed down
   D. wet down

   8.____

9. The apartment was left vacant.
   In this sentence, the word *vacant* means

   A. clean   B. empty   C. furnished   D. locked

   9.____

10. The caretaker spent the whole day doing various repairs.
    In this sentence, the word *various* means

    A. different   B. necessary   C. small   D. special

11. He came back to assist his partner.
    In this sentence, the word *assist* means

    A. call   B. help   C. stop   D. question

12. A person who is biased cannot be a good foreman.
    In this sentence, the word *biased* means

    A. easy-going   B. prejudiced
    C. strict   D. uneducated

13. The lecture for the new employees was brief.
    In this sentence, the word *brief* means

    A. educational   B. free
    C. interesting   D. short

14. He was asked to clarify the order.
    In this sentence, the word *clarify* means

    A. follow out   B. make clear
    C. take back   D. write out

15. The employee was commended by his foreman.
    In this sentence, the word *commended* means

    A. assigned   B. blamed   C. picked   D. praised

16. Before the winter, the lawnmower engine was dismantled.
    In this sentence, the word *dismantled* means

    A. oiled   B. repaired
    C. stored away   D. taken apart

17. They excavated a big hole on the project lawn.
    In this sentence, the word *excavated* means

    A. cleaned out   B. discovered
    C. dug out   D. filled in

18. The new man was told to sweep the exterior area.
    In this sentence, the word *exterior* means

    A. asphalt   B. nearby   C. outside   D. whole

19. The officer refuted the statement of the driver.
    As used in this sentence, the word *refuted* means MOST NEARLY

    A. disproved   B. elaborated upon
    C. related   D. supported

20. The mechanism of the parking meter is not intricate.
    As used in this sentence, the word *intricate* means MOST NEARLY

    A. cheap
    B. complicated
    C. foolproof
    D. strong

    20._____

21. The weight of each box fluctuates.
    As used in this sentence, the word *fluctuates* means MOST NEARLY

    A. always changes
    B. decreases
    C. increases gradually
    D. is similar

    21._____

22. The person chosen to investigate the new procedure should be impartial.
    As used in this sentence, the word *impartial* means MOST NEARLY

    A. experienced
    B. fair
    C. forward looking
    D. important

    22._____

23. Carelessness in the safekeeping of keys will not be tolerated.
    As used in this sentence, the word *tolerated* means MOST NEARLY

    A. forgotten
    B. permitted
    C. punished lightly
    D. understood

    23._____

24. The traffic was easily diverted.
    As used in this sentence, the word *diverted* means MOST NEARLY

    A. controlled
    B. speeded up
    C. stopped
    D. turned aside

    24._____

25. A transcript of the report was prepared in the office.
    As used in this sentence, the word *transcript* means MOST NEARLY

    A. brief
    B. copy
    C. record
    D. translation

    25._____

26. The change was authorized by the supervisor.
    As used in this sentence, the word *authorized* means MOST NEARLY

    A. completed   B. corrected   C. ordered   D. permitted

    26._____

27. The supervisor read the excerpt of the collector's report.
    According to this sentence, the supervisor read _____ the report.

    A. a passage from
    B. a summary of
    C. the original of
    D. the whole of

    27._____

28. During the probation period, the worker proved to be inept.
    The word *inept* means MOST NEARLY

    A. incompetent
    B. insubordinate
    C. satisfactory
    D. uncooperative

    28._____

29. The putative father was not living with the family.
    The word *putative* means MOST NEARLY

    A. reputed
    B. unemployed
    C. concerned
    D. indifferent

    29._____

30. The adopted child researched various documents of vital statistics in an effort to discover the names of his natural parents.
    The words *vital statistics* mean MOST NEARLY statistics relating to

    A. human life
    B. hospitals
    C. important facts
    D. health and welfare

31. Despite many requests for them, there was a scant supply of new blotters.
    The word *scant* means MOST NEARLY

    A. adequate
    B. abundant
    C. insufficient
    D. expensive

32. Did they replenish the supply of forms in the cabinet?
    The word *replenish* means MOST NEARLY

    A. straighten up
    B. refill
    C. sort out
    D. use

33. Employees may become bored if they are assigned diverse duties.
    The word *diverse* means MOST NEARLY

    A. interesting
    B. different
    C. challenging
    D. enjoyable

Questions 34-37.

DIRECTIONS: Each of Questions 34 through 37 consists of a capitalized word followed by four suggested meanings of the word. Select the word or phrase which means MOST NEARLY the same as the capitalized word.

34. PROFICIENCY

    A. vocation
    B. competency
    C. repugnancy
    D. prominence

35. BIBLIOGRAPHY

    A. description
    B. stenography
    C. photograph
    D. compilation of books

36. FIDELITY

    A. belief
    B. treachery
    C. strength
    D. loyalty

37. ACCELERATE

    A. adjust   B. press   C. quicken   D. strip

38. One of the machinists in your shop enjoys the reputation of being a great equivocator.
    This means MOST NEARLY that he

    A. takes pride and is happy in his work
    B. generally hedges and often gives misleading answers
    C. is a strong union man with great interest in his fellow workers' welfare
    D. is good at resolving disputes

39. When a person has the reputation of persistently making foolish or silly remarks, it may be said that he is

    A. inane
    B. meticulous
    C. a procrastinator
    D. a prevaricator

40. When two mechanics, called A and B, make measurements of the same workpiece and find significant discrepancies in their measurements, it is MOST NEARLY correct to state that

    A. mechanic B made an erroneous reading
    B. mechanic A was careless in making his measurements
    C. both mechanics made their measurements correctly
    D. there was considerable difference in the two sets of measurements

41. A foreman who *expedites* a job,

    A. abolishes it
    B. makes it bigger
    C. slows it down
    D. speeds it up

42. If a man is working at a *uniform* speed, it means he is working at a speed which is

    A. changing   B. fast   C. slow   D. steady

43. To say that a caretaker is *obstinate* means that he is

    A. cooperative
    B. patient
    C. stubborn
    D. willing

44. To say that a caretaker is *negligent* means that he is

    A. careless   B. neat   C. nervous   D. late

45. To say that something is *absurd* means that it is

    A. definite
    B. not clear
    C. ridiculous
    D. unfair

46. To say that a foreman is *impartial* means that he is

    A. fair   B. improving   C. in a hurry   D. watchful

47. A man who is *lenient* is one who is

    A. careless
    B. harsh
    C. inexperienced
    D. mild

48. A man who is *punctual* is one who is

    A. able   B. polite   C. prompt   D. sincere

49. If you think one of your men is too *awkward* to do a job, it means you think he is too

    A. clumsy   B. lazy   C. old   D. weak

50. A person who is *seldom* late, is late

    A. always   B. never   C. often   D. rarely

KEY (CORRECT ANSWERS)

1. D	11. B	21. A	31. C	41. D
2. A	12. B	22. B	32. B	42. D
3. B	13. D	23. B	33. B	43. C
4. D	14. B	24. D	34. B	44. A
5. C	15. D	25. B	35. D	45. C
6. D	16. D	26. D	36. D	46. A
7. B	17. C	27. A	37. C	47. D
8. C	18. C	28. A	38. B	48. C
9. B	19. A	29. A	39. B	49. A
10. A	20. B	30. A	40. D	50. D

TEST 2

DIRECTIONS: Each question or incomplete statement is followed by several suggested answers or completions. Select the one that BEST answers the question or completes the statement. *PRINT THE LETTER OF THE CORRECT ANSWER IN THE SPACE AT THE RIGHT.*

1. The Department of Health can certify that conditions in a housing accommodation are detrimental to life or health.
   As used in the above sentence, the word *detrimental* means MOST NEARLY

   A. injurious
   B. serious
   C. satisfactory
   D. necessary

   1.____

2. The Administrator shall have the power to revoke any adjustment in rents granted either the landlord or the tenant.
   As used in the above sentence, the word *revoke* means MOST NEARLY

   A. increase   B. decrease   C. rescind   D. restore

   2.____

Questions 3-5.

DIRECTIONS: Each of Questions 3 through 5 consists of a capitalized word followed by four suggested meanings of the word. Select the word which means MOST NEARLY the same as the capitalized word.

3. DOGMATISM

   A. dramatism
   B. positiveness
   C. doubtful
   D. tentativeness

   3.____

4. ELECTRODE

   A. officer
   B. electrolyte
   C. terminal
   D. positive

   4.____

5. EMIT

   A. return   B. enter   C. omit   D. discharge

   5.____

6. The word *inflammable* means MOST NEARLY

   A. burnable   B. acid   C. poisonous   D. explosive

   6.____

7. The word *disinfect* means MOST NEARLY

   A. deodorize   B. sterilize   C. bleach   D. dissolve

   7.____

8. He wanted to ascertain the facts before arriving at a conclusion.
   The word *ascertain* means MOST NEARLY

   A. disprove   B. determine   C. convert   D. provide

   8.____

9. Did the supervisor assent to her request for annual leave?
   The word *assent* means MOST NEARLY

   A. allude   B. protest   C. agree   D. refer

   9.____

10. The new worker was fearful that the others would rebuff her.
    The word *rebuff* means MOST NEARLY

    A. ignore   B. forget   C. copy   D. snub

11. The supervisor of that office does not condone lateness.
    The word *condone* means MOST NEARLY

    A. mind   B. excuse   C. punish   D. remember

12. Each employee was instructed to be as concise as possible when preparing a report.
    The word *concise* means MOST NEARLY

    A. exact   B. sincere   C. flexible   D. brief

13. The shovelers should not distribute the asphalt faster than it can be properly handled by the rakers.
    As used above, *distribute* means MOST NEARLY

    A. dump   B. pick-up   C. spread   D. heat

14. Any defective places should be cut out.
    As used above, *defective* means MOST NEARLY

    A. low   B. hard   C. soft   D. faulty

15. *Sphere of authority* is called

    A. constituency   B. dictatorial
    C. jurisdiction   D. vassal

16. Rollers are made in several sizes.
    As used above, *several* means MOST NEARLY

    A. large   B. heavy   C. standard   D. different

17. Sometimes a roller is run over an old surface to detect weak spots.
    As used above, *detect* means MOST NEARLY

    A. compact   B. remove   C. find   D. strengthen

18. Reconstruction of the old base is sometimes required as a preliminary operation.
    As used above, *preliminary* means MOST NEARLY

    A. first   B. necessary   C. important   D. local

19. If a man makes an *absurd* remark, he makes one which is MOST NEARLY

    A. misleading   B. ridiculous
    C. unfair   D. wicked

20. A worker who is *adept* at his job is one who is MOST NEARLY

    A. cooperative   B. developed
    C. diligent   D. skilled

21. If a man states a condition is *general,* he means it is MOST NEARLY

    A. artificial   B. prevalent
    C. timely   D. transient

Questions 22-50.

DIRECTIONS: Each of Questions 22 through 50 consists of a sentence in which a word is italicized. Of the four words following each sentence, select the word whose meaning is MOST NEARLY the same as the meaning of the italicized word.

22. The agent's first *assignment* was to patrol on Hicks Avenue.
    A. test B. sign C. job D. deadline

23. Agents get many *inquiries* from the public.
    A. complaints B. suggestions
    C. compliments D. questions

24. The names of all fifty states were written in *abbreviated* form.
    A. shortened B. corrected
    C. eliminated D. illegible

25. The meter was examined and found to be *defective*.
    A. small B. operating C. destroyed D. faulty

26. Agent Roger's reports are *legible*, but Agent Baldwin's are not.
    A. similar B. readable C. incorrect D. late

27. The time allowed, as shown by the meter, had *expired*.
    A. started B. broken C. ended D. violated

28. The busy *commercial* area is quiet in the evenings.
    A. deserted B. growing C. business D. local

29. The district office *authorized* the giving of summonses to illegally parked trucks.
    A. suggested B. approved
    C. prohibited D. recorded

30. Department property must be used *exclusively* for official business.
    A. occasionally B. frequently
    C. only D. properly

31. The District Commander *banned* driving in the area.
    A. detoured B. permitted
    C. encouraged D. prohibited

32. Two copies of the summons are *retained* by the Enforcement Agent.
    A. kept B. distributed
    C. submitted D. signed

33. The Agent *detected* a parking violation.
    A. cancelled B. discovered
    C. investigated D. reported

34. *Pedestrians* may be given summonses for violating traffic regulations.

    A. Bicycle riders
    B. Horsemen
    C. Motorcyclists
    D. Walkers

35. Parked cars are not allowed to *obstruct* traffic.

    A. direct
    B. lead
    C. block
    D. speed

36. It was *obvious* to the Agent that the traffic light was broken.

    A. uncertain
    B. surprising
    C. possible
    D. clear

37. The signs stated that parking in the area was *restricted* to vehicles of foreign diplomats.

    A. allowed
    B. increased
    C. desired
    D. limited

38. Each violation carries an *appropriate* fine.

    A. suitable
    B. extra
    C. light
    D. heavy

39. Strict enforcement of parking regulations helps to *alleviate* traffic congestion.

    A. extend
    B. build
    C. relieve
    D. increase

40. The Bureau has a rule which states that an Agent shall speak and act *courteously* in any relationship with the public.

    A. respectfully
    B. timidly
    C. strangely
    D. intelligently

41. City traffic regulations prohibit parking at *jammed* meters.

    A. stuck
    B. timed
    C. open
    D. installed

42. A *significant* error was made by the collector.

    A. doubtful
    B. foolish
    C. important
    D. strange

43. It is better to *disperse* a crowd.

    A. hold back
    B. quiet
    C. scatter
    D. talk to

44. Business groups wish to *expand* the program.

    A. advertise
    B. defeat
    C. enlarge
    D. expose

45. The procedure was *altered* to assist the storekeepers.

    A. abolished
    B. changed
    C. improved
    D. made simpler

46. The collector was instructed to *survey* the damage to the parking meter.

    A. examine
    B. give the reason for
    C. repair
    D. report

47. It is *imperative* that a collector's report be turned in after each collection.

    A. desired
    B. recommended
    C. requested
    D. urgent

48. The collector was not able to *extricate* the key.   48.____

    A. find
    B. free
    C. have a copy made of
    D. turn

49. Parking meters have *alleviated* one of our major traffic problems.   49.____

    A. created
    B. lightened
    C. removed
    D. solved

50. Formerly drivers with learners' permits could drive only on *designated* streets.   50.____

    A. dead-end   B. not busy   C. one way   D. specified

KEY (CORRECT ANSWERS)

1.	A	11.	B	21.	B	31.	D	41.	A
2.	C	12.	D	22.	C	32.	A	42.	C
3.	B	13.	C	23.	D	33.	B	43.	C
4.	C	14.	D	24.	A	34.	D	44.	C
5.	D	15.	C	25.	D	35.	C	45.	B
6.	A	16.	D	26.	B	36.	D	46.	A
7.	B	17.	C	27.	C	37.	D	47.	D
8.	B	18.	A	28.	C	38.	A	48.	B
9.	C	19.	B	29.	B	39.	C	49.	B
10.	D	20.	D	30.	C	40.	A	50.	D

TEST 3

DIRECTIONS: Each question or incomplete statement is followed by several suggested answers or completions. Select the one that BEST answers the question or completes the statement. *PRINT THE LETTER OF THE CORRECT ANSWER IN THE SPACE AT THE RIGHT.*

1. Sprinkler systems in buildings can retard the spread of fires.
   As used in this sentence, the word *retard* means MOST NEARLY

   A. quench   B. slow   C. reveal   D. aggravate

2. Although there was widespread criticism, the director refused to curtail the program.
   As used in this sentence, the word *curtail* means MOST NEARLY

   A. change   B. discuss   C. shorten   D. expand

3. Argon is an inert gas.
   As used in this sentence, the word *inert* means MOST NEARLY

   A. unstable   B. uncommon   C. volatile   D. inactive

4. The firemen turned their hoses on the shed and the main building simultaneously.
   As used in this sentence, the word *simultaneously* means MOST NEARLY

   A. in turn   B. without hesitation
   C. with great haste   D. at the same time

5. The officer was rebuked for his failure to act promptly. As used in this sentence, the word *rebuked* means MOST NEARLY

   A. demoted   B. reprimanded
   C. discharged   D. reassigned

6. Parkways in the city may be used to facilitate responses to fire alarms.
   As used in this sentence, the word *facilitate* means MOST NEARLY

   A. reduce   B. alter   C. complete   D. ease

7. Fire extinguishers are most effective when the fire is incipient.
   As used in this sentence, the word *incipient* means MOST NEARLY

   A. accessible   B. beginning
   C. red hot   D. confined

8. It is important to convey to new members the fundamentals of the procedure.
   As used in this sentence, the words *convey to* means MOST NEARLY

   A. prove for   B. confirm for
   C. suggest to   D. impart to

9. The explosion was a graphic illustration of the effects of neglect and carelessness.
   As used in this sentence, the word *graphic* means MOST NEARLY

   A. terrible   B. typical   C. unique   D. vivid

10. The worker was assiduous in all things relating to his duties.
    As used in this sentence, the word *assiduous* means MOST NEARLY

    A. aggressive   B. careless   C. persistent   D. cautious

11. A worker must be adept to be successful at his work. 11.____
    As used in this sentence, the word *adept* means MOST NEARLY

    A. ambitious   B. strong   C. agile   D. skillful

12. The extinguisher must be inverted before it will operate. As used in this sentence, the 12.____
    word *inverted* means MOST NEARLY

    A. turned over   B. completely filled
    C. lightly shaken   D. unhooked

13. Assume that the bridge operator may at times be assigned to the task of coordinating the 13.____
    bridge crew for the various routine jobs.
    As used in this sentence, the word *coordinating* means MOST NEARLY

    A. ordering   B. testing
    C. scheduling   D. instructing

14. The worker made an insignificant error. 14.____
    As used in this sentence, the word *insignificant* means MOST NEARLY

    A. latent   B. serious
    C. accidental   D. minor

15. An Assistant Supervisor should be attentive. 15.____
    As used in this sentence, the word *attentive* means MOST NEARLY

    A. watchful   B. prompt   C. negligent   D. willing

16. The Assistant Supervisor reported a cavity in the roadway. 16.____
    As used in this sentence, the word *cavity* means MOST NEARLY

    A. lump   B. wreck   C. hollow   D. oil-slick

17. Anyone working in traffic must be cautious. 17.____
    As used in this sentence, the word *cautious* means MOST NEARLY

    A. brave   B. careful   C. expert   D. fast

Questions 18-20.

DIRECTIONS: Each of Questions 18 through 20 consists of a capitalized word followed by four suggested meanings of the word. Select the word or phrase which means MOST NEARLY the same as the capitalized word.

18. OSMOSIS 18.____

    A. combining   B. diffusion
    C. ossification   D. incantation

19. COLLOIDAL 19.____

    A. mucinous   B. powdered   C. hairy   D. beautiful

20. PRETEXT

    A. ritual
    B. fictitious reason
    C. sermon
    D. truthful motive

21. *Easily broken or snapped* defines the word

    A. brittle   B. pliable   C. cohesive   D. volatile

22. *At right angles to a given line or surface* defines the word

    A. horizontal
    B. oblique
    C. perpendicular
    D. adjacent

23. *Tools with cutting edges for enlarging or shaping holes* are

    A. screwdrivers
    B. pliers
    C. reamers
    D. nippers

24. *An instrument used for measuring very small distances* is called a

    A. gage
    B. compass
    C. slide ruler
    D. micrometer

25. When the phrase *acrid smoke* is used, it refers to smoke that is

    A. irritating
    B. dense
    C. black
    D. very hot

26. The officer gave explicit directions on how the work was to be done.
    As used in this sentence, the word *explicit* means MOST NEARLY

    A. implied   B. clear   C. vague   D. brief

27. After the fire had been extinguished, the debris was taken outside and soaked.
    As used in this sentence, the word *debris* means MOST NEARLY

    A. wood   B. rubbish   C. couch   D. paper

28. The trapped man blanched when he saw the life net below him.
    As used in this sentence, the word *blanched* means MOST NEARLY

    A. turned pale
    B. sprang forward
    C. flushed
    D. fainted

29. The worker and his supervisor discussed the problem candidly.
    As used in this sentence, the word *candidly* means MOST NEARLY

    A. angrily
    B. frankly
    C. tolerantly
    D. understandingly

30. The truck came careening down the street.
    As used in this sentence, the word *careening* means MOST NEARLY

    A. with sirens screaming
    B. at a slow speed
    C. swaying from side to side
    D. out of control

31. The population of the province is fairly homogeneous.
    As used in this sentence, the word *homogeneous* means MOST NEARLY

    A. devoted to agricultural pursuits
    B. conservative in outlook
    C. essentially alike
    D. sophisticated

32. The reports of injuries during the past month are being tabulated.
    As used in this sentence, the word *tabulated* means MOST NEARLY

    A. analyzed
    B. placed in a file
    C. put in the form of a table
    D. verified

33. The terms offered were tantamount to surrender.
    As used in this sentence, the word *tantamount* means MOST NEARLY

    A. equivalent   B. opposite
    C. preferable   D. preliminary

34. The man's injuries were superficial.
    As used in this sentence, the word *superficial* means MOST NEARLY

    A. on the surface   B. not fatal
    C. free from infection D. not painful

35. This experience warped his outlook on life.
    As used in this sentence, the word *warped* means MOST NEARLY

    A. changed   B. improved
    C. strengthened   D. twisted

36. Hotel guests usually are transients.
    As used in this sentence, the word *transients* means MOST NEARLY

    A. persons of considerable wealth
    B. staying for a short time
    C. visitors from other areas
    D. untrustworthy persons

37. The pupil's work specimen was considered unsatisfactory because of his failure to observe established tolerances. As used in this sentence, the word *tolerances* means MOST NEARLY

    A. safety precautions
    B. regard for the rights of others
    C. allowable variations in dimensions
    D. amount of waste produced in an operation

38. Punishment was severe because the act was considered willful.
    As used in this sentence, the word *willful* means MOST NEARLY

    A. brutal   B. criminal
    C. harmful   D. intentional

39. The malfunctioning of the system was traced to a defective thermostat.
    As used in this sentence, the word *thermostat* means MOST NEARLY a device that reacts to changes in

    A. amperage
    B. water pressure
    C. temperature
    D. atmospheric pressure

40. His garden contained a profusion of flowers, shrubs, and bushes.
    As used in this sentence, the word *profusion* means MOST NEARLY

    A. abundance
    B. display
    C. representation
    D. scarcity

41. The inspector would not approve the work because it was out of plumb.
    As used in this sentence, the words *out of plumb* means MOST NEARLY not

    A. properly seasoned
    B. of the required strength
    C. vertical
    D. fireproof

42. The judge admonished the witness for his answer.
    As used in this sentence, the word *admonished* means MOST NEARLY

    A. complimented
    B. punished
    C. questioned
    D. warned

43. A millimeter is a measure of length.
    The length represented by *one millimeter* is

    A. one-thousandth of a meter
    B. one thousand meters
    C. one-millionth of a meter
    D. one million meters

44. It is not possible to misconstrue his letter.
    As used in this sentence, the word *misconstrue* means MOST NEARLY

    A. decipher
    B. forget
    C. ignore
    D. misinterpret

45. The wire connecting the two terminals must be kept taut.
    As used in this sentence, the word *taut* means MOST NEARLY without

    A. defects
    B. slack
    C. electrical charge
    D. pressure

46. Reaching the summit appeared beyond the capacity of the hikers.
    As used in this sentence, the word *summit* means MOST NEARLY

    A. canyon   B. peak   C. plateau   D. ravine

47. The plot was thwarted by the quick action of the police. As used in this sentence, the word *thwarted* means MOST NEARLY

    A. blocked
    B. discovered
    C. punished
    D. solved

48. An abrasive was required by the machinist to complete his task. 48._____
    As used in this sentence, the word *abrasive* means a substance used for

    A. coating
    B. lubricating
    C. measuring
    D. polishing

49. The facades of the building were dirty and grimy. 49._____
    As used in this sentence, the word *facades* means MOST NEARLY

    A. cellars
    B. fronts
    C. residents
    D. surroundings

50. Several firemen were injured by the detonation. 50._____
    As used in this sentence, the word *detonation* means MOST NEARLY

    A. accident   B. collapse   C. collision   D. explosion

KEY (CORRECT ANSWERS)

1. B	11. D	21. A	31. C	41. C
2. C	12. A	22. C	32. C	42. D
3. D	13. C	23. C	33. A	43. A
4. D	14. D	24. D	34. A	44. D
5. B	15. A	25. A	35. D	45. B
6. D	16. C	26. B	36. B	46. B
7. B	17. B	27. B	37. C	47. A
8. D	18. B	28. A	38. D	48. D
9. D	19. A	29. B	39. C	49. B
10. C	20. B	30. C	40. A	50. D

WORD MEANING

EXAMINATION SECTION
TEST 1

Questions 1-20.

DIRECTIONS: Each question consists of a statement. You are to indicate whether the statement is TRUE (T) or FALSE (F). *PRINT THE LETTER OF THE CORRECT ANSWER IN THE SPACE AT THE RIGHT.*

1. *To eliminate hand pumping* means NEARLY the same as *to do away with hand pumping.* 1.____

2. *Discarding a ladder with a cracked rung* means NEARLY the same as *repairing a ladder with a cracked rung.* 2.____

3. A *projecting* stub is USUALLY a stub which sticks out. 3.____

4. A *nitrogen deficiency* in the soil is an oversupply of nitrogen in the soil. 4.____

5. Saying that a soil has a heavy *texture* is NEARLY the same as saying that the soil has a deep color. 5.____

6. A *neutral* soil is one in which no useful plants will grow. 6.____

7. A plant which is *dormant* is USUALLY in an inactive period of growth. 7.____

8. Saying that sun is *detrimental* to ferns is NEARLY the same as saying that sun is harmful to ferns. 8.____

9. *Vendors are permitted only in certain park areas.* In this sentence, the word *vendors* means NEARLY the same as *sellers.* 9.____

10. *The Assistant Gardener was confident that he would be able to learn the new work quickly.* In this sentence, the word *confident* means NEARLY the same as *sure.* 10.____

11. *The employee's behavior on the job was improper.* In this sentence, the word *improper* means NEARLY the same as *good.* 11.____

12. *The foreman's oral instructions were always clear and to the point.* In this sentence, the word *oral* means NEARLY the same as *spoken.* 12.____

13. *A covering with paper will prevent excessive loss of moisture from the surface soil.* In this sentence, the word *excessive* means NEARLY the same as *unnecessary.* 13.____

14. *In making a permanent hotbed, the ground should be excavated to a depth of fifteen inches.* In this sentence, the word *excavated* means NEARLY the same as *dug out.* 14.____

15. *After the seed has been sown, an application of water will help it to germinate.* In this sentence, the word *germinate* means NEARLY the same as *start growing.* 15.____

16. *A sandy soil may be greatly improved through the incorporation of organic materials.* In this sentence, the word *incorporation* means NEARLY the same as *removal.* 16.____

17. *Manures are considered a concentrated form of fertilizer.* In this sentence, the word *concentrated* means NEARLY the same as *natural*.   17._____

18. *Ventilation of some kind must be given the plants.* In this sentence, the word *ventilation* means NEARLY the same as *heat*.   18._____

19. *When rain water enters soil, it penetrates air spaces.* In this sentence, the word *penetrates* means NEARLY the same as *fills*.   19._____

20. *The metal was corroded.* In this sentence, the word *corroded* means NEARLY the same as *polished*.   20._____

Questions 21-40.

DIRECTIONS: In answering Questions 21 through 40, select the lettered word which means MOST NEARLY the same as the capitalized word. *PRINT THE LETTER OF THE CORRECT ANSWER IN THE SPACE AT THE RIGHT.*

21. ACCURATE   21._____
    A. correct   B. useful   C. afraid   D. careless

22. ALTER   22._____
    A. copy   B. change   C. repeat   D. agree

23. DOCUMENT   23._____
    A. outline   B. agreement   C. blueprint   D. record

24. INDICATE   24._____
    A. listen   B. show   C. guess   D. try

25. INVENTORY   25._____
    A. custom   B. discovery   C. warning   D. list

26. ISSUE   26._____
    A. annoy   B. use up   C. give out   D. gain

27. NOTIFY   27._____
    A. inform   B. promise   C. approve   D. strengthen

28. ROUTINE   28._____
    A. path   B. mistake   C. habit   D. journey

29. TERMINATE   29._____
    A. rest   B. start   C. deny   D. end

30. TRANSMIT   30._____
    A. put in   B. send   C. stop   D. go across

31. QUARANTINE

    A. feed
    C. clean
    B. keep separate
    D. give an injection to

32. HERD

    A. group   B. pair   C. person   D. ear

33. SPECIES

    A. few   B. favorite   C. kind   D. small

34. INJURE

    A. hurt   B. need   C. protect   D. help

35. ANNOY

    A. like   B. answer   C. rest   D. bother

36. EXTINCT

    A. likely
    C. tired
    B. no longer exists
    D. gradually dying out

37. CONFINE

    A. fly about freely
    C. keep within limits
    B. free
    D. care

38. ENVIRONMENT

    A. distant
    C. disease
    B. surroundings
    D. lake

39. AVIARY

    A. pig pen
    C. elephant cage
    B. large bird cage
    D. snake pit

40. CRATE

    A. make   B. report   C. box   D. truck

KEY (CORRECT ANSWERS)

1. T	11. F	21. A	31. B
2. F	12. T	22. B	32. A
3. T	13. F	23. D	33. C
4. F	14. T	24. B	34. A
5. F	15. T	25. D	35. D
6. F	16. F	26. C	36. B
7. T	17. F	27. A	37. C
8. T	18. F	28. C	38. B
9. T	19. F	29. D	39. B
10. T	20. F	30. B	40. C

TEST 2

Questions 1-6.

DIRECTIONS: Questions 1 through 6 are to be answered on the basis of the following paragraph.

It is important that traffic signals be regularly and <u>effectively</u> maintained. Signals with <u>impaired</u> efficiency cannot be expected to command <u>desired</u> respect. Poorly maintained traffic signs create disrespect in the minds of those who are to obey them and thereby reduce the effectiveness and authority of the signs. Maintenance should receive <u>paramount</u> consideration in the design and purchase of traffic signal equipment. The <u>initial</u> step in a good maintenance program for traffic signals is the establishment of a maintenance record. This record should show the cost of operation and maintenance of different types of equipment. It should give complete information regarding signal operations and indicate where <u>defective</u> planning exists in maintenance programs.

1. The word *effectively,* as used in the above paragraph, means MOST NEARLY   1.____

   A. occasionally   B. properly
   C. expensively   D. cheaply

2. The word *impaired,* as used in the above paragraph, means MOST NEARLY   2.____

   A. reduced   B. increased   C. constant   D. high

3. The word *desired,* as used in the above paragraph, means MOST NEARLY   3.____

   A. public   B. complete   C. wanted   D. enough

4. The word *paramount,* as used in the above paragraph, means MOST NEARLY   4.____

   A. little   B. chief   C. excessive   D. some

5. The word *initial,* as used in the above paragraph, means MOST NEARLY   5.____

   A. first   B. final
   C. determining   D. most important

6. The word *defective,* as used in the above paragraph, means MOST NEARLY   6.____

   A. suitable   B. real   C. good   D. faulty

Questions 7-31.

DIRECTIONS: Each of Questions 7 through 31 consists of a capitalized word followed by four suggested meanings of the word. For each question, choose the word or phrase which means MOST NEARLY the same as the capitalized word.

7. ABOLISH   7.____

   A. count up   B. do away with
   C. give more   D. pay double for

8. ABUSE   8.____

   A. accept   B. mistreat   C. respect   D. touch

177

9. ACCURATE 9._____
   A. correct   B. lost   C. neat   D. secret

10. ASSISTANCE 10._____
    A. attendance   B. belief
    C. help   D. reward

11. CAUTIOUS 11._____
    A. brave   B. careful   C. greedy   D. hopeful

12. COURTEOUS 12._____
    A. better   B. easy   C. polite   D. religious

13. CRITICIZE 13._____
    A. admit   B. blame   C. check on   D. make dirty

14. DIFFICULT 14._____
    A. capable   B. dangerous   C. dull   D. hard

15. ENCOURAGE 15._____
    A. aim at   B. beg for   C. cheer on   D. free from

16. EXTENT 16._____
    A. age   B. size   C. truth   D. wildness

17. EXTRAVAGANT 17._____
    A. empty   B. helpful   C. over   D. wasteful

18. FALSE 18._____
    A. absent   B. colored
    C. not enough   D. wrong

19. INDICATE 19._____
    A. point out   B. show up
    C. shrink from   D. take to

20. NEGLECT 20._____
    A. disregard   B. flatten
    C. likeness   D. thoughtfulness

21. PENALIZE 21._____
    A. make   B. notice   C. pay   D. punish

22. POSTPONED 22._____
    A. put off   B. repeated   C. taught   D. went to

23. PUNCTUAL

    A. bursting   B. catching
    C. make a hole in   D. on time

23.____

24. RARE

    A. large   B. ride up   C. unusual   D. young

24.____

25. REVEAL

    A. leave   B. renew   C. soften   D. tell

25.____

26. EXCESSIVE

    A. excusable   B. immoderate
    C. ethereal   D. intentional

26.____

27. VOLUNTARY

    A. common   B. paid   C. sharing   D. willing

27.____

28. WHOLESOME

    A. cheap   B. healthful   C. hot   D. together

28.____

29. SERIOUS

    A. important   B. order   C. sharp   D. tight

29.____

30. TRIVIAL

    A. alive   B. empty   C. petty   D. troublesome

30.____

31. VENTILATE

    A. air out   B. darken
    C. last   D. take a chance

31.____

Questions 32-40.

DIRECTIONS: Each question consists of a statement. You are to indicate whether the statement is TRUE (T) or FALSE (F).

32. *The price of this merchandise fluctuates from day to day.* In this sentence, the word *fluctuates* means the OPPOSITE of *remains steady*.

32.____

33. *The patient was in acute pain.* In this sentence, the word *acute* means the OPPOSITE of *slight*.

33.____

34. *The essential data appear in the report.* In this sentence, the word *data* means the OPPOSITE of *facts*.

34.____

35. *The open lounge is spacious.* In this sentence, the word *spacious* means the OPPOSITE of *well-lighted*.

35.____

36. *The landscaping work was a prolonged task.* In this sentence, the word *prolonged* means NEARLY the same as *difficult*.

36.____

37. *A transparent removable cover was placed over the flower bed.* In this sentence, the word *transparent* means NEARLY the same as *wooden*. 37._____

38. *The prompt action of the employee saved many lives.* In this sentence, the word *prompt* means NEARLY the same as *quick*. 38._____

39. *The attendant's request for a vacation was approved.* In this sentence, the word *approved* means NEARLY the same as *refused*. 39._____

40. *The paycheck was received in the mail.* In this sentence, the *word received* means NEARLY the same as *lost*. 40._____

KEY (CORRECT ANSWERS)

1. B	11. B	21. D	31. A
2. A	12. C	22. A	32. T
3. C	13. B	23. D	33. T
4. B	14. D	24. C	34. F
5. A	15. C	25. D	35. F
6. D	16. B	26. B	36. F
7. B	17. D	27. D	37. F
8. B	18. D	28. B	38. T
9. A	19. A	29. A	39. F
10. C	20. A	30. C	40. F

TEST 3

Questions 1-50.

DIRECTIONS: Each question consists of a statement. You are to indicate whether the statement is TRUE (T) or FALSE (F). *PRINT THE LETTER OF THE CORRECT ANSWER IN THE SPACE AT THE RIGHT.*

1. *A few men were assisting the attendant.* In this sentence, the word *assisting* means NEARLY the same as *helping*. 1.____

2. *He opposed the idea of using a vacuum cleaner for this job.* In this sentence, the word *opposed* means NEARLY the same as *suggested*. 2.____

3. *Four employees were selected.* In this sentence, the word *selected* means NEARLY the same as *chosen*. 3.____

4. *This man is constantly supervised.* In this sentence, the word *constantly* means NEARLY the same as *rarely*. 4.____

5. *One part of soap to two parts of water is sufficient.* In this sentence, the word *sufficient* means NEARLY the same as *enough*. 5.____

6. *The fire protection system was inadequate.* In this sentence, the word *inadequate* means NEARLY the same as *very good*. 6.____

7. *The nozzle of the hose was clogged.* In this sentence, the word *clogged* means NEARLY the same as *brass*. 7.____

8. *He resembles the man who worked here before.* In this sentence, the word *resembles* means NEARLY the same as *replaces*. 8.____

9. *They eliminated a number of items.* In this sentence, the word *eliminated* means NEARLY the same as *bought*. 9.____

10. *He is a dependable worker.* In this sentence, the word *dependable* means NEARLY the same as *poor*. 10.____

11. *Some wood finishes color the wood and conceal the natural grain.* In this sentence, the word *conceal* means NEARLY the same as *hide*. 11.____

12. *Paint that is chalking sometimes retains its protective value.* In this sentence, the word *retains* means NEARLY the same as *keeps*. 12.____

13. *Wood and trash had accumulated.* In this sentence, the word *accumulated* means NEARLY the same as *piled up*. 13.____

14. An *inflammable* liquid is one that is easily set on fire. 14.____

15. *The amounts were then compared.* In this sentence, the word *compared* means NEARLY the same as *added*. 15.____

16. *The boy had fallen into a shallow pool.* In this sentence, the word *shallow* means NEARLY the same as *deep*. 16._____

17. *He acquired a new instrument.* In this sentence, the word *acquired* means NEARLY the same as *got*. 17._____

18. *Several men were designated for this activity.* In this sentence, the word *designated* means NEARLY the same as *laid off*. 18._____

19. *The drawer had been converted into a file.* In this sentence, the word *converted* means NEARLY the same as *changed*. 19._____

20. *The patient has recuperated.* In this sentence, the word *recuperated* means NEARLY the same as *died*. 20._____

21. *A rigid material should be used.* In this sentence, the word *rigid* means NEARLY the same as *stiff*. 21._____

22. *Only half the supplies were utilized.* In this sentence, the word *utilized* means NEARLY the same as *used*. 22._____

23. *In all these years, he had never obstructed any change.* In this sentence, the word *obstructed* means NEARLY the same as *suggested*. 23._____

24. *Conditions were aggravated when he left.* In this sentence, the word *aggravated* means NEARLY the same as *improved*. 24._____

25. *The autopsy room is now available.* In this sentence, the word *available* means NEARLY the same as *clean*. 25._____

26. *An investigation which precedes a report is one which comes before the report.* 26._____

27. *Another word was inserted.* In this sentence, the word *inserted* means NEARLY the same as *put in*. 27._____

28. *He reversed the recommended steps in the procedure.* In this sentence, the word *reversed* means NEARLY the same as *explained*. 28._____

29. *His complaint was about a trivial matter.* In this sentence, the word *trivial* means NEARLY the same as *petty*. 29._____

30. *Using the proper tool will aid a worker in doing a better job.* In this sentence, the word *aid* means NEARLY the same as *help*. 30._____

31. *The application form has a space for the name of the former employer.* In this sentence, the word *former* means NEARLY the same as *new*. 31._____

32. *The exterior of the building needed to be painted.* In this sentence, the word *exterior* means NEARLY the same as *inside*. 32._____

33. *The smoke from the fire was dense.* In this sentence, the word *dense* means NEARLY the same as *thick*. 33._____

34. *Vacations should be planned in advance.* In this sentence, vacations should be planned ahead of time. 34._____

35. *The employee denied that he would accept another job.* 35._____
In this sentence, the word *denied* means NEARLY the same as *admitted*.

36. *An annual report is made by the central stockroom.* In this sentence, the word *annual* means NEARLY the same as *monthly.* 36._____

37. *Salaries were increased in the new budget.* In this sentence, the word *increased* means NEARLY the same as *cut.* 37._____

38. *All excess oil is to be removed from tools.* In this sentence, the word *excess* means NEARLY the same as *extra.* 38._____

39. *The new employee did similar work on his last job.* In this sentence, the word *similar* means NEARLY the same as *interesting.* 39._____

40. *Helpful employees make favorable impressions on the public.* In this sentence, the word *favorable* means NEARLY the same as *poor.* 40._____

41. *Some plants are grown for the decorative value of their leaves.* In this sentence, the word *decorative* means NEARLY the same as *ornamental.* 41._____

42. *They made a circular flower garden.* In this sentence, the word *circular* means NEARLY the same as *square.* 42._____

43. *The gardener was a conscientious worker.* In this sentence, the word *conscientious* means NEARLY the same as *lazy.* 43._____

44. *The instructions received were contradictory.* In this sentence, the word *contradictory* means NEARLY the same as *alike.* 44._____

45. *His application for the job was rejected.* In this sentence, the word *rejected* means NEARLY the same as *accepted.* 45._____

46. *This plant reaches maturity quickly.* In this sentence, the word *maturity* means NEARLY the same as *full development.* 46._____

47. *The garden was provided with a system of underground irrigation.* In this sentence, the word *irrigation* means NEARLY the same as *watering.* 47._____

48. *In some plants, the flowers often appear before the foliage.* In this sentence, the word *foliage* refers to the leaves of the plant. 48._____

49. *The new horticultural society was organized through the merger of two previous groups.* In this sentence, the word *merger* means NEARLY the same as *breakup.* 49._____

50. *The stem of the plant measured three inches in diameter.* In this sentence, the word *diameter* means NEARLY the same as *height.* 50._____

KEY (CORRECT ANSWERS)

1. T	11. T	21. T	31. F	41. T
2. F	12. T	22. T	32. F	42. F
3. T	13. T	23. F	33. T	43. F
4. F	14. T	24. F	34. T	44. F
5. T	15. F	25. F	35. F	45. F
6. F	16. F	26. T	36. F	46. T
7. F	17. T	27. T	37. F	47. T
8. F	18. F	28. F	38. T	48. T
9. F	19. T	29. T	39. F	49. F
10. F	20. F	30. T	40. F	50. F

WORD MEANING

EXAMINATION SECTION
TEST 1

DIRECTIONS: Each question consists of a statement. You are to indicate whether the statement is TRUE (T) or FALSE (F). *PRINT THE LETTER OF THE CORRECT ANSWER IN THE SPACE AT THE RIGHT.*

1. *The foreman had received a few requests.* In this sentence, the word *requests* means NEARLY the same as *complaints*.   1._____

2. *The procedure for doing the work was modified.* In this sentence, the word *modified* means NEARLY the same as *discovered*.   2._____

3. *He stressed the importance of doing the job right.* In this sentence, the word *stressed* means NEARLY the same as *discovered*.   3._____

4. *He worked with rapid movements.* In this sentence, the word *rapid* means NEARLY the same as *slow*.   4._____

5. *The man resumed his work when the foreman came in.* In this sentence, the word *resumed* means NEARLY the same as *stopped*.   5._____

6. *The interior door would not open.* In this sentence, the word *interior* means NEARLY the same as *inside*.   6._____

7. *He extended his arm.* In this sentence, the word *extended* means NEARLY the same as *stretched out*.   7._____

8. *He answered promptly.* In this sentence, the word *promptly* means NEARLY the same as *quickly*.   8._____

9. *He punctured a piece of rubber.* In this sentence, the word *punctured* means NEARLY the same as *bought*.   9._____

10. *Education curbs crime.* In this sentence, the word *curb* means NEARLY the same as *checks*.   10._____

11. *Badges were distributed to the attendants.* In this sentence, the word *distributed* means NEARLY the same as *given out*.   11._____

12. *The attendant lifted the pail without assistance.* In this sentence, the word *assistance* means NEARLY the same as *delay*.   12._____

13. *The alert attendant notices unusual happenings.* In this sentence, the word *alert* means NEARLY the same as *busy*.   13._____

14. *Several bottles of ammonia were required for cleaning windows.* In this sentence, the word *required* means NEARLY the same as *needed*.   14._____

15. *The building had an efficient heating system.* In this sentence, the word *efficient* means NEARLY the same as *faulty*.   15._____

16. *An attendant never operates a motor vehicle.* In this sentence, the word *operates* means NEARLY the same as *fixes.*

17. *The new employee was praised for his work.* In this sentence, the word *praised* means NEARLY the same as *blamed.*

18. *Cooperation makes the work of all the employees easier.* In this sentence, the word *cooperation* means NEARLY the same as *working together.*

19. *All the people in the building had the same problems.* In this sentence, the word *problems* means NEARLY the same as *wages.*

20. *The employee was transferred to special work for the day.* In this sentence, the word *transferred* means NEARLY the same as *shifted.*

21. *Your supervisor will tell you of the different responsibilities of your job.* In this sentence, the word *responsibilities* means NEARLY the same as *tools.*

22. *A damper regulates the air flowing through a furnace.* In this sentence, the word *regulates* means NEARLY the same as *controls.*

23. *The wounded man was perspiring.* In this sentence, the word *perspiring* means NEARLY the same as *sweating.*

24. *This mop absorbs water better than a sponge.* In this sentence, the word *absorbs* means NEARLY the same as *spreads.*

25. *A metal box contained all the cleaning material.* In this sentence, the word *contained* means NEARLY the same as *held.*

26. *The stock of paper towels had gone down.* In this sentence, the word *stock* means NEARLY the same as *bond.*

27. *The Governor today urged all citizens to prevent fires.* In this sentence, the word *urged* means NEARLY the same as *ordered.*

28. *The news did not disturb the foreman.* In this sentence, the word *disturb* means NEARLY the same as *upset.*

29. *The Commissioner said that sixty men registered for the training course.* In this sentence, the word *registered* means NEARLY the same as *were eligible.*

30. *New York City attracts many people because of its opportunities.* In this sentence, the word *attracts* means NEARLY the same as *employs.*

31. *Five systems were suggested for helping the work of attendants.* In this sentence, the word *systems* means NEARLY the same as *methods.*

32. *It is not easy to select a foreman from such a fine group.* In this sentence, the word *select* means NEARLY the same as *pick.*

33. *The power of the public is in its freedom.* In this sentence, the word *power* means NEARLY the same as *strength.*

34. *The rescue was made quickly by the attendant.* In this sentence, the word *rescue* means NEARLY the same as *report*.

35. *The attendant avoided a quarrel.* In this sentence, the word *avoided* means NEARLY the same as *started*.

36. *A decaying branch is dangerous to the life of a tree.* In this sentence, the word *decaying* means NEARLY the same as *rotting*.

37. *Shearing helps keep the plants in the shape required.* In this sentence, the word *shearing* means NEARLY the same as *watering*.

38. *Some shrubs have vigorous growth and early flowering.* In this sentence, the word *vigorous* means NEARLY the same as *weak*.

39. *The lawn retained its healthy green color.* In this sentence, the word *retained* means NEARLY the same as *kept*.

40. *The soil is combined with an acid plant food.* In this sentence, the word *combined* means NEARLY the same as *mixed*.

41. *Gardening can be tiring without the right tools.* In this sentence, the word *tiring* means NEARLY the same as *amusing*.

42. *With the ground saturated, the roots may die.* In this sentence, the word *saturated* means NEARLY the same as *soaked*.

43. *Air can penetrate freely if holes are made in the soil.* In this sentence, the word *penetrate* means NEARLY the same as *follows*.

44. *With some plants, flowers precede the growth of leaves.* In this sentence, the word *precede* means NEARLY the same as *follow*.

45. *The gardener anticipated frost.* In this sentence, the word *anticipated* means NEARLY the same as *expected*.

46. *Tools are assembled when the job is finished.* In this sentence, the word *assembled* means NEARLY the same as *cleaned*.

47. *Part of the area was set aside for a miniature rock garden.* In this sentence, the word *miniature* means NEARLY the same as *beautiful*.

48. *Cheap tools are seldom durable.* In this sentence, the word *durable* means NEARLY the same as *long lasting*.

49. *Concrete walks are maintained clean easily.* In this sentence, the word *maintained* means NEARLY the same as *kept*.

50. *Each morning the assistant gardener was punctual in reporting to work.* In this sentence, the word *punctual* means NEARLY the same as *prompt*.

KEY (CORRECT ANSWERS)

1. F	11. T	21. F	31. T	41. F
2. T	12. F	22. T	32. T	42. T
3. F	13. F	23. T	33. T	43. F
4. F	14. T	24. F	34. F	44. F
5. F	15. F	25. T	35. F	45. T
6. T	16. F	26. F	36. T	46. F
7. T	17. F	27. F	37. F	47. F
8. T	18. T	28. T	38. F	48. T
9. F	19. F	29. F	39. T	49. T
10. T	20. T	30. F	40. T	50. T

TEST 2

DIRECTIONS: Each question consists of a statement. You are to indicate whether the statement is TRUE (T) or FALSE (F). *PRINT THE LETTER OF THE CORRECT ANSWER IN THE SPACE AT THE RIGHT.*

1. *Formal shearing destroys the plant's individuality.* In this sentence, the word *formal* means NEARLY the same as *irregular*. 1._____

2. *The entire tree is covered with a film which is flexible, colorless, and lasting.* In this sentence, the word *flexible* means NEARLY the same as *tough*. 2._____

3. *All of the equipment is mobile.* In this sentence, the word *mobile* means NEARLY the same as *movable*. 3._____

4. *Just enough asphalt adheres to make a mat.* In this sentence, the word *adheres* means NEARLY the same as *sticks*. 4._____

5. *Efforts at proper maintenance were nullified by this act.* In this sentence, the word *nullified* means NEARLY the same as *brought to nothing*. 5._____

6. Saying that a hose is *perforated* is another way of saying that a hose is *bent*. 6._____

7. *Do not injure the foliage of a plant* means NEARLY the same as *do not injure the plant's roots*. 7._____

8. *Pulverizing* soil is breaking it down into very small bits. 8._____

9. Humus is the part of the soil which is very often called clay in gardening practice. 9._____

10. *Aerating* a turf area is NEARLY the same as *sodding* the area. 10._____

11. *To mechanically agitate* means NEARLY the same as *to seed by mechanical power*. 11._____

12. *Ashes are transported from Department of Sanitation incinerators to points of ultimate disposal.* In this sentence, the word *ultimate* means NEARLY the same as *final*. 12._____

13. *In some areas where mechanical sweepers are used, supplementary manual cleaning is required.* In this sentence, the word *supplementary* means NEARLY the same as *additional*. 13._____

14. *It was stipulated that ferrous metals should be used.* In this sentence, the word *stipulated* means NEARLY the same as *agreed*. 14._____

15. *We find a different type of residue here.* In this sentence, the word *residue* means NEARLY the same as *inhabitant*. 15._____

16. *Several giant segments lay there.* In this sentence, the word *segments* means NEARLY the same as *parts*. 16._____

17. *The number of usable fill properties continues to dwindle.* In this sentence, the word *dwindle* means NEARLY the same as *multiply*. 17._____

18. *The salient provisions were given.* In this sentence, the word *salient* means NEARLY the same as *prominent*. 18._____

19. *Rate of putrefaction must be considered.* In this sentence the word *putrefaction* means NEARLY the same as *rotting*. 19.____

20. *The supervisor gave a brief talk on the importance on safety.* In this sentence, the word *brief* means NEARLY the same as *interesting*. 20.____

21. *The supervisor made a thorough study of the problem.*
In this sentence, the word *thorough* means NEARLY the same as *complete*. 21.____

22. *It is essential that all employees work together as a team.* In this sentence, the word *essential* means NEARLY the same as *absolutely necessary*. 22.____

23. *Employees are occasionally required to work overtime.* In this sentence, the word *occasionally* means NEARLY the same as *often*. 23.____

24. *The form is to be submitted in duplicate.* According to this sentence, three copies of the form are to be submitted. 24.____

25. *The benches should be wiped free of dirt and moisture each day.* In this sentence, *the word moisture* means NEARLY the same as *oil*. 25.____

26. *She omitted her name at the bottom of the application.* In this sentence, *the word omitted* means NEARLY the same as *left out*. 26.____

27. *The employee's excuse for being absent was absurd.* In this sentence, the word *absurd* means NEARLY the same as *sensible*. 27.____

28. *The attendant was instructed to reverse the mop head at the end of each stroke.* In this sentence, the word *reverse* means NEARLY the same as *clean*. 28.____

29. *The supervisor was in accord with the employee's suggestion.* In this sentence, the word *accord* means NEARLY the same as *agreement*. 29.____

30. *The mail clerk inserted the letter in the envelope.* In this sentence, the word *inserted* means NEARLY the same as *found*. 30.____

31. *If a tenant does not comply with the rules of the Housing Project, report this to your supervisor.* In this sentence, the words *comply with* mean NEARLY the same as *obey*. 31.____

32. *Surplus water on a floor should be wiped up with a mop.* In this sentence, the word *surplus* means NEARLY the same as *dirty*. 32.____

33. *An employee who is hurt should turn in an accident report immediately.* In this sentence, the *word immediately* means NEARLY the same as *right away*. 33.____

34. *A new employee is expected to learn his job gradually.*
In this sentence, the word *gradually* means NEARLY the same as *correctly*. 34.____

35. *The Commissioner said it was an immense job to keep New York City clean.* In this sentence, the word *immense* means NEARLY the same as *very big*. 35.____

36. *The foreman could tell, right away that the caretaker had swept the hall thoroughly.* In this sentence, the word *thoroughly* means NEARLY the same as *poorly*. 36.____

37. *The caretaker could not make permanent repairs.* In this sentence, the word *permanent* means NEARLY the same as *plumbing.* 37._____

38. *The employee requested a summer vacation.* In this sentence, the word *requested* means NEARLY the same as *asked for.* 38._____

39. *The caretaker could not open the door because the lock was jammed.* In this sentence, the word *jammed* means NEARLY the same as *loose.* 39._____

40. *Jones and Smith were rivals in the section's clean-up campaign.* In this sentence, the word *rivals* means NEARLY the same as *partners.* 40._____

41. *The caretaker persuaded the children to keep the playground clean.* In this sentence, the word *persuaded* means NEARLY the same as *warned.* 41._____

42. *All elevators should be operating during the morning rush hour to avoid crowding in the lobby.* In this sentence, the word *lobby* means NEARLY the same as *entrance hall.* 42._____

43. *The caretaker used a liquid polish on the brass trim.* In this sentence, the word *liquid* means NEARLY the same as *paste.* 43._____

44. *Report all minor accidents to your supervisor.* In this sentence, the word *minor* means NEARLY the same as *serious.* 44._____

45. *The attendant obtained the towels from the supply room.* In this sentence, the word *obtained* means NEARLY the same as *inspected.* 45._____

46. *Ten men were needed for the normal work of the section.* In this sentence, the word *normal* means NEARLY the same as *regular.* 46._____

47. *The swimming pool can accommodate 100 people.* In this sentence, the word *accommodate* means NEARLY the same as *hold without crowding.* 47._____

48. *The elevator operator did not recognize the new tenant.* In this sentence, the word *recognize* means NEARLY the same as *like.* 48._____

49. *The new playground swings were installed carefully.* In this sentence, the word *installed* means NEARLY the same as *put in.* 49._____

50. *Kerosene or benzine will ruin asphalt tile.* In this sentence, the word *ruin* means NEARLY the same as *spoil.* 50._____

4 (#2)

KEY (CORRECT ANSWERS)

1. F	11. F	21. T	31. T	41. F
2. F	12. T	22. T	32. F	42. T
3. T	13. T	23. F	33. T	43. F
4. T	14. T	24. F	34. F	44. F
5. T	15. F	25. F	35. T	45. F
6. F	16. T	26. T	36. F	46. T
7. F	17. F	27. F	37. F	47. T
8. T	18. T	28. F	38. T	48. F
9. F	19. T	29. T	39. F	49. T
10. F	20. F	30. F	40. F	50. T

TEST 3

DIRECTIONS: Each question consists of a statement. You are to indicate whether the statement is TRUE (T) or FALSE (F). *PRINT THE LETTER OF THE CORRECT ANSWER IN THE SPACE AT THE RIGHT.*

1. *His ideas about the best method of doing the work were flexible.* In this sentence, the word *flexible* means NEARLY the same as *unchangeable.* 1.____

2. *Many difficulties were encountered.* In this sentence, the word *encountered* means NEARLY the same as *met.* 2.____

3. *The different parts of the refuse must be segregated.* In this sentence, the word *segregated* means NEARLY the same as *combined.* 3.____

4. *The child was obviously hurt.* In this sentence, the word *obviously* means NEARLY the same as *accidentally.* 4.____

5. *Some kind of criteria for judging service necessity must be established.* In this sentence, the word *criteria* means NEARLY the same as *standards.* 5.____

6. *A small segment of the membership favored the amendment.* In this sentence, the word *segment* means NEARLY the same as *part.* 6.____

7. *The effectiveness of any organization depends upon the quality and integrity of its rank and file.* In this sentence, the word *integrity* means NEARLY the same as *quantity.* 7.____

8. *He adhered to his opinion.* In this sentence, the word *adhered* means NEARLY the same as *stuck to.* 8.____

9. *The suspects were interrogated at the police station.* In this sentence, *interrogated* means NEARLY the same as *identified.* 9.____

10. *Flanking the fireplace are shelves holding books.* In this sentence, the word *flanking* means NEARLY the same as *above.* 10.____

11. *He refused to comment on the current Berlin crisis.* In this sentence, the word *current* means NEARLY the same as *shocking.* 11.____

12. *Nothing has been done to remedy the situation.* In this sentence, the word *remedy* means NEARLY the same as *correct.* 12.____

13. *The reports had been ignored.* In this sentence, the word *ignored* means NEARLY the same as *prepared.* 13.____

14. *A firm was hired to construct the building.* In this sentence, the word *construct* means NEARLY the same as *build.* 14.____

15. *The Commissioner spoke about the operations of his department.* In this sentence, the word *operations* means NEARLY the same as *problems.* 15.____

16. *The increase in the number of accidents is negligible.* In this sentence, the word *negligible* means NEARLY the same as *serious.* 16.____

17. *He received monetary assistance.* In this sentence, the word *monetary* means NEARLY the same as *temporary.*   17.____

18. *Litigation delayed construction of the new incinerator.* In this sentence, the word *litigation* means NEARLY the same as *rising costs.*   18.____

19. *Proximity of the site is important.* In this sentence, the word *proximity* means NEARLY the same as *closeness.*   19.____

20. *At sanitary landfills, refuse is not dumped indiscriminately.* In this sentence, the word *indiscriminately* means NEARLY the same as *before burning.*   20.____

21. *Improvised equipment is seldom used.* In this sentence, the word *improvised* means NEARLY the same as *worn out.*   21.____

22. *At marine loading stations, refuse barges are loaded by gravity.* In this sentence, the word *gravity* means NEARLY the same as *shovel.*   22.____

23. *Many difficulties were encountered in the operation.* In this sentence, the word *encountered* means NEARLY the same as *met.*   23.____

24. *Traffic control facilitates the collection of waste in a large city.* In this sentence, the word *facilitates* means NEARLY the same as *eases.*   24.____

25. *Four persons were extricated immediately.* In this sentence, the word *extricated* means NEARLY the same as *treated.*   25.____

26. *Large objects produce extensive damage to mechanical equipment of furnaces.* In this sentence, the word *extensive* means NEARLY the same as *slight.*   26.____

27. *The car's headlights flickered on the dark street.* In this sentence, the word *flickered* means NEARLY the same as *shone brightly.*   27.____

28. *The sweeper was retained when the vacuum cleaners were installed.* In this sentence, the word *retained* means NEARLY the same as *kept.*   28.____

29. *Several men had dismantled the engine.* In this sentence, the word *dismantled* means NEARLY the same as *inspected.*   29.____

30. *The switch should be pushed down when the car approaches.* In this sentence, the word *approaches* means NEARLY the same as *comes near.*   30.____

31. *There is a possibility of ground water contamination.* In this sentence, the word *contamination* means NEARLY the same as *radioactivity.*   31.____

32. *The components of refuse must be segregated.* In this sentence, the word *components* means NEARLY the same as *containers.*   32.____

33. *The arrival of the tractor coincided with that of the dump truck.* In this sentence, the word *coincided* means NEARLY the same as *interfered.*   33.____

34. *Every idea sent to the Employee Suggestion Program is appraised.* In this sentence, the word *appraised* means NEARLY the same as *judged.*   34.____

35. *An adjacent garage maintained snow equipment.* In this sentence, the word *adjacent* means NEARLY the same as *neighboring*.   35.____

36. *Check all facts before analyzing a report.* In this sentence, the word *analyzing* means NEARLY the same as *submitting*.   36.____

37. *The abatement of odors affects living conditions.* In this sentence, the word *abatement* means NEARLY the same as *reduction*.   37.____

38. *For proper growth, the plant needs plenty of water, supplemented with liquid manure.* In this sentence, the word *supplemented* means NEARLY the same as *replaced*.   38.____

39. *One reason why aphids are undesirable is that they transmit plant diseases.* In this sentence, the word *transmit* means NEARLY the same as *pass on*.   39.____

40. *When the trees are young, the spaces between them may be utilized for other plantings.* In this sentence, the word *utilized* means NEARLY the same as *used*.   40.____

41. *The cuttings will take root readily.* In this sentence, the word *readily* means NEARLY the same as *quickly*.   41.____

42. *The seedlings should be transplanted at least once to stimulate growth.* In this sentence, the word *stimulate* means NEARLY the same as *encouraged*.   42.____

43. *The water evaporates through cracks in the soil.* In this sentence, the word *evaporates* means NEARLY the same as *flows in*.   43.____

44. *Hardy, native vines were planted.* In this sentence, the word *hardy* means NEARLY the same as *few*.   44.____

45. *The insects were present in moderate numbers.* In this sentence, the word *moderate* means NEARLY the same as *large*.   45.____

46. *The beetle is injurious to garden crops.* In this sentence, the word *injurious* means NEARLY the same as *harmful*.   46.____

47. *With proper care, the plants will survive the winter.* In this sentence, the word *survive* means NEARLY the same as *live through*.   47.____

48. *An arbor should be inconspicuous.* In this sentence, the word *inconspicuous* means NEARLY the same as *made of wood*.   48.____

49. *The plants are indifferent as to soil.* In this sentence, the word *indifferent* means NEARLY the same as *not particular*.   49.____

50. *The plant produces fragrant flowers.* In this sentence, the word *fragrant* means NEARLY the same as *sweet smelling*.   50.____

KEY (CORRECT ANSWERS)

1. F	11. F	21. F	31. F	41. T
2. T	12. T	22. F	32. F	42. T
3. F	13. F	23. T	33. F	43. F
4. F	14. T	24. T	34. T	44. F
5. T	15. F	25. F	35. T	45. F
6. T	16. F	26. F	36. F	46. T
7. F	17. F	27. F	37. T	47. T
8. T	18. F	28. T	38. F	48. F
9. F	19. T	29. F	39. T	49. T
10. F	20. F	30. T	40. T	50. T

READING COMPREHENSION UNDERSTANDING AND INTERPRETING WRITTEN MATERIAL

COMMENTARY

The ability to read and understand written materials—texts, publications, newspapers, orders, directions, expositions—is a skill basic to a functioning democracy and to an efficient business or viable government.

That is why almost all examinations—for beginning, middle, and senior levels—test reading comprehension, directly or indirectly.

The reading test measures how well you understand what you read. This is how it is done: You read a short paragraph and five statements. From the five statements, you choose the one statement, or answer, that is BEST supported by, or best matches, what is said in the paragraph.

SAMPLE QUESTIONS

DIRECTIONS: Each question has five suggested answers, lettered A, B, C, D, and E. Decide which one is the BEST answer. *PRINT THE LETTER OF THE CORRECT ANSWER IN THE SPACE AT THE RIGHT.*

1. The prevention of accidents makes it necessary not only that safety devices be used to guard exposed machinery but also that mechanics be instructed in safety rules which they must follow for their own protection and that the light in the plant be adequate.
   The paragraph BEST supports the statement that industrial accidents
   A. are always avoidable
   B. may be due to ignorance
   C. usually result from inadequate machinery
   D. cannot be entirely overcome
   E. result in damage to machinery

1.____

ANALYSIS

Remember what you have to do:
- First - Read the paragraph
- Second - Decide what the paragraph means
- Third - Read the five suggested answers.
- Fourth - Select the one answer which BEST matches what the paragraph says or is BEST supported by something in the paragraph. (Sometimes you may have to read the paragraph again in order to be sure which suggested answer is best.

This paragraph is talking about three steps that should be taken to prevent industrial accidents
1. Use safety devices on machines
2. Instruct mechanics in safety rules
3. provide adequate lighting

SELECTION

With this in mind, let's look at each suggested answer. Each one starts with "Industrial accidents…"

SUGGESTED ANSWER A
Industrial accidents (A) are always avoidable.
(The paragraph talks about how to avoid accidents, but does not say that accidents are always avoidable.)

SUGGESTED ANSWER B
Industrial accidents (B) may be due to ignorance.
(One of the steps given in the paragraph to prevent accidents is to instruct mechanics on safety rules. This suggests that lack of knowledge or ignorance of safety rules causes accidents. This suggested answer sounds like a good possibility for being the right answer.)

SUGGESTED ANSWER C
Industrial accidents (C) usually result from inadequate machinery.
(The paragraph does suggest that exposed machines cause accidents, but it doesn't say that it is the usual cause of accidents. The word usually makes this a wrong answer.)

SUGGESTED ANSWER D
Industrial accidents (D) cannot be entirely overcome.
(You may know from your own experience that this is a true statement. But that is not what the paragraph is talking about. Therefore, it is NOT the correct answer.)

SUGGESTED ANSWER E
Industrial accidents (E) result in damage to machinery.
(This is a statement that may or may not be true, but in any case it is NOT covered by the paragraph.)

Looking back, you see that the one suggested answer of the five given that BEST matches what the paragraph says is: Industrial accidents (B) may be due to ignorance.

The CORRECT answer then is B.

Be sure to read ALL the possible answers before you make your choice. You may think that none of the five answers is really good, but choose the BEST one of the five.

---

2. Probably few people realize, as they drive on a concrete road, that steel is used to keep the surface flat in spite of the weight of the busses and trucks. Steel bars, deeply embedded in the concrete, provide sinews to take the stresses so that the stresses cannot crack the slab or make it wavy.
    The paragraph BEST supports the statement that a concrete road
    A. is expensive to build
    B. usually cracks under heavy weights
    C. looks like any other road
    D. is used only for heavy traffic
    E. is reinforced with other material

2.____

ANALYSIS

This paragraph is commenting on the fact that
1. few people realize, as they drive on a concrete road, that steel is deeply embedded
2. steel keeps the surface flat
3. steel bars enable the road to take the stresses without cracking or becoming wavy

SELECTION

Now read and think about the possible answers:
A. A concrete road is expensive to build. (Maybe so but that is not what the paragraph is about.)
B. A concrete road usually cracks under heavy weights. (The paragraph talks about using steel bars to prevent heavy weights from cracking concrete roads. It says nothing about how usual it is for the roads to crack. The word usually makes this suggested answer wrong.)
C. A concrete road looks like any other road. (This may or may not be true. The important thing to note is that it has nothing to do with what the paragraph is about.)
D. A concrete road is used only for heavy traffic. (This answer at least has something to do with the paragraph—concrete roads are used with heavy traffic—but it does not say "used only.")
E. A concrete road is reinforced with other material. (This choice seems to be the correct one on two counts: First, the paragraph does suggest that concrete roads are made

stronger by embedding steel bars in them. This is another way of saying "concrete roads are reinforced with steel bars." Second, by the process of elimination, the other four choices are ruled out as correct answers simply because they do not apply.)

You can be sure that not all the reading questions will be so easy as these.

HINTS FOR ANSWERING READING QUESTIONS

1. Read the paragraph carefully. Then read each suggested answer carefully. Read every word, because often one word can make the difference between a right and a wrong answer.

2. Choose that answer which is supported in the paragraph itself. Do not choose an answer which is a correct statement unless it is based on information in the paragraph.

3. Even though a suggested answer has many of the words used in the paragraph, it may still be wrong.

4. Look out for words—such as *always*, *never*, *entirely*, or *only*—which tend to make a suggested answer wrong.

5. Answer first those questions which you can answer most easily. Then work on the other questions.

6. If you can't figure out the answer to the question, guess.

READING COMPREHENSION
UNDERSTANDING AND INTERPRETING WRITTEN MATERIAL
EXAMINATION SECTION
TEST 1

DIRECTIONS: Read the following passages, and select the MOST appropriate word from the five alternatives provided for each deleted word. *PRINT THE LETTER OF THE CORRECT ANSWER IN THE SPACE AT THE RIGHT.*

PASSAGE I

Bridges are built to allow a continuous flow of highway and railway traffic across water lying in their paths. But engineers cannot forget the fact that river traffic, too, is essential to or economy. The role of 1 is important. To keep these vessels moving freely, bridges are built high enough, when possible, to let them pass underneath. Sometimes, however, channels must accommodate very tall ships. It may be uneconomical to build a tall enough bridge. The 2 would be too high. To save money, engineers build movable bridges.

1. A. wind B. boats C. weight 1.____
   D. wires E. experience

2. A. levels B. cost C. standards 2.____
   D. waves E. deck

In the swing bridge, the middle part pivots or swings open. When the bridge is closed, this section joins the two ends of the bridge, blocking tall vessels. But this section 3. When swung open, it is perpendicular to the ends of the bridge, creating two free channels for river traffic. With swing bridges, channel width is limited by the bridge's piers. The largest swing bridge provides only a 75-meter channel. Such channels are sometimes too 4. In such cases, a bascule bridge may be built.

3. A. stands B. floods C. wears 3.____
   D. turns E. supports

4. A. narrow B. rough C. long 4.____
   D. deep E. straight

Bascule bridges are drawbridges with two arms that swing upward. They provide an opening as wide as the span. They are also versatile. These bridges are not limited to being fully opened or fully closed. They can be 5 in many ways. They can be fixed at different angles to accommodate different vessels.

5. A. approached B. crossed C. lighted 5.____
   D. planned E. positioned

In vertical lift bridges, the center remains horizontal. Towers at both ends allow the center to be lifted like an elevator. One interesting variation of this kind of bridge was built during World War II. A lift bridge was desired, but there were wartime shortages of the steel and machinery needed for the towers. It was hard to find enough 6. An ingenious engineer designed the bridge so that it did not have to be raised above traffic. Instead it was 7. It could be submerged seven meters below the river surface. Ships sailed over it.

6. A. work   B. material   C. time   6.____
   D. power   E. space

7. A. burned   B. emptied   C. secured   7.____
   D. shared   E. lowered

PASSAGE II

Before anesthetics were discovered, surgery was carried out under very severe time restrictions. Patients were awake, tossing and screaming in terrible pain. Surgeons were forced to hurry in order to constrain suffering and minimize shock. 8 was essential. Haste, however, did not make for good outcomes in surgery. No surprise then, that the 9 were often poor.

8. A. Blood   B. Silence   C. Speed   8.____
   D. Water   E. Money

9. A. quarters   B. teeth   C. results   9.____
   D. materials   E. families

The discovery of anesthetics happened, in part, by accident. During the early 1800's, nitrous oxide and ether were used for entertainment. At "either frolics" in theaters, volunteers would breathe these gases, become lightheaded, and run around the stage laughing and dancing. By chance, a Connecticut dentist saw such a 10. One volunteer banged his leg against a sharp edge. But he did not 11. He paid no attention to his wound, as though he felt nothing. This gave the dentist the idea of using gas to kill pain,

10. A. show   B. machine   C. face   10.____
    D. source   E. growth

11. A. dream   B. recover   C. succeed   11.____
    D. agree   E. notice

At first, using the "open drip method," ether and chloroform were filtered through a cotton pad placed over the mouth and nose. This direct dose was difficult to regulate and irritating to the nose and throat. Patients would hold their breath, cough, or gag. This made it impossible for them to relax, let alone sleep. Consequently, surgery was often 12. It couldn't begin until the patient had quieted and the anesthesia had taken hold.

12. A. delayed   B. required   C. blamed   12.____
    D. observed   E. repeated

Today's procedures are safer and more accurate. In the "closed method," a fixed amount of gas is released from sealed bottles into an inhalator bag when the patient exhales. He inhales this gas through tubes with his next breath. In this way, the gas is 13. The system carefully regulates how much gas reached the patient.

13. A. heated B. controlled C. cleaned 13.____
    D. selected E. wasted

For dentistry and minor operations, patients need not be asleep. Newer anesthetics can be used which deaden nerves only in the affected part of the body. These 14 anesthetics offer several advantages. For instance, since the anesthesia is fairly light and patients remain awake, they can cooperate with their doctors.

14. A. local B. natural C. ancient
    D. heavy E. three

PASSAGE III

An indispensable element in the development of telephony was the continual improvement of telephone station instruments, those operating units located at the clients premises. Modern units normally consist of a transmitter, receiver, and transformer. They also contain a bell or equivalent summoning device, a mechanism for controlling the unit's connection to the client's line, and various associated items, like dials. All of these 15 have changed over the years. The transmitter, especially, has undergone enormous refinement during the last century.

15. A. parts B. costs C. services 15.____
    D. models E. routes

Bell's original electromagnetic transmitter functioned likewise as receiver, the same instrument being held alternately to mouth and ear. But having to 16 the instrument this way was inconvenient. Suggestions understandably emerged for mounting the transmitter and receiver onto a common handle, thereby creating what are now known as handsets. Transmitter and receiver were, in fact, later 17 his way. Combination handsets were produced for commercial utilization late in the nineteenth century, but prospects for their acceptance were uncertain as the initial quality of transmissions with the handsets was disappointing. But 18 transmissions followed. With adequately high transmission standards attained, acceptance of handsets was virtually assured.

16. A. store B. use C. test 16.____
    D. strip E. clean

17. A. grounded B. marked C. covered 17.____
    D. priced E. coupled

18. A. shorter B. fewer C. better 18.____
    D. faster E. cheaper

Among the most significant improvements in transmitters has been the enormous amplification (up to a thousandfold) of speech sounds. This increased 19 has benefited telecommunications enormously. Nineteenth century telephone conversations frequently were only marginally audible whereas nowadays even murmured conversations can be transmitted successfully, barring unusual atmospheric or electronic disturbances.

19. A. distance B. speed C. market 19.____
    D. volume   E. number

Vocal quality over nineteenth century instruments was distorted, the speaker not readily identifiable. By comparison, current sound is characterized by considerably greater naturalism. Modern telephony produces speech sounds more nearly resembling an individual's actual voice. Thus, it is easier to 20 the speaker. A considerable portion of this improvement is attributable to practical applications of laboratory investigations concerning the mechanisms of human speech and audition. These 21 have exerted a profound influence. Their results prompted technical innovations in modern transmitter design which contributed appreciably to the excellent communication available nowadays.

20. A. time   B. help   C. bill   20.____
    D. stop   E. recognize

21. A. studies   B. rates   C. materials   21.____
    D. machines E. companies

PASSAGE IV

The dramatic events of December 7, 1941, plunged this nation into war. The full 22 of the war we cannot even now comprehend, but one of the effects stands out in sharp relief —the coming of the air age. The airplane, which played a relatively 23 part in World War I, has already soared to heights undreamed of save by the few with mighty vision.

In wartime the airplane is the 24 on wings and the battleship that flies. To man in his need it symbolizes deadly extremes; friend or foe; deliverance or 25.

It is a powerful instrument of war revolutionizing military strategy, but its peacetime role is just as 26. This new master of time and space, fruit of man's inventive genius, has come to stay, smalling the earth and smoothing its surface.

To all of us, then, to youth, and to 27 alike comes the winged challenge to get ourselves ready—to 28 ourselves for living in an age which the airplane seems destined to mold.

22. A. destruction B. character C. history   22.____
    D. import   E. picture

23. A. important   B. dull   C. vast   23.____
    D. unknown   E. minor

24. A. giant   B. ant   C. monster   24.____
    D. artillery   E. robot

25. A. ecstasy   B. bombardment C. death   25.____
    D. denial   E. survival

5 (#1)

26. A. revolting   B. revolutionary   C. residual   26.____
     D. reliable   E. regressive

27. A. animals   B. nations   C. women   27.____
     D. men   E. adult

28. A. distract   B. engage   C. determine   28.____
     D. deter   E. orient

PASSAGE V

Let us consider how voice training may contribute to 29 development and an improved social 30.

In the first place, it has been fairly well established that individuals tend to become what they believe 31 people think them to be.

When people react more favorably toward us because our voices 32 the impression that we are friendly, competent, and interesting, there is a strong tendency for us to develop those 33 in our personality.

If we are treated with respect by others, we soon come to have more respect for 34.

Then, too, one's own consciousness of having a pleasant, effective voice of which he does not need to be ashamed contributes materially to a feeling of poise, self-confidence, and a just pride in himself.

A good voice, like good clothes, can do much for an 35 that otherwise might be inclined to droop.

29. A. facial   B. material   C. community   29.____
     D. personality   E. physical

30. A. adjustment   B. upheaval   C. development   30.____
     D. bias   E. theories

31. A. some   B. hostile   C. jealous   31.____
     D. inferior   E. destroy

32. A. betray   B. imply   C. destroy   32.____
     D. transfigure   E. convey

33. A. detects   B. qualities   C. techniques   33.____
     D. idiosyncrasies E. quirks

34. A. others   B. their children C. their teachers 34.____
     D. ourselves   E. each other

35. A. mind   B. heart   C. brain   35.____
     D. feeling   E. ego

PASSAGE VI

How are symphony orchestras launched, kept going, and built up in smaller communities? Recent reports from five of them suggest that, though the 36 changes, certain elements are fairly common. One thing shines out; 37 is essential.

Also, aside from the indispensable, instrumentalists who play, the following personalities, either singly, or preferably in 38 seem to be the chief needs; a conductor who wants to conduct so badly he will organize his own orchestra if it is the only way he can get one; a manager with plenty of resourcefulness in rounding up audiences and finding financial support; an energetic community leader, generally a woman, who will take up locating the orchestra as a 39; and generous visiting soloists who will help draw those who are 40 that anything local can be used.

36. A. world   B. pattern   C. reason   36.____
    D. scene   E. cast

37. A. hatred   B. love   C. enthusiasm 37.____
    D. participation E. criticism

38. A. combination B. particular C. isolation 38.____
    D. sympathy   E. solitary

39. A. chore   B. duty   C. hobby   39.____
    D. delight   E. career

40. A. convinced B. skeptical   C. happy   40.____
    D. unhappy   E. unsure

KEY (CORRECT ANSWERS)

1.	B	11.	E	21.	A	31.	E
2.	B	12.	A	22.	D	32.	E
3.	D	13.	B	23.	E	33.	B
4.	A	14.	A	24.	D	34.	D
5.	E	15.	A	25.	C	35.	E
6.	B	16.	B	26.	B	36.	B
7.	E	17.	E	27.	E	37.	C
8.	C	18.	C	28.	E	38.	A
9.	C	19.	D	29.	D	39.	C
10.	A	20.	E	30.	A	40.	B

READING COMPREHENSION
UNDERSTANDING AND INTERPRETING WRITTEN MATERIAL
EXAMINATION SECTION
TEST 1

DIRECTIONS: Each question or incomplete statement is followed by several suggested answers or completions. Select the one that BEST answers the question or completes the statement. *PRINT THE LETTER OF THE CORRECT ANSWER IN THE SPACE AT THE RIGHT.*

Question 1.
DIRECTIONS: Question 1 is to be answered on the basis of the following passage.

Skiing has recently become one of the more popular sports in the United States. Because of its popularity, thousands of winter vacationers are flying north rather than south. In many areas, reservations are required months ahead of time.

I discovered the accommodation shortage through an unfortunate experience. On a sunny Saturday morning, I set out from Denver for the beckoning slopes of Aspen, Colorado. After passing signs for other ski areas, I finally reached my destination. Naturally, I lost no time in heading for the nearest tow. After a stimulating afternoon of miscalculated stem turns, I was famished. Well, one thing led to another, and it must have been eight o'clock before I concerned myself with a bed for my bruised and aching bones.

It took precisely one phone call to ascertain the lack of lodgings in the Aspen area. I had but one recourse. My auto and I started the treacherous jaunt over the pass and back towards Denver. Along the way, I went begging for a bed. Finally, a jolly tavernkeeper took pity, and for only thirty dollars a night allowed me the privilege of staying in a musty, dirty, bathless room above his tavern.

1. The author's problem would have been avoided if he had
   A. not tired himself out skiing
   B. taken a bus instead of driving
   C. arranged for food as soon as he arrived
   D. arranged for accommodations well ahead of his trip
   E. answer cannot be determined from the information given

1.____

Question 2.
DIRECTIONS: Question 2 is to be answered on the basis of the following passage.

Helen Keller was born in 1880 in Tuscumbia, Alabama. When she was two years old, she lost her sight and hearing as the result of an illness. In 1886, she became the pupil of Anne Sullivan, who taught Helen to see with her fingertips, to *hear* with her feet and hands, and to communicate with other people. Miss Sullivan succeeded in arousing Helen's curiosity and interest by spelling the names of objects into her hand. At the end of three years, Helen had mastered the manual and the braille alphabet and could read and write.

2. When did Helen Keller lose her sight and hearing?

2.____

Question 3.
DIRECTIONS: Question 3 is to be answered on the basis of the following passage.

Sammy got to school ten minutes after the school bell had rung. He was breathing hard and had a black eye. His face was dirty and scratched. One leg of his pants was torn.

Tommy was late to school, too; however, he was only five minutes late. Like Sammy, he was breathing hard, but he was happy and smiling.

3. Sammy and Tommy had been fighting. 3.____
   Who probably won?
   A. Sammy
   B. Tommy
   C. Cannot tell from story
   D. The teacher
   E. The school

Question 4.
DIRECTIONS: Question 4 is to be answered on the basis of the following passage.

This is like a game to see if you can tell what the nonsense word in the paragraph stands for. The nonsense word is just a silly word for something that you know very well. Read the paragraph and see if you can tell what the underlined nonsense word stands for.

You can wash your hands and face in zup. You can even take a bath in it. When people swim, they are in the zup. Everyone drinks zup.

4. Zup is PROBABLY
   A. milk   B. pop   C. soap   D. water   E. soup

Question 5.
DIRECTIONS: Question 5 is to be answered on the basis of the following passage.

After two weeks of unusually high-speed travel, we reached Xeno, a small planet whose population, though never before visited by Earthmen, was listed as *friendly* in the INTERSTELLAR GAZETTEER.

On stepping lightly (after all, the gravity of Xeno is scarcely more than twice that of our own moon) from our spacecraft, we saw that *friendly* was an understatement. We were immediately surrounded by Frangibles of various colors, mostly pinkish or orange, who held out their *hands* to us. Imagine our surprise when their *hands* actually merged with ours as we tried to shake them!

Then, before we could stop them (how could we have stopped them?), two particularly pink Frangibles simply stepped right into two eminent scientists among our party, who immediately lit up with the same pink glow. While occupied in this way, the scientists reported afterwards they suddenly discovered they *knew* a great deal about Frangibles and life on Xeno..

Apparently, Frangibles could take themselves apart atomically and enter right into any other substance. They communicated by thought waves, occasionally merging *heads* for greater clarity. Two Frangibles who were in love with each other would spend most of their time merged into one; they were a bluish-green color unless they were having a love's quarrel, when they turned gray.

5. In order to find out about an object which interested him, what would a Frangible MOST likely do? 5.____
   A. Take it apart
   B. Enter into it
   C. Study it scientifically
   D. Ask earth scientists about it
   E. Wait to see if it would change color

Question 6.
DIRECTIONS: Question 6 is to be answered on the basis of the following passage.

This is like a game to see if you can tell what the nonsense word in the paragraph stands for. The nonsense word is just a silly word for something that you know very well. Read the paragraph and see if you can tell what the underlined nonsense word stands for.

Have you ever smelled a <u>mart</u>? They smell very good. Bees like <u>marts</u>. They come inn many colors. <u>Marts</u> grow in the earth, and they usually bloom in the spring.

6. <u>Marts</u> are PROBABLY
   A. bugs   B. flowers   C. perfume   D. pies   E. cherries

Question 7.
DIRECTIONS: Question 7 is to be answered on the basis of the following passage.

Christmas was only a few days away. The wind was strong and cold. The walks were covered with snow. The downtown streets were crowded with people. Their faces were hidden by many packages as they went in one store after another. They all tried to move faster as they looked at the clock.

7. When did the story PROBABLY happen? 7.____
   A. November 28   B. December 1   C. December 21
   D. December 25   E. December 2

Question 8.
DIRECTIONS: Question 8 is to be answered on the basis of the following passage.

THE WAYFARER

The Wayfarer,
Perceiving the pathway to truth,
Was struck with astonishment.
It was thickly grown with weeds.
Ha, he said,
I see that no one has passed here
In a long time.
Later he saw that each weed
Was a singular knife,
Well, he mumbled at last,
Doubtless there are other roads.

8. *I see that no one has passed here in a long time.* 8.____
   What do the above lines from the poem mean?
   A. The way of truth is popular.
   B. People are fascinated by the truth.
   C. Truth comes and goes like the wind.
   D. The truth is difficult to recognize.
   E. Few people are searching for the truth.

Question 9.
DIRECTIONS: Question 9 is to be answered on the basis of the following passage.

Any attempt to label an entire generation is unrewarding, and yet the generation which went through the last war, or at least could get a drink easily once it was over, seems to possess a uniform, general quality which demands an adjective. It was John Kerouac, the author of a fine, neglected novel, THE TOWN AND THE CITY, who final came up with it. It was several years ago, when the face was harder to recognize, but he had a sharp, sympathetic eye, and one day he said, *You know, this is really a beat generation.* The origins of the word *beat* are obscure, but the meaning is only too clear to most Americans. More than mere weariness, it implies the feeling of having been used, of being raw. It involves a sort of nakedness of mind, and, ultimately of soul; a feeling of being reduced to the bedrock of consciousness. In short, it means being undramatically pushed up against the wall of oneself. A man is beat whenever he goes for broke and waters the sum of his resources on a single number; and the young generation has done that continually from early youth.

9. What does the writer suggest when he mentions a *fine, neglected novel*? 9.____
   A. Kerouac had the right idea about the war.
   B. Kerouac had a clear understanding of the new post-war generation.
   C. Kerouac had not received the recognition of THE TOWN AND THE CITY that was deserved.
   D. Kerouac had the wrong idea about the war.
   E. All of the above

Questions 10-11.
DIRECTIONS: Questions 10 and 11 are to be answered on the basis of the following passage.

One spring, Farmer Brown had an unusually good field of wheat. Whenever he say any birds in this field, he got his gun and shot as many of them as he could. In the middle of the summer, he found that his wheat was being ruined by insects. With no birds to feed on them, the insects had multiplied very fast. What Farmer Brown did not understand was this: A bird is not simply an animal that eats food the farmer may want for himself. Instead, it is one of many links in the complex surroundings, or environment, in which we live.

How much grain a farmer can raise on an acre of ground depends on many factors. All of these factors can be divided into two big groups. Such things as the richness of the soil, the amount of rainfall, the amount of sunlight, and the temperature belong together in one of these groups. This group may be called nonliving factors. The second group may be called living factors. The living factors in any plant's environment are animals and other plants. Wheat, for example, may be damaged by wheat rust, a tiny plant that feeds on wheat, or it may be eaten by plant-eating animals such as birds or grasshoppers…

It is easy to see that the relations of plants and animals to their environment are very complex, and that any change in the environment is likely to bring about a whole series of changes.

10. What does the passage suggest a good farmer should understand about nature? 10.____
    A. Insects are harmful to plants.
    B. Birds are not harmful to plants.
    C. Wheat may be damaged by both animals and other plants.
    D. The amount of wheat he can raise depends on two factors: birds and insects.
    E. A change in one factor of plants' surroundings may cause other factors to change.

11. What important idea about nature does the writer want us to understand? 11.____
    A. Farmer Brown was worried about the heavy rainfall.
    B. Nobody needs to have such destructive birds around.
    C. Farmer Brown did not want the temperature to change.
    D. All insects need not only wheat rust but grasshoppers.
    E. All living things are dependent on other living things.

Question 12.
DIRECTIONS: Question 12 is to be answered on the basis of the following passage.

For a 12-year-old, I've been around a lot because my father's in the Army. I have been to New York and to Paris. When I was nine, my parents took me to Rome. I didn't like Europe very much because the people don't speak the same language as I do. When I am older, my mother says I can travel by myself. I think I will like that. Ever since I was 13, I have wanted to go to Canada.

12. Why can't everything this person said be TRUE? 12.____
    A. 12-year-olds can't travel alone.
    B. No one can travel that much in 12 years.
    C. There is a conflict in the ages used in the passage.
    D. 9-year-olds can't travel alone.
    E. He is a liar.

Question 13.
DIRECTIONS: Question 13 is to be answered on the basis of the following passage.

Between April and October, the Persian Gulf is dotted with the small boats of pearl divers. Some seventy-five thousand of them are busy diving down and bringing up pearl-bearing oysters. These oysters are not the kind we eat. The edible oyster produces pearls of little or no value. You may have heard tales of divers who discovered pearls and sold them for great sums of money. These stories are entertaining but not accurate.

13. The Persian Gulf has many   13.____
    A. large boats of pearl divers
    B. pearl divers who eat oysters
    C. edible oysters that produce pearls
    D. non-edible oysters that produce pearls
    E. edible oysters that do not produce pearls

Question 14.
DIRECTIONS: Question 14 is to be answered on the basis of the following passage.

Art says that the polar ice cap is melting at the rate of 3% per year. Bert says that this isn't true because the polar ice cap is really melting at the rate of 7% per year.

14. We know for certain that   14.____
    A. Art is wrong.   B. Bert is wrong.
    C. they are both wrong   D. they both might be right
    E. they can't both be right

Question 15.
DIRECTIONS: Question 15 is to be answered on the basis of the following passage.

FORTUNE AND MEN'S EYES
                                                       Shakespeare

When, in disgrace with fortune and men's eyes,
I all alone beweep my outcast state,
And trouble deaf heaven with my bootless cries,
And look upon myself and curse my fate,
Wishing me like to one more rich in hope,
Featured like him, like him with friends possessed
Desiring this man's art, and that man's scope,
With what I most enjoy contented least;
Yet in these thoughts myself almost despising,
Haply I think on thee; and then my state,
Like to the lark at break of day arising
From sullen earth, sings hymns at heaven's gate;
For thy sweet love remembered, such wealth brings
That then I scorn to change my state with kings.

15. What saves this man from wishing to be different than he is?   15.____
    A. Such wealth brings   B. Hymns at heaven's gate
    C. The lark at break of day   D. Thy sweet love remembered
    E. Change my state with kings

Question 16.
DIRECTIONS: Question 16 is to be answered on the basis of the following passage.

My name is Gregory Gotrocks, and I live in Peoria, Illinois. I sell tractors. In June 1952, the Gotrocks Tractor Company (my dad happens to be the president) sent me to Nepal-Tibet to check on our sales office there.

Business was slow, and I had a lot of time to kill. I decided to see Mt. Everest so that I could tell everyone back in Peoria that I had seen it.

It was beautiful; I was spellbound. I simply had to see what the view looked like from the top. So I started up the northwest slope. Everyone know that this is the best route to take. It took me three long hours to reach the top, but the climb was well worth it.

16. Gregory Gotrocks went to see Mt. Everest so that he could 16._____
    A. see some friends
    B. sell some tractors
    C. take a picture of it
    D. plant a flag at its base
    E. entertain his friends back home

Questions 17-18.
DIRECTIONS: Questions 17 and 18 are to be answered on the basis of the following passage.

Suburbanites are not irresponsible. Indeed, what is striking about the young couples' march along the abyss is the earnestness and precision with which they go about it. They are extremely budget-conscious. They can rattle off most of their monthly payments down to the last penny; one might say that even their impulse buying is deliberately planned. They are conscientious in meeting obligations and rarely do they fall delinquent in their accounts.

They are exponents of what could be called <u>budgetism</u>. This does not mean that they actually keep formal budgets—quite the contrary. The beauty of budgetism is that one doesn't have to keep a budget at all. It's done automatically. In the new middle-class rhythms of life, obligations are homogenized, for the overriding aim is to have oneself precommitted to regular, unvarying monthly payments on all the major items,

Americans used to be divided into three sizable groups: those who thought of money obligations in terms of the week, of the month, and of the year. Many people remain at both ends of the scale; but with the widening of the middle class, the mortgage payments are firmly geared to a thirty-day cycle, and any dissonant peaks and valleys are anathema. Just as young couples are now paying winter fuel bills in equal monthly fractions through the year, so they seek to spread out all the other heavy seasonal obligations they can anticipate. If vendors will not oblige by accepting equal monthly installments, the purchasers will smooth out the load themselves by floating loans.

It is, suburbanites cheerfully explain, a matter of psychology. They don't trust themselves. In self-entrapment is security. They try to budget so tightly that there is no unappropriated funds, for they know these would burn a hole in their pocket. Not merely out of greed for goods, then, do they commit themselves; it is protection they want, too. And though it would be extreme to say that they go into debt to be secure, carefully chartered debt does give them a certain peace of mind—and in suburbia this is more coveted than luxury itself.

17. What is the *abyss* along which the young couples are marching? 17._____
    A. Nuclear war
    B. Unemployment
    C. Mental breakdown
    D. Financial disaster
    E. Catastrophic illness

18. What conclusion does the author reach concerning carefully chartered debt 18._____
    among young couples in the United States today?
    It
    A. is a symbol of love
    B. bring marital happiness
    C. helps them to feel secure
    D. enables them to acquire wealth
    E. provides them with material goods

Question 19.
DIRECTIONS: Question 19 is to be answered on the basis of the following passage. Read the verse and fill in the space at the right the object described in the verse.

You see me when I'm right or wrong;
My face I never hide.
My hands move slowly round and round
And o'er me minutes glide.

19.   A.   Book   B.   Clock   C.   Record   D.   Table   E.   Lock   19.____

Question 20-22.
DIRECTIONS: Questions 20 through 22 are to be answered on the basis of the following passage.

   Until about thirty years ago, the village of Nayon seems to have been a self-sufficient agricultural community with a mixture of native and sixteenth century Spanish customs. Lands were abandoned when too badly eroded. The balance between population and resources allowed a minimum subsistence. A few traders exchanged goods between Quito and the villages in the tropical barrancas, all within a radius of ten miles. Houses had dirt floors, thatched roofs, and pole walls that were sometimes plastered with mud. Guinea pigs ran freely about each house and were the main meat source. Most of the population spoke no Spanish. Men wore long hair and concerned themselves chiefly with farming.
   The completion of the Guayaquil-Quito railway in 1908 brought the first real contacts with industrial civilization to the high inter-Andean valley. From this event gradually flowed not only technological changes but new ideas and social institutions. Feudal social relationships no longer seemed right and immutable; medicine and public health improved; elementary education became more common; urban Quito began to expand; and finally, and perhaps least important so far, modern industries began to appear, although even now on a most modest scale.
   In 1948-49, the date of our visit, only two men wore their hair long; and only to old-style houses remained. If guinea pigs were kept, they were penned; their flesh was now a luxury food, and beef the most common meat. Houses were of adobe or fired brick, usually with tile roofs, and often contained five or six rooms, some of which had plank or brick floors. Most of the population spoke Spanish. There was no resident priest, but an appointed government official and a policeman represented authority. A six-teacher school provided education. Clothing was becoming citified; for men it often included overalls for work and a tailored suit, white shirt, necktie, and felt hat for trips to Quito. Attendance at church was low, and many festivals had been abandoned. Volleyball or soccer was played weekly in the plaza by young men who sometimes wore shorts, blazers, and berets. There were few shops, for most purchases were made in Quito, and from there came most of the food, so that there was a far more varied diet than twenty-five years ago. There were piped water and sporadic health services; in addition, most families patronized Quito doctors in emergencies.
   The crops and their uses had undergone change. Maize, or Indian corn, was still the primary crop, but very little was harvested as grain. Almost all was sold in Quito as green corn to eat boiled on the cob, and a considerable amount of the corn eaten as grain in Nayon was imported. Beans, which do poorly here, were grown on a small scale for household consumption. Though some squash was eaten, most was exported. Sweet potatoes, tomatoes, cabbage, onions, peppers, and, at lower elevations, sweet yucca, and arrowroot were grown extensively for export; indeed, so export-minded was the community that it was almost

impossible to buy locally grown produce in the village. People couldn't be bothered with retail scales.

20. Why was there primitiveness and self-containment in Nayon before 1910? 20.____
    A. Social mores
    B. Cultural tradition
    C. Biological instincts
    D. Geographical factors
    E. Religious regulations

21. By 1948, the village of Nayon was 21.____
    A. a self-sufficient village
    B. out of touch with the outside world
    C. a small dependent portion of a larger economic unit
    D. a rapidly growing and sound social and cultural unit
    E. a metropolis

22. Why was Nayon originally separated from its neighbors? 22.____
    A. Rich arable land
    B. Long meandering streams
    C. Artificial political barriers
    D. Broad stretches of arid desert
    E. Deep rugged gorges traversed by rock trails

Question 23.
DIRECTIONS: Question 23 is to be answered on the basis of the following passage. Read the verse and fill in the space at the right the object described in the verse.

I have two eyes and when I'm worn
I give the wearer four.
I'm strong or weak or thick or thin
Need I say much more?

23. A. Clock   B. Eyeglasses   C. Piano   23.____
    D. Thermometer   E. I don't know

Question 24.
DIRECTIONS: Question 24 is to be answered on the basis of the following passage.

Scarlet fever begins with fever, chills, headache, and sore throat. A doctor diagnoses the illness as scarlet fever when a characteristic rash erupts on the skin. This rash appears on the neck and chest in three to five days after the onset of the illness and spreads rapidly over the body. Sometimes the skin on the palm of the hands and soles of the feet shreds in flakes.
Scarlet fever is usually treated with penicillin and, in severe cases, a convalescent serum. The disease may be accompanied by infections of the ear and throat, inflammation of the kidneys, pneumonia, and inflammation of the heart.

24. How does the author tell us that scarlet fever may be a serious disease? 24.____
    A. He tells how many people die of it.
    B. He tells that he once had the disease.
    C. He tells that hands and feet may fall off.

D. He tells how other infections may come with scarlet fever.
E. None of the above

Question 25.
DIRECTIONS: Question 25 is to be answered on the basis of the following passage. Read the verse and fill in the space at the right the object described in the verse.

I have no wings but often fly;
I come in colors many.
From varied nationalities
Respect I get a-plenty.

25. A. Deck of cards   B. Eyeglasses   C. Flag   25.____
     D. Needles   E. None of the above

KEY (CORRECT ANSWERS)

1.	D		11.	E
2.	B		12.	C
3.	B		13.	D
4.	D		14.	E
5.	B		15.	D
6.	B		16.	E
7.	C		17.	D
8.	E		18.	C
9.	C		19.	B
10.	E		20.	D

21.	C
22.	E
23.	B
24.	D
25.	C

READING COMPREHENSION
UNDERSTANDING AND INTERPRETING WRITTEN MATERIAL
EXAMINATION SECTION
TEST 1

DIRECTIONS: Each question has five suggested answers, lettered A to E. Decide which one is the BEST answer. *PRINT THE LETTER OF THE CORRECT ANSWER IN THE SPACE AT THE RIGHT.*

1. Some specialists are willing to give their services to the Government entirely free of charge; some feel that a nominal salary, such as will cover traveling expenses, is sufficient for a position that is recognized as being somewhat honorary in nature; many other specialists value their time so highly that they will not devote any of it to public service that does not repay them at a rate commensurate with the fees that they can obtain from a good private clientele.
   The paragraph BEST supports the statement that the use of specialists by the Government
   A. is rare because of the high cost of securing such persons
   B. may be influenced by the willingness of specialists to serve
   C. enables them to secure higher salaries in private fields
   D. has become increasingly common during the past few years
   E. always conflicts with private demands for their services

1.____

2. The fact must not be overlooked that only about one-half of the international trade of the world crosses the oceans. The other half is merely exchanges of merchandise between countries lying alongside each other or at least within the same continent.
   The paragraph BEST supports the statement that
   A. the most important part of any country's trade is transoceanic
   B. domestic trade is insignificant when compared with foreign trade
   C. the exchange of goods between neighboring countries is not considered international trade
   D. foreign commerce is not necessarily carried on by water
   E. about one-half of the trade of the world is international

2.____

3. Individual differences in mental traits assume importance in fitting workers to jobs because such personal characteristics are persistent and are relatively little influenced by training and experience.
   The paragraph BEST supports the statement that training and experience
   A. are limited in their effectiveness in fitting workers to jobs
   B. do not increase a worker's fitness for a job
   C. have no effect upon a person's mental traits
   D. have relatively little effect upon the individual's chances for success
   E. should be based on the mental traits of an individual

3.____

4. The competition of buyers tends to keep prices up, the competition of sellers to send them down. Normally, the pressure of competition among sellers is stronger than that among buyers since the seller has his article to sell and must get rid of it, whereas the buyer is not committed to anything.
The paragraph BEST supports the statement that low prices are caused by
   A. buyer competition
   B. competition of buyers with sellers
   C. fluctuations in demand
   D. greater competition among sellers than among buyers
   E. more sellers than buyers

4._____

5. In seventeen states, every lawyer is automatically a member of the American Bar Association. In some other states and localities, truly representative organizations of the Bar have not yet come into being, but are greatly needed.
The paragraph IMPLIES that
   A. representative Bar Associations are necessary in states where they do not now exist
   B. every lawyer is required by law to become a member of the Bar
   C. the Bar Association is a democratic organization
   D. some states have more lawyers than others
   E. every member of the American Bar Association is automatically a lawyer in seventeen states

5._____

KEY (CORRECT ANSWERS)

1. B
2. D
3. A
4. D
5. A

TEST 2

DIRECTIONS: Each question has five suggested answers, lettered A to E. Decide which one is the BEST answer. *PRINT THE LETTER OF THE CORRECT ANSWER IN THE SPACE AT THE RIGHT.*

1. We hear a great deal about the new education, and see a great deal of it in action. But the school house, though prodigiously magnified in scale, is still very much the same old school house.
   The paragraph IMPLIES
   A. the old education was, after all, better than the new
   B. although the modern school buildings are larger than the old ones, they have not changed very much in other respects
   C. the old school houses do not fit in with modern educational theories
   D. a fine school building does not make up for poor teachers
   E. schools will be schools

   1._____

2. No two human beings are of the same pattern—not even twins and the method of bringing out the best in each one necessarily according to the nature of the child.
   The paragraph IMPLIES that
   A. individual differences should be considered in dealing with children
   B. twins should be treated impartially
   C. it is an easy matter to determine the special abilities of children
   D. a child's nature varies from year to year
   E. we must discover the general technique of dealing with children

   2._____

3. Man inhabits today a world very different from that which encompassed even his parents and grandparents. It is a world geared to modern machinery—automobiles, airplanes, power plants; it is linked together and served by electricity.
   The paragraph IMPLIES that
   A. the world has no changed much during the last few generations
   B. modern inventions and discoveries have brought about many changes in man's way of living
   C. the world is run more efficiently today than it was in our grandparents' time
   D. man is much happier today than he was a hundred years ago
   E. we must learn to see man as he truly is, underneath the veneers of man's contrivances

   3._____

4. Success in any study depends largely upon the interest taken in that particular subject by the student. This being the case, each teacher earnestly hopes that her students will realize at the vey onset that shorthand can be made an intensely fascinating study.
   The paragraph IMPLIES that
   A. Everyone is interested in shorthand
   B. success in a study is entirely impossible unless the student finds the study very interesting

   4._____

219

C. if a student is eager to study shorthand, he is likely to succeed in it
D. shorthand is necessary for success
E. anyone who is not interested in shorthand will not succeed in business

5. The primary purpose of all business English is to move the reader to agreeable and mutually profitable action. This action may be indirect or direct, but in either case a highly competitive appeal for business should be clothed with incisive diction tending to replace vagueness and doubt with clarity, confidence, and appropriate action.
The paragraph IMPLIES that the
   A. ideal business letter uses words to conform to the reader's language level
   B. business correspondent should strive for conciseness in letter writing
   C. keen competition of today has lessened the value of the letter as an appeal for business
   D. writer of a business letter should employ incisive diction to move the reader to compliant and gainful action
   E. the writer of a business letter should be himself clear, confident, and forceful

KEY (CORRECT ANSWERS)

1. B
2. A
3. B
4. C
5. D

TEST 3

DIRECTIONS: Each question has five suggested answers, lettered A to E. Decide which one is the BEST answer. *PRINT THE LETTER OF THE CORRECT ANSWER IN THE SPACE AT THE RIGHT.*

1. To serve the community best, a comprehensive city plan must coordinate all physical improvements, even at the possible expense of subordinating individual desires, to the end that a city may grow in a more orderly way and provide adequate facilities for its people
   The paragraph IMPLIES that
   A. city planning provides adequate facilities for recreation
   B. a comprehensive city plan provides the means for a city to grow in a more orderly fashion
   C. individual desires must always be subordinated to civic changes
   D. the only way to serve a community is to adopt a comprehensive city plan
   E. city planning is the most important function of city government

   1.____

2. Facility in writing letters, the knack of putting into these quickly written letters the same personal impression that would mark an interview, and the ability to boil down to a one-page letter the gist of what might be called a five- or ten-minute conversation —all these are essential to effective work under conditions of modern business organization.
   The paragraph IMPLIES that
   A. letters are of more importance in modern business activities than ever before
   B. letters should be used in place of interviews
   C. the ability to write good letters is essential to effective work in modern business organization
   D. business letters should never be more than one page in length
   E. the person who can write a letter with great skill will get ahead more readily than others

   2.____

3. The general rule is that it is the city council which determines the amount to be raised by taxation and which therefore determines, within the law, the tax rates. As has been pointed out, however, no city council or city authority has the power to determine what kind of taxes should be levied.
   The paragraph IMPLIES that
   A. the city council has more authority than any other municipal body
   B. while the city council has a great deal of authority in the levying of taxes, its power is not absolute
   C. the kinds of taxes levied in different cities vary greatly
   D. the city council appoints the tax collectors
   E. the mayor determines the kinds of taxes to be levied

   3.____

221

4. The growth of modern business has made necessary mass production, mass distribution, and mass selling. As a result, the problems of personnel and industrial relations have increased so rapidly that grave injustice in the handling of personal relationships have frequently occurred. Personnel administration is complex because, as in all human problems, many intangible elements are involved. Therefore a thorough, systematic, and continuous study of the psychology of human behavior is essential to the intelligent handling of personnel.
The paragraph IMPLIES that
   A. complex modern industry makes impossible the personal relationships which formerly existed between employer and employee
   B. mass decisions are successfully applied to personnel problems
   C. the human element in personnel administration makes continuous study necessary to is intelligent application
   D. personnel problems are less important than the problems of mass production and mass distribution
   E. since personnel administration is so complex and costly, it should be subordinated to the needs of good industrial relations

4.____

5. The Social Security Act is striving toward the attainment of economic security for the individual and for his family. It was stated, in outlining this program, that security for the individual and for the family concerns itself with three factors: (1) decent homes to live in; (2) development of the natural resources of the country so as to afford the fullest opportunity to engage in productive work; and (3) safeguards against the major misfortunes of life. The Social Security Act is concerned with the third of these factors —"safeguards against misfortunes which cannot be wholly eliminated in this man-made world of ours."
The paragraph IMPLIES that the
   A. Social Security Act is concerned primarily with supplying to families decent homes in which to live
   B. development of natural resources is the only means of offering employment to the masses of the unemployed
   C. Social Security Act has attained absolute economic security for the individual and his family
   D. Social Security Act deals with the first (1) factor as stated in the paragraph above
   E. Social Security Act deals with the third (3) factor as stated in the paragraph above

5.____

KEY (CORRECT ANSWERS)

1. B
2. C
3. B
4. C
5. E

TEST 4

DIRECTIONS: Each question has five suggested answers, lettered A to E. Decide which one is the BEST answer. *PRINT THE LETTER OF THE CORRECT ANSWER IN THE SPACE AT THE RIGHT.*

PASSAGE 1

Free unrhymed verse has been practiced for some thousands of years and reaches back to the incantation which linked verse with the ritual dance. It provided a communal emotion; the aim of the cadenced phrases was to create a state of mind. The general coloring of free rhythms in the poetry of today is that of speech rhythm, composed in the sequence of the musical phrase, not in the sequence of the metronome, the regular beat. In the twenties, conventional rhyme fell into almost complete disuse. This liberation from rhyme became as well a liberation of rhyme. Freed of its exacting task of supporting lame verse, it would be applied with greater effect where wanted for some special effect. Such break in the tradition of rhymed verse had the healthy effect of giving it a fresh start, released from the hampering convention of too familiar cadences. This refreshing and subtilizing of the use of rhythm can be seen everywhere in the poetry today.

1. The title below that BEST expresses the ideas of this paragraph is: 1.____
   A. Primitive Poetry
   B. The Origin of Poetry
   C. Rhyme and Rhythm in Modern Verse
   D. Classification of Poetry
   E. Purposes in All Poetry

2. Free verse had its origin in primitive   2.____
   A. fairytales   B. literature   C. warfare
   D. chants   E. courtship

3. The object of early free verse was to   3.____
   A. influence the mood of the people   B. convey ideas
   C. produce mental pictures   D. create pleasing sounds
   E. provide enjoyment

PASSAGE 2

Control of the Mississippi had always been goals of nations having ambitions in the New World. LaSalle claimed it for France in 1682. Iberville appropriated it to France when he colonized Louisiana in 1700. Bienville founded New Orleans, its principal port, as a French city in 1718. The fleur-de-lis were the blazon of the delta country until 1762. Then Spain claimed all of Louisiana. The Spanish were easy neighbors. American products from western Pennsylvania and the Northwest Territory were barged down the Ohio and Mississippi to New Orleans; here they were reloaded on ocean-going vessels that cleared for the great seaports of the world.

2 (#4)

4. The title below that BEST expresses the ideas of this paragraph is: 4.____
   A. Importance of Seaports
   B. France and Spain in the New World
   C. Early Control of the Mississippi
   D. Claims of European Nations
   E. American Trade on the Mississippi

5. Until 1762, the lower Mississippi area was held by 5.____
   A. England   B. Spain   C. the United States
   D. France   E. Indians

6. In doing business with Americans, the Spaniards were 6.____
   A. easy to outsmart
   B. friendly to trade
   C. inclined to charge high prices for use of their ports
   D. shrewd
   E. suspicious

PASSAGE 3

Our humanity is by no means so materialistic as foolish talk is continually asserting it to be. Judging by what I have learned about men and women, I am convinced that there is far more in them of idealistic willpower than ever comes to the surface of the world. Just as the water of streams is small in amount compared to that which flows underground, so the idealism which becomes visible is small in amount compared with that which men and women bear locked in their hearts, unreleased or scarcely released. To unbind what is bound, to bring the underground waters to the surface—mankind is waiting and longing for men who can do that.

7. The title below that BEST expresses the ideas of the paragraph is: 7.____
   A. Releasing Underground Riches
   B. The Good and Bad in Man
   C. Materialism in Humanity
   D. The Surface and the Depths of Idealism
   E. Unreleased Energy

8. Human beings are more idealistic than 8.____
   A. the water in underground streams
   B. their waiting and longing proves
   C. outward evidence shows
   D. the world
   E. other living creatures

PASSAGE 4

The total impression made by any work of fiction cannot be rightly understood without a sympathetic perception of the artistic aims of the writer. Consciously or unconsciously, he has accepted certain facts, and rejected or suppressed other facts, in order to give unity to the particular aspect of human life which he is depicting. No novelist possesses the impartiality, the indifference, the infinite tolerance of nature. Nature displays to use, with complete unconcern, the beautiful and the ugly, the precious and the trivial, the pure and the impure. But a writer must select the aspects of nature and human nature which are demanded by the work in hand. He is forced to select, to combine, to create.

9. The title below that BEST expresses the ideas of this paragraph is: 9.____
   A. Impressionists in Literature
   B. Nature as an Artist
   C. The Novelist as an Imitator
   D. Creative Technic of the Novelist
   E. Aspects of Nature

10. A novelist rejects some facts because they   10.____
    A. are impure and ugly
    B. would show he is not impartial
    C. are unrelated to human nature
    D. would make a bad impression
    E. mar the unity of his story

11. It is important for a reader to know   11.____
    A. the purpose of the author
    B. what facts the author omits
    C. both the ugly and the beautiful
    D. something about nature
    E. what the author thinks of human nature

PASSAGE 5

If you watch a lamp which is turned very rapidly on and off, and you keep your eyes open, "persistence of vision" will bridge the gaps of darkness between the flashes of light, and the lamp will seem to be continuously lit. This "topical afterglow" explains the magic produced by the stroboscope, a new instrument which seems to freeze the swiftest motions while they are still going on, and to stop time itself dead in its tracks. The "magic" is all in the eye of the beholder.

12. The "magic" of the stroboscope is due to   12.____
    A. continuous lighting
    B. intense cold
    C. slow motion
    D. behavior of the human eye
    E. a lapse of time

13. "Persistence of vision" is explained by   13.____
    A. darkness
    B. winking
    C. rapid flashes
    D. gaps
    E. after impression

KEY (CORRECT ANSWERS)

1.	C	6.	B	11.	A
2.	D	7.	D	12.	D
3.	A	8.	C	13.	E
4.	C	9.	D		
5.	D	10.	E		

TEST 5

DIRECTIONS: Each question has five suggested answers, lettered A to E. Decide which one is the BEST answer. *PRINT THE LETTER OF THE CORRECT ANSWER IN THE SPACE AT THE RIGHT.*

PASSAGE 1

During the past fourteen years, thousands of top-lofty United States elms have been marked for death by the activities of the tiny European elm bark beetle. The beetles, however, do not do fatal damage. Death is caused by another importation, Dutch elm disease, a fungus infection which the beetles carry from tree to tree. Up to 1941, quarantine and tree-sanitation measures kept the beetles and the disease pretty well confined within 510 miles around metropolitan New York. War curtailed these measures and made Dutch elm disease a wider menace. Every household and village that prizes an elm-shaded lawn or commons must now watch for it. Since there is as yet no cure for it, the infected trees must be pruned or felled, and the wood must be burned in order to protect other healthy trees.

1. The title below that BEST expresses the ideas of this paragraph is:
   A. A Menace to Our Elms
   B. Pests and Diseases of the Elm
   C. Our Vanishing Elms
   D. The Need to Protect Dutch Elms
   E. How Elms are Protected

2. The danger of spreading the Dutch elm disease was increased by
   A. destroying infected trees
   B. the war
   C. the lack of a cure
   D. a fungus infection
   E. quarantine measures

3. The European elm bark beetle is a serious threat to our elms because it
   A. chews the bark
   B. kills the trees
   C. is particularly active on the eastern seaboard
   D. carries infection
   E. cannot be controlled

PASSAGE 2

It is elemental that the greater the development of man, the greater the problems he has to concern him. When he lived in a cave with stone implements, his mind no less than his actions was grooved into simple channels. Every new invention, every new way of doing things posed fresh problems for him. And, as he moved along the road, he questioned each step, as indeed he should, for he trod upon the beliefs of his ancestors. It is equally elemental to say that each step upon this later road posed more questions than the earlier ones. It is only the educated man who realizes the results of his actions; it is only the thoughtful one who questions his own decisions.

4. The title below that BEST expresses the ideas of this paragraph is: 4.____
   A. Channels of Civilization
   B. The Mark of a Thoughtful Man
   C. The Cave Man in Contrast with Man Today
   D. The Price of Early Progress
   E. Man's Never-Ending Challenge

PASSAGE 3

Spring is one of those things that man has no hand in, any more than he has a part in sunrise or the phases of the moon. Spring came before man was here to enjoy it, and it will go right on coming even if man isn't here some time in the future. It is a matter of solar mechanics and celestial order. And for all our knowledge of astronomy and terrestrial mechanics, we haven't yet been able to do more than bounce a radar beam off the moon. We couldn't alter the arrival of the spring equinox by as much as one second, if we tried.

Spring is a matter of growth, of chlorophyll, of bud and blossom. We can alter growth and change the time of blossoming in individual plants; but the forests still grow in nature's way, and the grass of the plains hasn't altered its nature in a thousand years. Spring is a magnificent phase of the cycle of nature; but man really hasn't any guiding or controlling hand in it. He is here to enjoy it and benefit by it. And April is a good time to realize it; by May perhaps we will want to take full credit.

5. The title below that BEST expresses the ideas of this passage is: 5.____
   A. The Marvels of the Spring Equinox
   B. Nature's Dependence on Mankind
   C. The Weakness of Man Opposed to Nature
   D. The Glories of the World
   E. Eternal Growth

6. The author of the passage states that 6.____
   A. man has a part in the phases of the moon
   B. April is a time for taking full-credit
   C. April is a good time to enjoy nature
   D. man has a guiding hand in spring
   E. spring will cease to be if civilization ends

PASSAGE 4

The walled medieval town was as characteristic of its period as the cut of a robber baron's beard. It sprang out of the exigencies of war, and it was not without its architectural charm, whatever is hygienic deficiencies may have been. Behind its high, thick walls not only the normal inhabitants but the whole countryside fought and cowered in an hour of need. The capitals of Europe now forsake the city when the sirens scream and death from the sky seems imminent. Will the fear of bombs accelerate the slow decentralization which began with the automobile and the wide distribution of electrical energy and thus reverse the medieval flow to the city?

7. The title below that BEST expresses the ideas in this paragraph is: 7._____
   A. A Changing Function of the Town
   B. The Walled Medieval Town
   C. The Automobile's Influence on City Life
   D. Forsaking the City
   E. Bombs Today and Yesterday

8. Conditions in the Middle Ages made the walled town   8._____
   A. a natural development
   B. the most dangerous of all places
   C. a victim of fires
   D. lacking in architectural charm
   E. healthful

9. Modern conditions may   9._____
   A. make cities larger
   B. make cities more hygienic
   C. protect against floods
   D. cause people to move from population centers
   E. encourage good architecture

PASSAGE 5

The literary history of this nation began when the first settler from abroad of sensitive mind paused in his adventure long enough to feel that he was under a different sky, breathing new air and that a New World was all before him with only his strength and Providence for guides. With him began a new emphasis upon an old theme in literature, the theme of cutting loose and faring forth, renewed, under the powerful influence of a fresh continent for civilized literature, whose other flow has come from a nostalgia for the rich culture of Europe, so much of which was perforce left behind.

10. The title below that BEST expresses the ideas of this paragraph is: 10._____
    A. America's Distinctive Literature   B. Pioneer Authors
    C. The Dead Hand of the Past   D. Europe's Literary Grandchild
    E. America Comes of Age

11. American writers, according to the author, because of their colonial experiences   11._____
    A. were antagonistic to European writers
    B. cut loose from Old World influences
    C. wrote only on New World events and characters
    D. created new literary themes
    E. gave fresh interpretation to an old literary idea

KEY (CORRECT ANSWERS)

1. A
2. B
3. D
4. E
5. C
6. C
7. A
8. A
9. D
10. A
11. E

TEST 6

DIRECTIONS: Each question has five suggested answers, lettered A to E. Decide which one is the BEST answer. *PRINT THE LETTER OF THE CORRECT ANSWER IN THE SPACE AT THE RIGHT.*

1. Any business not provided with capable substitutes to fill all important positions is a weak business. Therefore, a foreman should train each man not on to perform his own particular duties but also to do those of two or three positions.
   The paragraph BEST supports the statement that
   A. dependence on substitutes is a sign of weak organization
   B. training will improve the strongest organization
   C. the foreman should be the most expert at any particular job under him
   D. every employee can be trained to perform efficiency work other than his own
   E. vacancies in vital positions should be provided for in advance

   1.____

2. The coloration of textile fabrics composed of cotton and wool generally requires two processes, as the process used in dyeing wool is seldom capable of fixing the color upon cotton. The usual method is to immerse the fabric in the requisite baths to dye the wool and then to treat the partially dyed material in the manner found suitable for cotton.
   The paragraph BEST supports the statement that the dyeing of textile fabrics composed of cotton and wool is
   A. less complicated than the dyeing of wool alone
   B. more successful when the material contains more cotton than wool
   C. not satisfactory when solid colors are desired
   D. restricted to two colors for any one fabric
   E. usually based upon the methods required for dyeing the different materials

   2.____

3. The serious investigator must direct his whole effort toward success in his work. If he wishes to succeed in each investigation, his work will be by no means easy, smooth, or peaceful; on the contrary, he will have to devote himself completely and continuously to a task that requires all his ability.
   The paragraph BEST supports the statement that an investigator's success depends most upon
   A. ambition to advance rapidly in the service
   B. persistence in the face of difficulty
   C. training and experience
   D. willingness to obey orders without delay
   E. the number of investigations which he conducts

   3.____

4. Honest people in one nation find it difficult to understand the viewpoint of honest people in another. State departments and their ministers exist for the purpose of explaining the viewpoints of one nation in terms understood by another. Some of their most important work lies in this direction.

   4.____

The paragraph BEST supports the statement that
- A. people of different nations may not consider matters in the same light
- B. it is unusual for many people to share similar ideas
- C. suspicion prevents understanding between nations
- D. the chief work of state departments is to guide relations between nations united by a common cause
- E. the people of one nation must sympathize with the viewpoints of others

5. Economy once in a while is just not enough. I expect to find it at every level of responsibility, from cabinet member to the newest and youngest recruit. Controlling waste is something like bailing a boat; you have to keep at it. I have no intention of easing up on my insistence on getting a dollar of value for each dollar we spend.
   The paragraph BEST supports the statement that
   - A. we need not be concerned about items which cost less than a dollar
   - B. it is advisable to buy the cheaper of two items
   - C. the responsibility of economy is greater at high levels than at low levels
   - D. economy becomes easy with practice
   - E. economy is a continuing responsibility

KEY (CORRECT ANSWERS)

1. E
2. E
3. B
4. A
5. E

TEST 7

DIRECTIONS: Each question has five suggested answers, lettered A to E. Decide which one is the BEST answer. *PRINT THE LETTER OF THE CORRECT ANSWER IN THE SPACE AT THE RIGHT.*

1. On all permit imprint mail the charge for postage has been printed by the mailer before he presents it for mailing and pays the postage. Such mail of any class is mailable only at the post office that issued a permit covering it. Since the postage receipts for such mail represent only the amount of permit imprint mail detected and verified, employees in receiving, handling, and outgoing sections must be alert constantly to route such mail to the weighing section before it is handled or dispatched.
The paragraph BEST supports the statement that, at post offices where permit mail is received for dispatch,
    A. dispatching units make a final check on the amount of postage payable on permit imprint mail
    B. employees are to check the postage chargeable on mail received under permit
    C. neither more nor less postage is to be collected than the amount printed on permit imprint mail
    D. the weighing section is primarily responsible for failure to collect postage on such mail
    E. unusual measures are taken to prevent unstamped mail from being accepted

1.____

2. Education should not stop when the individual has been prepared to make a livelihood and to live in modern society. Living would be mere existence were there were no appreciation and enjoyment of the riches of art, literature, and science.
The paragraph BEST supports the statement that true education
    A. is focused on the routine problems of life
    B. prepares one for full enjoyment of life
    C. deals chiefly with art, literature, and science
    D. is not possible for one who does not enjoy scientific literature
    E. disregards practical ends

2.____

3. Insured and c.o.d. air and surface mail is accepted with the understanding that the sender guarantees any necessary forwarding or return postage. When such mail is forwarded or returned, it shall be rated up for collection of postage; except that insured or c.o.d. air mail weighing 8 ounces or less and subject to the 40 cents an ounce rate shall be forwarded by air if delivery will be advanced, and returned by surface means without additional postage.
The paragraph BEST supports the statement that the return postage for undeliverable insured mail is
    A. included in the original prepayment on air mail parcels
    B. computed but not collected before dispatching surface patrol post mail to sender

3.____

233

C. not computed or charged for any air mail that is returned by surface transportation
D. included in the amount collected when the sender mails parcel post
E. collected before dispatching for return if any amount due has been guaranteed

4. All undeliverable first-class mail, except first-class parcels and parcel post paid with first-class postage, which cannot be returned to the sender, is sent to a dead-letter branch. Undeliverable matter of the third- and fourth-classes of obvious value for which the sender does not furnish return postage and undeliverable first-class parcels and parcel-post matter bearing postage of the first-class, which cannot be returned, is sent to a dead parcel-post branch.
The paragraph BEST supports the statement that matter that is sent to a dead parcel-post branch includes all undeliverable 4.____
   A. mail, except for first-class letter mail, that appears to be valuable
   B. mail, except that of the first-class, on which the sender failed to prepay the original mailing costs
   C. parcels on which the mailer prepaid the first-class rate of postage
   D. third- and fourth-class matter on which the required return postage has not been paid
   E. parcels on which first-class postage has been prepaid, when the sender's address is not known

5. Civilization started to move rapidly when man freed himself of the shackles that restricted his search for truth.
The passage BEST supports the statement that the progress of civilization 5.____
   A. came as a result of man's dislike for obstacles
   B. did not begin until restrictions on learning were removed
   C. has been aided by man's efforts to find the truth
   D. is based on continually increasing efforts
   E. continues at a constantly increasing rate

KEY (CORRECT ANSWERS)

1. B
2. B
3. B
4. E

TEST 8

DIRECTIONS: Each question has five suggested answers, lettered A to E. Decide which one is the BEST answer. *PRINT THE LETTER OF THE CORRECT ANSWER IN THE SPACE AT THE RIGHT.*

1. E-mails should be clear, concise, and brief. Omit all unnecessary words. The parts of speech most often used in e-mails are nouns, verbs, adjectives, and adverbs. If possible, do without pronouns, prepositions, articles, and copulative verbs. Use simple sentences, rather than complex and compound.
    The paragraph BEST supports the statement that in writing e-mails one should always use
    A. common and simple words
    B. only nouns, verbs, adjectives, and adverbs
    C. incomplete sentences
    D. only words essential to the meaning
    E. the present tense of verbs

    1.____

2. The function of business is to increase the wealth of the country and the value and happiness of life. It does this by supplying the material needs of men and women. When the nation's business is successfully carried on, it renders public service of the highest value.
    The paragraph BEST supports the statement that
    A. all businesses which render public service are successful
    B. human happiness is enhanced only by the increase of material wants
    C. the value of life is increased only by the increase of wealth
    D. the material needs of men and women are supplied by well-conducted business
    E. business is the only field of activity which increases happiness

    2.____

3. In almost every community, fortunately, there are certain men and women known to be public-spirited. Others, however, may be selfish and act only as their private interests seem to require.
    The paragraph BEST supports the statement that those citizens who disregard others are
    A. fortunate   B. needed
    C. found only in small communities   D. not known
    E. not public spirited

    3.____

KEY (CORRECT ANSWERS)

1. D
2. D
3. E

MATHEMATICS
EXAMINATION SECTION
TEST 1

DIRECTIONS: Each question or incomplete statement is followed by several suggested answers or completions. Select the one that BEST answers the question or completes the statement. *PRINT THE LETTER OF THE CORRECT ANSWER IN THE SPACE AT THE RIGHT.*

Questions 1-60.

DIRECTIONS: For problems 1 through 22, compute an answer for each. For problems 23 through 60, select an answer from among the four choices given.

1. Add: 215
        86
     193

   1.____

2. From 761, subtract 257.

   2.____

3. Multiply: 206
       ×57

   3.____

4. Divide: $25\overline{)4175}$

   4.____

5. Divide: 408 ÷ 4

   5.____

6. Multiply: 1/2 × 3/4

   6.____

7. Add: 3.4 and 1.16

   7.____

8. Find the product of 3.4 and 7.8.

   8.____

9. If 12.36 is divided by 6, what is the quotient?

   9.____

10. What is 2/3 of 300?

   10.____

11. Subtract: 9.67
          4.85

   11.____

12. Divide: 8 ÷ 1/3

   12.____

13. If John spends $6.45, how much change should he receive from a $10 bill?

   13.____

14. What is the average (mean) of 81, 72, and 78?

   14.____

15. How many cubic centimeters are in the volume of a rectangular box 6 cm long, 4 cm wide, and 4 cm high?

15.____

16. What is the perimeter of a rectangle with length 6 and width 2?

16.____

17. A number of test scores are arranged as follows: 58, 65, 65, 75, 85, 85, 99. What is the median score?

17.____

18. Solve for x: $4x + 1 = 17$.

18.____

19. Solve for x: $\frac{6}{10} = \frac{x}{30}$

19.____

20. A team lost 40% of its games. If the team played 30 games, how many games were lost?

20.____

21. On a map, 1 centimeter represents 12 kilometers. How many kilometers does 2 ½ centimeters on the map represent?

21.____

22. What is the area of a square with each side of length 5?

22.____

23. ☐ - 186 = 54

   Which number makes this open sentence TRUE?
   A. 132 B. 238 C. 240 D. 250

23.____

24. The sum of 3/5 and 2/3 is
   A. 5/8 B. 5/15 C. 19/15 D. 6/8

24.____

25. What is he LEAST common denominator of the fractions 1/2, 2/3, and 5/6?
   A. 36 B. 18 C. 12 D. 6

25.____

26. Which of the following has the same value as 17/5?
   A. 12 B. 2 2/5 C. 3 2/5 D. 5 2/3

26.____

27. When written as a percent, the fraction 3/4 is
   A. 25% B. 66 2/3% C. 75% D. 86 1/2%

27.____

28. If 45,534 people were at a football game, what would be the total attendance reported to the nearest thousand?
   A. 40,000 B. 46,000 C. 47,000 D. 50,000

28.____

29. Which number represents seventy thousand eight hundred?
   A. 7,080 B. 70,080 C. 70,800 D. 78,000

29.____

30. When listed in order from smallest to largest, which fraction would be the FIRST?
   A. 1/5 B. 1/2 C. 1/3 D. 1/4

30.____

31. The cost of a telephone call was listed as:
    $1.00 for the first 3 minutes
    $0.30 for each additional minute
    What would be the total cost of a telephone call that was 6 minutes long?
    A. $1.80   B. $1.90   C. $2.00   D. $2.80

31._____

32. If A and B are points on the circle, then AB is a(n)
    AB is a(n)
    A. arc
    B. chord
    C. diameter
    D. radius

32._____

33. In the triangle ABC, what is the ratio of AB to BC?
    A. 5:6
    B. 5:7
    C. 7:5
    D. 6:5

33._____

34. Which number has the GREATEST value?
    A. .0824   B. .1032   C. .125   D. .091

34._____

35. Mr. White had a balance of $325.15 in his checking account. If he made a deposit of $75, what would be the amount of the new balance in his checking account?
    A. $250.15   B. $324.40   C. $325.90   D. $400.15

35._____

36. The sum of -11 and -8 is
    A. -19   B. -3   C. 3   D. 19

36._____

37. One day in March the highest temperature was 8 degrees C and the lowest was -3 degrees C.
    What was the total number of degree difference between the highest and lowest temperatures that day?
    A. 8   B. 11   C. 3   D. 5

37._____

38. The expression 10^3 is equal to
    A. -0   B. 300   C. 1,000   D. 10,000

38._____

39. On the accompanying graph, point A has coordinates
    A. (0,3)
    B. (1,3)
    C. (3,0)
    D. (3,1)

39._____

40. The circle graph to the right shows how each tax dollar is spent in Salt Lake City.
    What is the LARGEST part of the tax dollar spent for?
    A. Repairs
    B. Salaries
    C. Education
    D. Parks

    40.____

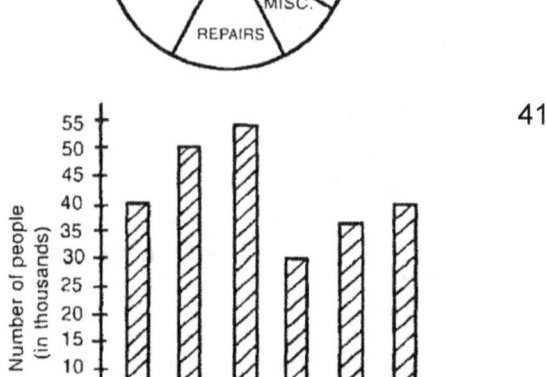

41. The graph to the right shows the number of people attending each game of the World Series one year.
    On which day did the FEWEST number of people attend a World Series game?
    A. Friday
    B. Monday
    C. Tuesday
    D. Thursday

    41.____

42. The graph to the right represents the relationship between distance traveled and flying time for a certain airplane.
    How many hours of flying time did the airplane require to travel 450 miles?
    A. 2 1/2
    B. 2
    C. 3
    D. 3 1/2

    42.____

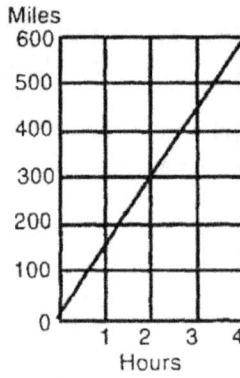

43. Which is the prime number?
    A. 21   B. 99   C. 101   D. 125

    43.____

44. Mr. Ford bought a t-shirt for $15.00 and had to pay a 7% sales tax.
    If he gave the clerk $20, what should his change be?
    A. $1.05   B. $3.95   C. $4.95   D. $16.05

    44.____

45. Of carpeting costs $9.50 a square meter, what is the total cost of carpeting an entire room floor which is 3 meters by 4 meters?
    A. $133   B. $114   C. $85.50   D. $66.50

    45.____

46. Ruby buys a television set with a $25 downpayment and 6 installment payments of $20.
    The total cost of the television set is
    A. $95   B. $120   C. $145   D. $150

    46.____

5 (#1)

47. Carver High School has an enrollment of 50 freshmen, 40 sophomores, 60 juniors, and 30 seniors.
What is the ratio of the number of jurors to the total enrollment?
A. 1:6　　　　B. 1:4　　　　C. 2:3　　　　D. 1:3

47._____

48. The area pf a circle with a radius of 5 centimeters is
A. 10π cm²　　B. 20π cm²　　C. 25π cm²　　D. 100π cm²

48._____

49. The circumference of a circle with a radius of 4 is
A. 2π　　　　B. 4π　　　　C. 8π　　　　D. 16π

49._____

50. Which of the following is a picture of a cylinder?
A.　　　　B.　　　　C.　　　　D.

50._____

51. A nail is placed against a ruler as shown in the above drawing.
How many centimeters long is the nail?
A. 7.0　　　　B. 6.5　　　　C. 6.0　　　　D. 5.5

51._____

52. Each race began at 11:00 A.M. The winner ran the course in 2 hours and 19 minutes.
At what time did the winner cross the finish line?
A. 8:41 A.M.　　B. 12:19 P.M.　　C. 1:19 P.M.　　D. 2:19 P.M.

52._____

53. Each house above represents 10,000 homes.
What is the total number of homes represented by the figures?
A. 40,500　　　B. 45,000　　　C. 405,000　　　D. 450,000

53._____

54. A radio is sold in a store for $54.50. The same radio can be ordered through the mail for $24.50 plus $1.50 for postage.
How much would be saved by buying the radio through the mail?
A. $28.50　　　B. $30.00　　　C. $30.50　　　D. $53.00

54._____

55. A stereo which usually sells for $450 is on sale for 1/3 off. 55.____
    What is the sale price?

56. Mary has a board 12 1/2 inches long. 56.____
    If she cuts 1 1/4 inches off the board, how long will the board be?
       A. 10 1/4 inches   B. 11 inches   C. 11 1/4 inches   D. 11 1/2 inches

57. If 3 cases of canned fruit cost $27, then 1 of these cases would cost 57.____
       A. $81   B. $18   C. $3   D. $9

58. Carlo earns $18 per hour at a part-time job. 58.____
    How much does he earn in a day when he works 5 1/2 hours?
       A. $90   B. $99   C. $108   D. $112.50

59. How many kilometers are there in the 10,000 meter run? 59.____
       A. 1   B. 2   C. 10   D. 100

60. What is the probability of obtaining a head when a coin is tossed? 60.____
       A. 1   B. 1/2   C. 1/3   D. 1/4

KEY (CORRECT ANSWERS)

1.	494	11.	4.82	21.	30	31.	B	41.	C	51.	B
2.	504	12.	24	22.	25	32.	B	42.	C	52.	C
3.	11,742	13.	$3.55	23.	C	33.	B	43.	C	53.	B
4.	167	14.	77	24.	C	34.	C	44.	B	54.	A
5.	102	15.	96	25.	D	35.	D	45.	B	55.	C
6.	3/8	16.	16	26.	C	36.	A	46.	C	56.	C
7.	4.56	17.	75	27.	C	37.	B	47.	D	57.	D
8.	26.52	18.	4	28.	C	38.	C	48.	C	58.	B
9.	2.06	19.	18	29.	C	39.	B	49.	C	59.	C
10.	20	20.	12	30.	A	40.	C	50.	A	60.	B

SOLUTIONS TO PROBLEMS

1. $215 + 86 + 193 = 494$

2. $761 - 257 = 504$

3. $(206)(57) = 11{,}742$

4. $4175 \div 25 = 167$

5. $408 \div 4 = 102$

6. $(\frac{1}{2})(\frac{3}{4}) = \frac{3}{8}$

7. $3.40 + 1.16 = 4.56$

8. $(3.4)(7.8) = 26.52$

9. $12.36 \div 6 = 2.06$

10. $\frac{2}{3}(30) = 20$

11. $9.67 - 4.85 = 4.82$

12. $8 \div \frac{1}{3} = (8)(\frac{3}{1}) = 24$

13. $\$10 - \$6.45 = \$3.55$

14. $(81+72+78) \div 3 = 77$

15. Volume = $(6)(4)(4) = 96$ cubic cen.

16. Perimeter = $(2)(6+2) = 16$

17. Median = $(7+1)/2 = 4^{th}$ score = 75

18. If $4x + 1 = 17$, then $4x = 16$. Solving, $x = 4$

19. If $\frac{6}{10} = \frac{x}{30}$, then $10x = 180$. Solving, $x = 18$

20. $(.40)(30) = 12$ games lost

21. $(2\frac{1}{2})(12) = 30$ kilometers

22. Area = $5^2 = 25$

8 (#1)

23. Missing number = 54 + 186 = 240

24. $\frac{3}{5} + \frac{2}{3} = \frac{9}{15} + \frac{10}{15} = \frac{19}{15}$

25. Least common denominator of $\frac{1}{2}$, $\frac{2}{3}$, and $\frac{5}{6}$ is 6.

26. $\frac{17}{5} = 3\frac{2}{5}$

27. $\frac{3}{4} = (\frac{3}{4})(100)\% = 75\%$

28. 46,534 is 47,000 to the nearest thousand

29. Seventy thousand eight hundred = 70,800

30. $\frac{1}{5}$ is smaller than $\frac{1}{2}$, $\frac{1}{3}$, and $\frac{1}{4}$

31. Total cost = $1.00 + (3)(.30) = $1.90

32. AB is a chord since it joins 2 points on the circle but does not pass through the center.

33. AB:BC = 5:7

34. .125 is larger than .0824, .1032, and .091

35. New balance = $325.15 + $75 = $400.15

36. (-11) + (-8) = -19

37. 8 – (-3) = 11 degrees difference

38. 10^3 = (10)(10)(10) = 1000

39. Point A has coordinates (1,3)

40. Education represents the largest section.

41. On Tuesday, about 30,000 people attended the World Series. This was the lowest attendance figure in the chart.

42. On the graph, 450 miles corresponds to 3 hours.

43. 101 is prime since it can only be divided evenly by itself and 1.

44. $15 + (.07)($15) = $16.05. Then, $20 - $16.05 = $3.95

9 (#1)

45. Total cost = ($9.50)(3)(4) = $114.00

46. Total cost = $25 + (6)($20) = $145

47. Juniors: total enrollment = 60:180 = $\frac{1}{3}$

48. Area = $(\pi)(5cm)^2 = 25\pi$ cm^2

49. Circumference = $(2\pi)(4) = 8\pi$

50. Selection A represents a cylinder. (The other 3 selections are cube, cone, triangular prism.)

51. Length of nail = 6.5 cm

52. 11:00 A.M. + 2 hrs. 19 min. = 1:19 P.M.

53. (10,000)(4.5) = 45,000

54. Amount saved = $54.50 - $24.50 - $1.50 = $28.50

55. Sale price = $450 − $(\frac{1}{3})$($450) = $300

56. $12\frac{1}{2}$" - $1\frac{1}{4}$" = $11\frac{1}{4}$ inches

57. 1 case costs $27 ÷ 3 = $9

58. ($18)(5 ½) = $99

59. Since 1 km = 1000m, 10 kilometers = 10,000 meters

60. In tossing a coin, the probability of getting a head = $\frac{1}{2}$

BASIC MATHEMATICS
EXAMINATION SECTION
TEST 1

DIRECTIONS: Each question or incomplete statement is followed by several suggested answers or completions. Select the one that BEST answers the question or completes the statement. *PRINT THE LETTER OF THE CORRECT ANSWER IN THE SPACE AT THE RIGHT.*

1. Add: 5,796 + 6 + 243 + 24   1.____
   A. 6,069   B. 6,079   C. 6,169   D. 6,179

2. Subtract: 8,007 - 6,898   2.____
   A. 1,109   B. 1,119   C. 1,209   D. 2,109

3. Multiply: 3,876 x 904   3.____
   A. 364,344   B. 3,493,904
   C. 3,494,904   D. 3,503,904

4. Divide: $76\overline{)58,976}$ 4.____
   A. 775   B. 776   C. 786   D. 876

5. Combine: (+4) + (-3) - (-7)   5.____
   A. -6   B. +6   C. +8   D. +14

6. Simplify: [(-8) x (-6)] ÷ (-3)   6.____
   A. -16   B. -14   C. +14   D. +16

7. Add: 1 3/5 + 3 7/8   7.____
   A. 4 10/40   B. 4 10/13   C. 4 19/40   D. 5 19/40

8. Subtract: 4 3/8 - 2 2/3   8.____
   A. 1 17/24   B. 2 1/24   C. 2 1/5   D. 2 17/24

9. Multiply: 3 2/3 x 5 1/2   9.____
   A. 15 1/3   B. 16 1/3   C. 20 1/6   D. 21 1/6

10. Divide: $7\frac{1}{2} \div 2\frac{1}{4}$ 10.____
    A. 3/10   B. 3 1/3   C. 3 1/2   D. 16 7/8

11. Add: 434.7 + .04 + 7.107   11.____
    A. .441847   B. .442207   C. 441.847   D. 442.207

247

12. Subtract: 986.4 - 34.87

    A. 6.377   B. 63.77   C. 951.53   D. 9,515.3

12.____

13. Multiply: 5.96 × 87.4

    A. 51.0904   B. 52.0904   C. 510.904   D. 520.904

13.____

14. Divide: $.034\overline{)6.698}$

    A. 19.2   B. 19.7   C. 192   D. 197

14.____

15. Add: $.7 + \frac{1}{2}$

    A. .12   B. 1.2   C. 7/2   D. 15/2

15.____

16. What is 5.5% of 75?

    A. 4.125   B. 13.65   C. 41.25   D. 412.5

16.____

17. 12 is what percent of 6?

    A. $\frac{1}{2}$%   B. 5%   C. 50%   D. 200%

17.____

18. 14 is 28% of _____.

    A. 2   B. 5   C. 50   D. 500

18.____

19. A record player sells for $92.00. It is discounted 15% for a special sale. What is the sale price?

    A. $13.80   B. $68.20   C. $77.00   D. $78.20

19.____

20.

Table A - Acme Mortgage Company
$320 Loan - 3/4 of 1% Interest

Month	Payment	Principal Paid/Month	Interest Paid/Month
1	$ 27.98	$ 25.58	$ 2.40
2	27.98	25.77	2.21
3	27.98	25.96	2.02
4	27.98	26.15	1.83
5	27.98	26.35	1.63
6	27.98	26.55	1.43
7	27.98	26.75	1.23
8	27.98	26.95	1.03
9	27.98	27.15	.83
10	27.98	27.35	.63
11	27.98	27.56	.42
12	27.93	27.77	.16
Total	$335.82	$ 320.00	$ 15.82

20.____

Acme Mortgage Company charges 3/4 of 1% (.0075) on the unpaid balance per month. Bowman Mortgage Company charges 9% per year on the total loan. Which company charges the LEAST amount of interest on a $320 loan held for one year?

    A. Acme charges the least amount.
    B. Bowman charges the least amount.
    C. Acme and Bowman charge the same.
    D. Insufficient information to determine.

21. Percent of Auto Insurance Discounts for High School Students with Certain Grade Point Averages

Policy Coverage	Grade Point Averages Percent of Discount		
	A	B	C
Liability	33 1/3%	33 1/3%	10%
Comprehensive	20%	10%	-
Collision	25%	20%	-

Frank Verna has a B average. The regular 6-month amounts to be paid for insurance before discount follow:

    Liability $18.00
    Comprehensive $20.00
    Collision $60.00
    Total $98.00

How much does Frank pay for insurance for 6 months?

    A. $20.00   B. $58.00   C. $78.00   D. $156.00

22. Mr. Martinez had a fire in his home. Repairing the damage will cost about $900. His home is valued at $14,000 and is insured for $12,000. Mr. Martinez had paid $32.00 a year for ten years for his insurance. The insurance company has agreed to pay the full amount of the claim ($900).
Which of the following statements are TRUE?
    I. The amount of the claim is more than what has been paid to the company.
    II. The insurance company should pay $14,000 for this claim.
    III. If the house had been completely burned, the insurance company would pay $14,000.
    IV. The maximum claim Mr. Martinez could collect is $12,000
The CORRECT answer is:

    A. I, II   B. I, III   C. II, III   D. I, IV

23. When two coins are tossed, what is the chance that both will be heads? 1 in

    A. 1   B. 2   C. 3   D. 4

24. If 4 teams are in a football league, how many games are necessary to allow each team to play every team one time? _____ games.

    A. 6   B. 9   C. 12   D. 16

25. Five people donated money to the Red Cross. The donations were: $52.00, $76.00, $18.00, $94.00, and $120.00.
    What was the AVERAGE donation?

    A. $70   B. $72   C. $76   D. $360

26. From the following statements, determine the CORRECT conclusion.
    I. If Lauraine is a red-head, then Lauraine is hot-tempered.
    II. Lauraine is not hot-tempered.
    The CORRECT answer is:

    A. Lauraine is a red-head.
    B. Lauraine is not a red-head.
    C. Lauraine could be a red-head.
    D. All red-heads are hot-tempered.

27. The graph represents the way the Jones family spends its money (budget). What is the monthly income if they are spending $4080 per year for food?
    A. $1,020
    B. $1,360
    C. $4,080
    D. $16,320

    (Pie chart: Rent $\frac{1}{4}$, Food $\frac{1}{4}$, Furniture $\frac{1}{16}$, Medical $\frac{1}{16}$, Car $\frac{1}{16}$, Saving $\frac{1}{8}$, Clothing $\frac{3}{16}$)

28.
	S	M	T	W	T	F	S
Charlie Simms	?	8	8	8	8	8	3
Jim Chow	2	9	8	8	9	9	4

    Time and one-half is paid on Saturdays and for hours worked beyond 8 hours each day. Double-time is paid for Sunday work.
    Mr. Simms would have to work how many hours on Sunday to earn as much as Mr. Chow?

    Regular time - $2.00/hour
    Time and one-half - $3.00/hour
    Double time - $4.00/hour

    _____ hours.

    A. 2   B. 5   C. 6   D. 20

29. Jane Gunther wrote checks for these items:
    $16.95 for a hair dryer
    $125.50 for a car payment
    $33.68 for television repair
    $21.59 for a dress
    Jane had a beginning check balance (before she wrote the checks) of $351.76. She also deposited $41.50 into her account.
    After the checks were written and the deposit made, what was her new balance?

    A. $154.04   B. $195.54   C. $196.54   D. $239.22

30. Given the formula I = PRT:
    If I = 24, R = .05, T = 3, find P.

    A. .00625   B. 1.6   C. 3.6   D. 160.0

31. Fencing is needed to enclose a piece of land 26 meters on a side.
    How much fencing is needed?
    _____ meters.
    A. 52
    B. 98
    C. 104
    D. 676

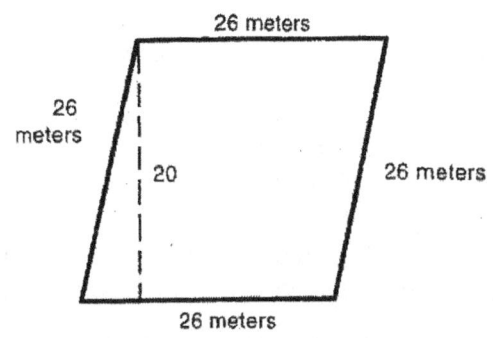

32. The area of figure A is 12 square units, and the area of B is 18 square units.
    What is the area of figure C?
    _____ square units.
    A. 16
    B. 16 1/2
    C. 17
    D. 17 1/2

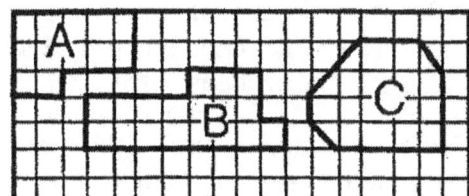

33. Using a 3 gallon spray can with a mixture rate of 1 teaspoon of insecticide per quart of water and an application rate of 1 gallon of mixture per 100 square feet, how much water and how much insecticide will be needed to spray an 85 feet by 10 feet lawn?
    _____ teaspoons of insecticide and _____ gallons of water.

    A. 34; 8 1/2   B. 34; 11   C. 17; 8 1/2   D. 24; 6

34. Bill Mata will carpet his living room which has the following dimensions. If Bill pays $6.00 per square yard for the carpet, how much will it cost to carpet his living room?
    (9 square feet = 1 square yard)
    A. $192
    B. $216
    C. $1,728
    D. $1,944

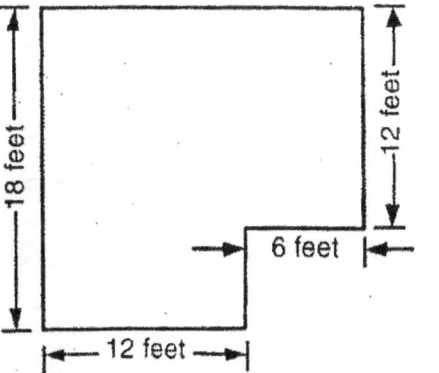

35. A cube is painted red and then divided into 27 smaller cubes.
    How many of the smaller cubes are painted on one side only?
    A. 4
    B. 6
    C. 8
    D. 10

36. John and Frank wish to pour a cement walk 108 feet long, 4 feet wide, and 3 inches deep.
   If ready-mix concrete can be delivered on weekdays for $19.50 a cubic yard and on weekends for $22.50 a cubic yard, how much would they save on the complete job if they decide on Thursday rather than on the weekend? (1 cubic yard = 27 cubic feet)

   A. $3.00   B. $12.00   C. $36.00   D. $78.00

37. Antifreeze may be purchased in different size containers for different prices:
   8 oz. can - 43¢
   10 oz. can - 51¢
   12 oz. can - 62¢
   If exactly 15 pints of antifreeze are needed, how many cans of each size are needed for the cost to be minimum? (16 oz. = 1 pint)

   A. 12 - 10 oz. cans and 10 - 12 oz. cans
   B. 24 - 10 oz. cans
   C. 18 - 12 oz. cans and 3-8 oz. cans
   D. 20 - 12 oz. cans

38. From the graph, assuming the growth rate in the senior class is constant, how many students will be seniors in 2006?

   A. 225
   B. 250
   C. 300
   D. 375

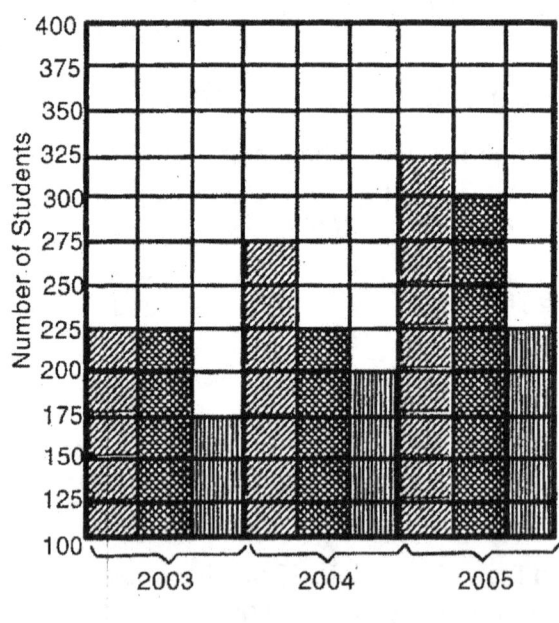

39.

Population in U.S. 1880-1980

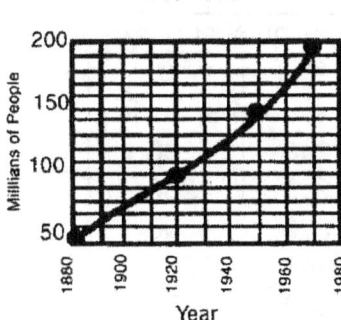

Percentage of the U.S. Population Over 65

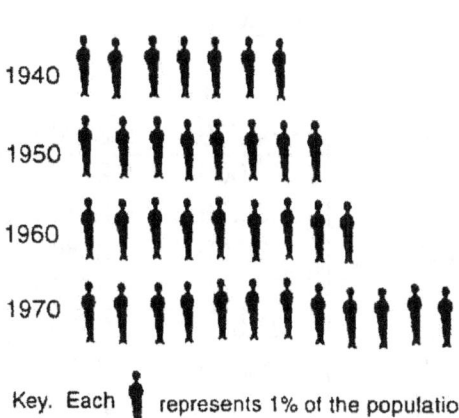

Key. Each ♂ represents 1% of the population

In looking at the two graphs, which of the following conclusions are TRUE?
  I. Both graphs show population growth.
  II. Both graphs cover exactly the same time period.
  III. The percentage of *over 65* population remains the same over the 1940 to 1970 period.
  IV. If you were in the retail business, you might expect greater sales to the *over 65* population in 1970 than in 1940.
  V. In the general population of about 200 million people in 1970, 24 million were over 65.
  VI. In 1920, there were only about 7 million people *over 65* out of about 100 million people.

The CORRECT answer is:

A. I, III, IV
C. II, III, VI
B. II, IV, V
D. I, IV, V

40. Jerry Martin owns a home with a market value of $180,000. Its assessed value is 25% of the market value. The tax rate is $5.00 per $100 of assessed value.
What is the amount of his tax?

A. $225.00   B. $2,250.00   C. $4,500.00   D. $6,750.00

41. You are governor of the state and you need an additional 500 million dollars in tax money. To raise the money, an increase in sales tax is required.
What information would be MOST helpful in determining the new tax rate?
  I. Average income per person in the state
  II. Number of people out of work
  III. Population of the state over 18 years of age
  IV. Birth rate in the state
  V. Percent of income spent on taxable goods
  VI. Percent of income spent on non-taxable goods
  VII. Number of people filing income tax returns

The CORRECT answer is:

A. I, IV, VI
C. V, VI
B. II, III, VII
D. I, V

42. Income Tax Table

If adjusted gross income is-		And the number of exemptions is -					
		1	2	3	4	5	6
At least	But less than	Your tax is -					
$24,500	$24,750	$2360	$1240	$230	$0	$0	$0
24,750	25,000	2400	1280	260	0	0	0
25,000	25,250	2440	1320	300	0	0	0
25,250	25,500	2480	1360	330	0	0	0
25,500	25,750	2530	1390	370	0	0	0
25,750	26,000	2570	1430	400	0	0	0
26,000	26,250	2610	1470	440	0	0	0
26,250	26,500	2650	1510	470	0	0	0
26,500	26,750	2700	1550	510	0	0	0
26,750	27,000	2740	1590	540	0	0	0
27,000	27,250	2780	1630	580	0	0	0
27,250	27,500	2820	1670	610	0	0	0
27,500	27,750	2870	1710	650	0	0	0
27,750	28,000	2910	1750	680	0	0	0
28,000	28,250	2950	1790	720	0	0	0
28,250	28,500	2990	1830	760	0	0	0
28,500	28,750	3040	1870	790	0	0	0

Jerry Ladd earned $28,390.00 during the year. To find his adjusted gross income, he must reduce the amount earned by the standard 10% deduction. He had only one exemption, himself.
How much tax did Jerry pay?

A. $1390   B. $1830   C. $2530   D. $2990

43.

Weight in Ounces	2 oz.	4 oz.	12 oz.	21 oz.
Price	5¢	7¢	15¢	24¢

Using the above table, predict the price if the weight is 32 ounces.

A. 27¢   B. 28¢   C. 29¢   D. 35¢

44. Given [(0,2), (1,4), (2,6),...(5,y)].
What is the value of y?

A. 8   B. 10   C. 12   D. 14

45. If the larger of two numbers is two and one-half times the smaller number, what fraction is the smaller of the larger?

A. 3/4   B. 4/5   C. 5/8   D. 2/5

46. John can save 75¢ a week. He has $3.75 in the bank now. How many weeks will it take him to have a total deposit of $12?

A. 16   B. 9   C. 11   D. 17

47. Using the approximation of 3.14 for pi, find the area of a circle whose diameter is 20 inches.
    _____ square inches.

    A. 31.4   B. 314   C. 628   D. 1256

    47.____

48. Express .045 as a percent.

    A. 45%   B. 4.5%   C. .45%   D. .045%

    48.____

49. Twenty is what percent of 50?

    A. 40   B. 60   C. 25   D. 16 2/3

    49.____

50. Two hundred twenty-five percent of 160 is

    A. 80   B. 350   C. 360   D. 440

    50.____

KEY (CORRECT ANSWERS)

1. A	11. C	21. C	31. C	41. C
2. A	12. C	22. D	32. C	42. C
3. D	13. D	23. D	33. A	43. D
4. B	14. D	24. A	34. A	44. C
5. C	15. B	25. B	35. B	45. D
6. A	16. A	26. B	36. B	46. C
7. D	17. D	27. D	37. B	47. B
8. A	18. C	28. B	38. B	48. B
9. C	19. D	29. B	39. D	49. A
10. B	20. A	30. D	40. B	50. C

SOLUTIONS TO PROBLEMS

1. $5796 + 6 + 243 + 24 = 6069$

2. $8007 - 6898 = 1109$

3. $(3876)(904) = 3,503,904$

4. $58,976 \div 76 = 776$

5. $(+4) + (-3) - (-7) = 4 - 3 + 7 = +8$

6. $[(-8)(-6)] \div -3 = 48 \div -3 = -16$

7. $1\frac{3}{5} + 3\frac{7}{8} = 1\frac{24}{40} + 3\frac{35}{40} = 4\frac{59}{40} = 5\frac{19}{40}$

8. $4\frac{3}{8} - 2\frac{2}{3} = 4\frac{9}{24} - 2\frac{16}{24} = 3\frac{33}{24} - 2\frac{16}{24} = 1\frac{17}{24}$

9. $(3\frac{2}{3})(5\frac{1}{2}) = (\frac{11}{3})(\frac{11}{2}) = \frac{121}{6} = 20\frac{1}{6}$

10. $7\frac{1}{2} \div 2\frac{1}{4} = \frac{15}{2} \div \frac{9}{4} = (\frac{15}{2})(\frac{4}{9}) = \frac{60}{18} = 3\frac{1}{3}$

11. $434.7 + .04 + 7.107 = 441.847$

12. $986.4 - 34.87 = 951.53$

13. $(5.96)(87.4) = 520.904$

14. $6.698 \div .034 = 197$

15. $.7 + \frac{1}{2} = .7 + .5 = 1.2$

16. $(.055)(75) = 4.125$

17. $\frac{12}{6} = 2 = 200\%$

18. $14 \div .28 = 50$

19. $\$92 - (.15)(\$92) = \$78.20$

20. Acme's interest charge = $15.82, whereas Bowman's interest charge = $(.09)(\$320)$ = $28.80. Thus, Acme charges less.

11 (#1)

21. $(\$18.00)(66\frac{2}{3}\%) + (\$20.00)(90\%) + (\$60.00)(80\%) = \$78.00$

22. Statements I and IV are correct. For 10 years, he has paid $320, but collected $900 on his claim. Also, since the insured value of the home is $12,000, he could not collect more than that amount on any claim.

23. Probability of 2 heads = (1/2) (1/2) = 1/4, which means 1 in 4.

24. The number of required games = (4)(3) ÷ 2 = 6

25. Average donation = ($52.00 + $76.00 + $18.00 + $94.00 + $120.00) ÷ 5 = $72

26. The correct conclusion is B: Lauraine is not a redhead. Let p = Lauraine is a redhead, q = Lauraine is hot-tempered. The given statement says: *If p, then q.* The contrapositive, which is also true, says, *If not q, then not p.* This corresponds to statement B.

27. Let x = monthly income. Then, $4080 = Solving, x = $16,320.

28. Mr. Chow's earnings = (2)($4) + (40)($2) + (7)($3) = $109.
For Monday through Saturday, Mr. Simms' earnings =
(40)($2) + (3)($3) = $89. Thus, Mr. Simms would need to earn
109 - 89 = $20 on Sunday. This means Sunday's time =
$20 ÷ $4 = 5 hours.

29. New balance = $351.76 + $41.50 - $16.95 - $125.50 - $33.68 - $21.59 = $195.54.

30. 24 = (P)(.05)(3), 24 = .15P, so P = 160

31. Fencing: (26)(4) = 104 meters.

32. Area of $C = (4)(5) - (\frac{1}{2})(1)(1) - (\frac{1}{2})(2)(2) - (\frac{1}{2})(1)(1) = 17$

33. (85)(10) = 850 sq.ft. = 8.5 gallons of water. Now, 8.5 gallons = 34 quarts, so 34 teaspoons of insecticide are needed.

34. Area = (12)(6) + (12)(18) = 288 sq.ft. = 32 sq.yds. Total cost = (32)($6) = $192

35. There are 6 cubes painted red on only one side. They are found in the center of each face of the original cube.

36. $(108)(4)(\frac{1}{4}) = 108$ cu.ft. = 4 cu.yds. Savings would be ($22.50)(4) - ($19.50)(4) = $12.00

37. 15 pints = 240 oz. The costs for each selection are:
For A: (12)(.51) + (10)(.62) = $12.32; for B: (24)(.51) = $12.24; for
C: (18)(.62) + (3)(.43) = $12.45; for D: (20)(.62) = $12.40.
So, selection B is the minimum cost.

38. The number of seniors in 2003, 2004, 2005 are 175, 200, and 225, respectively. If growth is constant, the number of seniors in 2006 is 250.

39. Statements I, IV, V are correct. Statement II is wrong because the 1st graph covers 1800-1970, whereas the 2nd graph covers 1940-1970. Statement III is wrong because the *over 65* population increases in percent from 7% in 1940 to 12% in 1970.

40. (25%)($180,000) = $45,000 assessed value. Amount of tax = ($5.00)($45,000 ÷ $100) = $2,250

41. For increasing sales tax, it would be helpful in knowing the respective percent of incor spent on taxable vs. non-taxable goods.

42. Adjusted gross income = ($28390)(.90) = $25551.00. On the tax chart, this figure lies between $25500 and $25750. Using the column for 1 exemption, the tax is $2530.

43. Using 2 oz. = .05, note that each additional oz. = 1 cent more. So, 32 oz. = .05 + .30 = .35.

44. (5,y) represents the sixth point in this sequence. Thus, the corresponding y value = (2)(6) = 12

45. Let x = smaller number, 2.5x = larger number.

    Then, $\dfrac{x}{2.5x} = \dfrac{1}{2.5} = \dfrac{10}{25} = \dfrac{2}{5}$

46. $12 - $3.75 = $8.25. Then, $8.25 ÷ .75 = 11 weeks

47. Radius = 10 in. Area = (3.14)(10^2) = 314 sq.in.

48. .045 = 4.5%

49. $\dfrac{20}{50} = 40\%$

50. (225%)(160) = (2.25)(160) = 360

BASIC MATHEMATICS
EXAMINATION SECTION
TEST 1

DIRECTIONS: Each question or incomplete statement is followed by several suggested answers or completions. Select the one that BEST answers the question or completes the statement. *PRINT THE LETTER OF THE CORRECT ANSWER IN THE SPACE AT THE RIGHT.*

1. 534
   18
   +1291

    A. 1733　B. 1743　C. 1833　D. 1843　E. 1853

    1.____

2. (17×23) − 16 + 20 =
    A. 459　B. 427　C. 411　D. 395　E. 355

    2.____

3. 3/7 + 5/11 =
    A. 33/35　B. 4/9　C. 8/18　D. 68/77　E. 15/77

    3.____

4. 4832 ÷ 6 =
    A. 905 1/3　B. 805 1/3　C. 95 1/3　D. 95　E. 85 1/3

    4.____

5. 62.3 − 4.9 =
    A. 5.74　B. 7.4　C. 57.4　D. 58.4　E. 67.4

    5.____

6. 3/5 × 4/9 =
    A. 4/15　B. 7/45　C. 27/20　D. 12/14　E. 15/4

    6.____

7. 14/16 − 5/16 =
    A. 8/16　B. 9/16　C. 11/16　D. 8　E. 9

    7.____

8. 5.03 + 2.7 + 40 =
    A. .570　B. 4.773　C. 5.70　D. 11.73　E. 47.73

    8.____

9. 5.37 × 21.4 =
    A. 11491.8　　B. 1149.18　　C. 114.918
    D. 11,4918　　E. 1.14918

    9.____

10. 5 1/4 + 2 7/8 =
    A. 8 1/4　B. 8 1/8　C. 7 2/3　D. 7 1/4　E. 7 1/8

    10.____

11. −14 + 5 =
    A. −19　B. −9　C. 9　D. 19　E. 70

    11.____

12. 2/7 of 28 =
    A. 98   B. 16   C. 14   D. 8   E. 4

13. 2/5 =
    A. .10   B. .20   C. .25   D. .40   E. .52

14. 20% of _____ is 38.
    A. 7.6   B. 19   C. 76   D. 190   E. 760

15. $\frac{8.4}{400}$ =
    A. .0021   B. .021   C. .21   D. 2.1   E. 21

16. $\frac{4}{5} = \frac{?}{60}$
    A. 240   B. 48   C. 20   D. 15   E. 12

17. What is the area of the rectangle shown at the right?
    A. 47 mm²
    B. 94 mm²
    C. 240 mm²
    D. 480 mm²
    E. 960 mm²

18. What number does ☐ represent in the following equation: 25 - ☐ - ☐ - ☐ - ☐ = 13?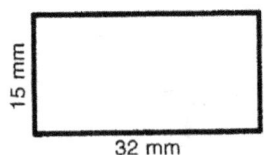
    A. 13   B. 12   C. 7   D. 4   E. 3

19. Approximate lengths are given in the right triangles shown at the right. What does length x equal?
    A. 48
    B. 39
    C. 37
    D. 35
    E. 32

    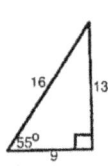 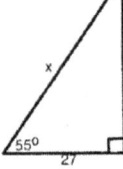

20. What is the perimeter of the triangle shown at the right?
    A. 10 × 15 × 17
    B. 10 + 15 + 17
    C. 1/2 × 10 × 15
    D. 1/2 × 10 × 17
    E. 1/2(10+15+17)

    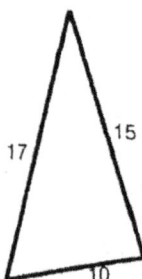

21. Which of the following expressions will give the same answer as 45 × 9?
    A. 5 × 3³   B. (4×9)+(5×9)   C. (40+9) × 5
    D. (45×3) + (45×3)   E. (45×10) − (45×1)

22. Find the average of 19, 21, 21, 22, and 27. 22.____
    A. 23 B. 22 C. 21 D. 20 E. 19

23. In the triangle at the right, how many degrees is <T? 23.____
    A. 75°
    B. 85°
    C. 95°
    D. 114°
    E. 180°

24. 24.____

    About how long is the paper clip?
    A. 5 cm B. 4 cm C. 3 cm D. 2 cm E. 1 cm

25. Five stores sell the same size cans of tomato soup. Their prices are listed below. 25.____
    Which sells the soup for the LOWEST price per can? _____ cans for _____.
    A. 6; 99¢ B. 6; 90¢ C. 5; 93¢ D. 3; 56¢ E. 3; 50¢

26. Rock star Peter Giles receives $1.97 royalty on each of his albums that is sold. 14,127 albums are sold. 26.____
    Estimate how much Peter Giles will receive.
    A. $7,000 B. $14,000 C. $20,000 D. $26,000 E. $28,000

27. An amplifier is advertised for 20% off the list price of $430. 27.____
    What is the sale price?
    A. $516 B. $454 C. $354 D. $344 E. $215

28. If 9 dozen eggs cost $3.60, what do 25 dozen eggs cost? 28.____
    A. $90.00 B. $10.00 C. $9.00 D. $2.54 E. $40

29. The distance between New York State and San Antonio is 1,860 miles. If a jet averages 465 miles per hour, how many hours will it take to travel the distance? 29.____
    A. 9 B. 5 C. 4 D. 3 E. 2

30. In a high school homeroom of 32 students, 24 are girls. 30.____
    What percent are girls?
    A. 3/4% B. 24% C. 25% D. 75% E. 80%

31. Which problem could give the answer shown on the calculator?
    A. 2 + .3
    B. 2 × 3/10
    C. 2 × 1/3
    D. 33333 + .2
    E. 7 ÷ 3

32. Cost of Eating at Home
    (One Week)

Age	Male	Female
6-11 yrs.	$14	$14
12-19 yrs.	$19	$15
20-54 yrs.	$20	$16
55 and Up	$14	$14

    According to the above table, how much will it cost in a typical week for the 3 members of the Wright family to eat at home? Mr. Wright is 56 years old; Mrs. Wright, 52; and their son, Harry, 17.
    A. $125   B. $52   C. $49   D. $42   E. $40

33. According to the above table shown in Question 32, how much does it cost in a typical four-week month to feed a 12-year-old girl?
    A. $4   B. $16   C. $48   D. $64   E. $78

34. Reverend Whilhite jogs for 1½ hours each day, 6 days a week. If he burns 800 calories per hour of jogging, how many calories does he burn in a week?
    A. 4800   B. 5600   C. 7200   D. 8400   E. 9000

35. Ground meat costs 90¢ per pound.
    How much does the meat on the scale cost?
    A. $1.80
    B. $1.60
    C. $1.54
    D. $1.44
    E. $.90

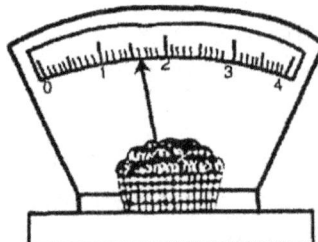

36. According to the graph at the right, about when did the weekly wages for a minimum wage worker go over $100?
    A. 2005
    B. 2010
    C. 2014
    D. 2019
    E. 2020

Weekly wages For a Minimum-Wage Employee

36._____

37. According to the bar graph at the right, what is the approximate height of the Crystal Beach Comet?
    A. 40 ft.
    B. 90 ft.
    C. 92 ft.
    D. 94 ft.
    E. 98 ft.

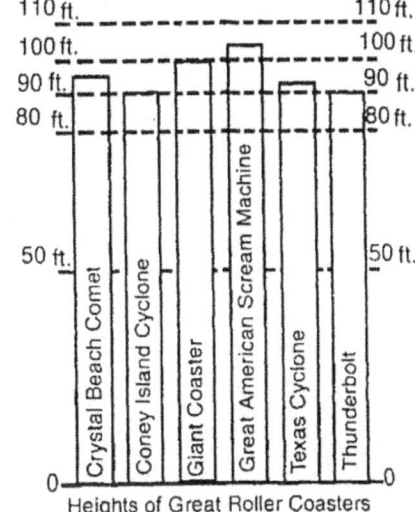
Heights of Great Roller Coasters

37._____

38. According to the bar graph shown in Question 37, what is the difference in height between the tallest and shortest roller coasters? _____ feet.
    A. 5   B. 10   C. 15   D. 20   E. 50

38._____

39. How much change will you receive from a $10 bill when you buy 4 grapefruits at 90¢ each and 3 apples at 40¢ each?
    A. $6.20   B. $5.20   C. $4.80   D. $4.20   E. $4.00

39._____

40. A medical supplier packages medicine in boxes. The cost of packaging is computed with the flow chart at the right.
What is the cost of packaging medicine in a box that is 30 cm long, 20 cm wide, and 20 cm high?
   A. $.20
   B. $.24
   C. $2.00
   D. $2.40
   E. $3.00

40.____

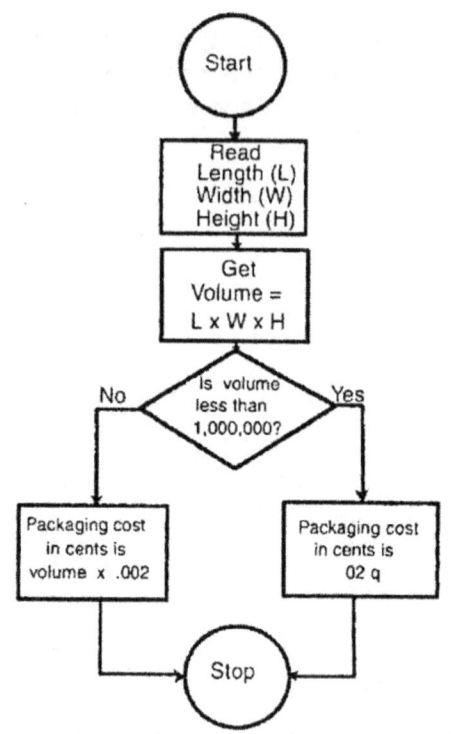

KEY (CORRECT ANSWERS)

1.	D	11.	B	21.	E	31.	E
2.	D	12.	D	22.	B	32.	C
3.	D	13.	D	23.	B	33.	D
4.	B	14.	D	24.	C	34.	C
5.	C	15.	B	25.	B	35.	D
6.	A	16.	B	26.	E	36.	C
7.	B	17.	D	27.	D	37.	D
8.	E	18.	E	28.	B	38.	C
9.	C	19.	A	29.	C	39.	B
10.	B	20.	B	30.	D	40.	A

7 (#1)

SOLUTIONS TO PROBLEMS

1. 534 + 18 + 1291 = 1843

2. (17×23) − 16 + 20 = 391 − 16 + 20 = 395

3. $\frac{3}{7} + \frac{5}{11} = \frac{33}{77} + \frac{35}{77} = \frac{68}{77}$

4. $4832 \div 6 = 805\frac{1}{3}$

5. 62.3 − 4.9 = 57.4

6. $\frac{3}{5} \times \frac{4}{9} = \frac{12}{45} = \frac{4}{15}$

7. $\frac{14}{16} \cdot \frac{5}{16} = \frac{9}{16}$

8. 5.03 + 2.7 + 40 = 47.73

9. 5.37 × 21.4 = 114.918

10. $5\frac{1}{4} + 2\frac{7}{8} = 7\frac{9}{8} = 8\frac{1}{8}$

11. -14 + 5 = -9

12. $\frac{2}{7}$ of 28 = $(\frac{2}{7})(\frac{28}{1})$ = 8

13. $\frac{2}{5}$ = .40 as a decimal

14. Let x = missing number. Then, .20x = 38. Solving, x = 190

15. $\frac{84}{400}$ = .021

16. Let x = missing number. Then, $\frac{4}{5} = \frac{x}{60}$. 5x = 240, so x = 48

17. Area = (15)(32) = 480mm^2

18. Let x = ☐. Then, 25 − 4x = 13. So, -4x = -12. Solving, x = 3.

19. $\frac{9}{27} = \frac{16}{x}$. Then, 9x = 432. Solving, x = 48.

20. Perimeter = 17 + 10 + 15 = 42

21. 45 × 9 = 405 = (45×10)-(45×1)

22. 19 + 21 + 21 + 22 + 27 = 110. Then, 110 ÷ 5 = 22

23. ∠T = 180° - 50° - 45° = 85°

24. The paper clip's length is about 5 – 2 = 3 cm.

25. For A: price per can = $\frac{.99}{6}$ = .165
    For B: price per can = $\frac{.90}{6}$ = .15
    For C: price per can = $\frac{.93}{5}$ = 186
    For D: price per can = $\frac{.56}{3}$ = .18$\overline{6}$
    For E: price per can = $\frac{.50}{3}$ = .1$\overline{6}$

    Lowest price is for B.

26. $1.97 = $2.00. Then, ($2.00)(14,127) = $28,254 = $28,000

27. Sale price = ($430)(.80) = $344

28. Let x = cost. Then, 9x = $90, so x = $10.00

29. $\frac{1860}{465}$ = 4 hours

30. $\frac{24}{32}$ = 75%

31. $\frac{7}{3}$ = 2.$\overline{3}$ = 2.33333 on the calculator shown

32. Total cost = $14 + $16 + $19 = $49

33. Cost = ($16)(4) = $64

34. (800)(1$\frac{1}{2}$)(6) = 7200 calories

35. (.90)(1.6) = $1.44

36. Around 2015, the minimum weekly wages exceeded $100.

37. The Crystal Beach Comet's height is about 94 ft.

38. Tallest = 105 ft. and the shortest = 90 ft. Difference = 15 ft.

39. $10 – (3)(.90) – (3)(.40) = $5.20 change.

40. (30)(20)(20) = 12,000 cm³. Since 12,000 < 1,000,000, the price is 20 cents.

INTERPRETING STATISTICAL DATA GRAPHS, CHARTS, AND TABLES

EXAMINATION SECTION

TEST 1

DIRECTIONS: Each question or incomplete statement is followed by several suggested answers or completions. Select the one that BEST answers the question or completes the statement. *PRINT THE LETTER OF THE CORRECT ANSWER IN THE SPACE AT THE RIGHT.*

Questions 1-12.

DIRECTIONS: Questions 1 through 12 are to be answered SOLELY on the basis of the information given in the graph and chart below.

ENROLLMENT IN POSTGRADUATE STUDIES

——— Sciences   -o-o-o-o Social sciences
-x-x-x Humanities   ⁓⁓⁓⁓ Professions

Fields	Subdivisions	2014	2015
Sciences	Math	10,000	12,000
	Physical Science	22,000	24,000
	Behavioral Science	32,000	35,000
Humanities	Literature	26,000	34,000
	Philosophy	6,000	8,000
	Religion	4,000	6,000
	Arts	10,000	16,000
Social Services	History	36,000	46,000
	Sociology	8,000	14,000
Professions	Law	2,000	2,000
	Medicine	6,000	8,000
	Business	30,000	44,000

2 (#1)

1. The number of students enrolled in the social sciences and in the humanities was the same in
   A. 2012 and 2014
   B. 2010 and 2014
   C. 2014 and 2015
   D. 2011 and 2014

   1._____

2. A comparison of the enrollment of students in the various postgraduate studies shows that in every year from 2010 through 2015, there were MORE students enrolled in _____ than in the _____.
   A. professions; sciences
   B. humanities; professions
   C. social sciences, professions
   D. humanities; sciences

   2._____

3. The number of students enrolled in the humanities was GREATER than the number of students enrolled in the professions by the same amount in _____ of the years.
   A. two
   B. three
   C. four
   D. five

   3._____

4. The one field of postgraduate study to show a DECREASE in enrollment in one year compared to the year immediately preceding is
   A. humanities
   B. sciences
   C. professions
   D. social sciences

   4._____

5. If the proportion of arts students to all humanities students was the same in 2012 as in 2015, then the number of arts students in 2012 was
   A. 7,500
   B. 13,000
   C. 15,000
   D. 5,000

   5._____

6. In which field of postgraduate study did enrollment INCREASE by 20 percent from 2012 to 2013?
   A. Humanities
   B. Professions
   C. Sciences
   D. Social sciences

   6._____

7. The GREATEST increase in overall enrollment took place between
   A. 2010 and 2011
   B. 2012 and 2013
   C. 2013 and 2014
   D. 2013 and 2015

   7._____

8. Between 2012 and 2015, the combined enrollment of the sciences and social sciences INCREASED by
   A. 40,000
   B. 48,000
   C. 50,000
   D. 54,000

   8._____

9. If the enrollment in the social sciences had decreased from 2014 to 2015 at the same rate as from 2013 to 2014, then the social science enrollment in 2015 would have differed from the humanities enrollment in 2015 MOST NEARLY by
   A. 6,000
   B. 8,000
   C. 12,000
   D. 22,000

   9._____

10. In the humanities, the GREATEST percentage increase in enrollment from 2014 to 2015 was in
    A. literature
    B. philosophy
    C. religion
    D. arts

    10._____

268

11. If the proportion of behavioral science students to the total number of students in the sciences was the same in 2011 as in 2014, then the increase in behavioral science enrollment from 2011 to 2015 was
    A. 5,000   B. 7,000   C. 10,000   D. 14,000

11._____

12. If enrollment in the professions increased at the same rate from 2015 to 2016 as from 2014 to 2015, the enrollment in the professions in 2001 would be MOST NEARLY
    A. 85,000   B. 75,000   C. 60,000   D. 55,000

12._____

KEY (CORRECT ANSWERS)

1.	B	7.	D
2.	C	8.	A
3.	B	9.	D
4.	D	10.	D
5.	A	11.	C
6.	C	12.	B

TEST 2

DIRECTIONS: Each question or incomplete statement is followed by several suggested answers or completions. Select the one that BEST answers the question or completes the statement. *PRINT THE LETTER OF THE CORRECT ANSWER IN THE SPACE AT THE RIGHT.*

Questions 1-5.

DIRECTIONS: Questions 1 through 5 involve calculations of annual grade averages for college students who have just completed their junior year. These averages are to be based on the following table showing the number of credit hours for each student during the year at each of the grade levels: A, B, C, D, and F. How these letter grades may be translated into numerical grades is indicated in the first column of the table.

Grade Value	Credit Hours – Junior Year					
	King	Lewis	Martin	Nonkin	Ottly	Perry
A = 95	12	23	9	15	6	3
B = 85	9	12	9	12	18	6
C = 75	6	6	9	3	3	21
D = 65	3	3	3	3	-	-
F = 0	-	-	3	-	-	-

Calculating a grade average for an individual student is a four-step process:
  I. Multiply each grade value by the number of credit hours for which the student received that grade.
  II. Add these multiplication products for each student.
  III. Add the student's total credit hours.
  IV. Divide the multiplication product total by the total number of credit hours.
  V. Round the result, if there is a decimal place, to the nearest whole number. A number ending in .5 would be rounded to the next higher number.

EXAMPLE:
Using student King's grades as an example, his grade average can be calculated by going through the following four steps:
  I. 95 × 12 = 1140   III. 12
  II. 85 × 9 = 765   9
  III. 75 × 6 = 450   6
  IV. 65 × 3 = 195   3
  V. 0 × 0 = 0   0
                                     30 TOTAL CREDIT HOURS
  II. TOTAL = 2550

  IV. Divide 2550 by 30: $\frac{2550}{30} = 85$.

King's grade average is 85.

1. The grade average of Lewis is   1.____
   A. 83   B. 84   C. 85   D. 86

2 (#2)

2. The grade average of Martin is
   A. 72 B. 73 C. 74 D. 75

3. The grade average of Nonkin is
   A. 85 B. 86 C. 87 D. 88

4. Student Ottly must attain a grade average of 90 in each of his years in college to be accepted into the graduate school of his choice.
   If, in summer school during his junior year, he takes two three-credit courses and receives a grade of 95 in each one, his grade average for his junior year will then be MOST NEARLY
   A. 87 B. 88 C. 89 D. 90

5. If Perry takes an additional three-credit course during the year and receives a grade of 95, his grade average will be increased to APPROXIMATELY
   A. 79 B. 80 C. 81 D. 82

KEY (CORRECT ANSWERS)

1. C
2. D
3. C
4. B
5. B

TEST 3

DIRECTIONS: Each question or incomplete statement is followed by several suggested answers or completions. Select the one that BEST answers the question or completes the statement. *PRINT THE LETTER OF THE CORRECT ANSWER IN THE SPACE AT THE RIGHT.*

Questions 1-5.

DIRECTIONS: Questions 1 through 5 are to be answered SOLELY on the basis of the following information and chart.

The following table gives pertinent data for six different applicants with regard to: Grade averages, which are expressed on a scale running from 0 (low) to 4 (high); Scores on qualifying test, which run from 200 (low) to 800 (high); Related work experience, which is expressed in number of months; Personal references, which are related from 1 (low) to 5 (high).

Applicant	Grade Average	Test Score	Work Experience	Reference
Jones	2.2	620	24	3
Perez	3.5	650	0	5
Lowitz	3.2	420	2	4
Uncker	2.1	710	15	2
Farrow	2.8	560	0	3
Shapiro	3.0	560	12	4

An administrative Assistant is in charge of the initial screening process for the program. This process requires classifying applicants into the following four groups:

A. SUPERIOR CANDIDATES: Unless the personal reference rating is lower than 3, all applicants with grade averages of 3.0 or higher and test scores of 600 or higher are classified as superior candidates.

B. GOOD CANDIDATES: Unless the personal reference rating is lower than 3, all applicants with one of the following combinations of grade averages and test scores are classified as good candidates:
1. Grade average of 2.5 to 2.9 and test score of 600 or higher;
2. Grade average of 3.0 or higher and test score of 550 to 599.

C. POSSIBLE CANDIDATES: Applicants with one of the following combinations of qualifications are classified as possible candidates:
1. Grade average of 2.5 to 2.9 and test score of 550 to 599 and a personal reference rating of 3 or higher;
2. Grade average of 2.0 to 2.4 and test score of 500 or higher and at least 21 months' work experience and a personal reference rating of 3 or higher;
3. A combination of grade average and test score that would otherwise qualify as superior or good but a personal reference score lower than 3.

D. REJECTED CANDIDATES: Applicants who do not fall in any of the above groups are to be rejected.

EXAMPLE:
　　　Jones' grade average of 2.2 does not meet the standard for either a superior candidate (grade average must be 3.0 or higher) or a good candidate (grade average must be 2.5 to 2.9). Grade average of 2.2 does not qualify Jones as a possible candidate if Jones has a test score of 500 or higher, at least 21 months' work experience, and a personal reference rating of 3 or higher. Since Jones has a test score of 620, 24 months' work experience, and a reference rating of 3, Jones is a possible candidate. The answer is C.

Answer Questions 1 through 5 as explained above, indicating for each whether the applicant should be classified as a
- A. Superior candidate
- B. Good candidate
- C. Possible candidate
- D. Rejected candidate

1. Perez
2. Lowitz
3. Uncker
4. Farrow
5. Shapiro

KEY (CORRECT ANSWERS)

1. A
2. D
3. D
4. C
5. B

www.ingramcontent.com/pod-product-compliance
Lightning Source LLC
Chambersburg PA
CBHW082031300426
44117CB00015B/2445